W9-CJE-126

THE BEST OF
NEW ENGLAND HUMOR

BOOKS BY JIM BRUNELLE

MAINE ALMANAC

'OVER TO HOME AND FROM AWAY'

THE BEST OF
NEW ENGLAND
HUMOR

... or pretty darn close

JIM BRUNELLE

YANKEE BOOKS

CAMDEN · MAINE

Cover and design by Lurelle Cheverie, Rockport, Maine

Typeset by Camden Type 'n Graphics, Camden, Maine

Printed and bound by St. Mary's Press, Hollywood, Maryland

Library of Congress Cataloging-in-Publication Data

The Best of New England humor—or pretty darn close / |compiled| by
Jim Brunelle.
    p.   cm.
    ISBN 0-89909-226-8
    1. New England—Humor.   2. American wit and humor.   I. Brunelle,
Jim.
PN6231.N557B47   1990

90-43568

This book is dedicated to the memory of

William M. Clark
(1913–1988)

who, because he was such a fine writer,
taught me the pleasures of editing,
and, because he was such a fine human
being, the pleasures of friendship.

Contents

CONTENTS

FUNNY STUFF

GROWING UP

CONTENTS

BRAHMINS

PASSING THROUGH

Acknowledgments

■ Anthologies are by nature a cooperative effort and this one is no exception. Librarians, for instance, play a central role in the collecting process, and all those I came in contact with went out of their way to make this a cheerful project. I am especially grateful to Stella J. Scheckter of the New Hampshire State Library for leading me to the humorous histories of Will M. Cressy. The staffs of the Portland Public Library and the Maine State Library were also particularly helpful. On a more personal level, I wish to thank my friend Betty Clark, widow of Bill Clark, for several favors, including the loan of that most indispensable of anthological devices—a copier. My wife Ellen supplied not only great quantities of spiritual encouragement but devoted hours to the often frustrating business of tracking down reprint permissions. Which leads up to the most pertinent acknowledgments—the contribution of the writers involved. ■

Foreword

■ Basically, there are two New Englands, northern and southern, with plenty of shared schizophrenia between them. Northern New England—Maine, New Hampshire, Vermont—can be categorized generally as rural; southern New England—Massachusetts, Connecticut, Rhode Island—as urban and suburban. The humorous literary and oral traditions of these two regions reflect those qualities. Generally speaking.

The types are familiar and firmly fixed. The Connecticut Yankee and the Maine Yankee may both trade on rurality for their wit, but the one is garrulous and the other taciturn. When the Bostonian tells a story the Vermonter becomes an ignorant hayseed; when the Vermonter tells a story the Bostonian is a pompous ignoramus.

Usually in such a match there's no contest; the Vermonter will inevitably prevail, if only because there are still more bumpkins than brahmins among us. Sophistication is far more susceptible to ridicule than innocence. Pomposity, of course, merely invites deflation.

The trouble with most humorous anthologies is that the compiler is often moved to analysis, the effect of which is poisonous to the material that follows. Someone once offered the following definition: "Humor is stuff that is funny." Let's leave it at that. Like pornography, you know it when you see it; like art, you know what you like. Who needs to be told what humor is about?

For this collection, at most I can claim to have done my best under the chains of individual bias to pick stuff I think the reader will find funny. The selections that follow are, for the most part, personal favorites. I did make some allowance for geographical and historical roundness. Call it padding if you will, although that was not the motive; other favorites—Seba Smith, Artemus Ward—were dropped in service to the same editorial balancing act. The idea was to assemble a representative collection of New England humor (and humor by New Englanders) covering a period of roughly three centuries, reflecting certain generational, regional, and cultural differences that have contributed to the vitality and character of this corner of America.

Finally, since I've been shameless enough to kidnap Mark Twain for the "introduction" to this collection, I've taken one other liberty. The piece is a composite, made without benefit of footnotes or ellipses. For those who really must know, the sources are listed in an appendix.

JIM BRUNELLE
Cape Elizabeth, 1990

Introduction
by Mark Twain

■ There is no more sin in publishing an entire volume of nonsense than there is in keeping a candy store with no hardware in it. It lies wholly with the customer whether he will injure himself by means of either, or will derive from them the benefits which they will afford him if he uses the possibilities judiciously. A successful book is not made of what is in it, but what is left out of it. Humor is out of place in a dictionary.

Humor is only a fragrance, a decoration. Often it is merely an odd trick of speech and of spelling, and presently the fashion passes and the fame along with it. There are those who say a novel should be a work of art solely, and you must not preach in it, you must not teach in it. That may be true as regards novels, but it is not true as regards humor. Humor must not professedly teach, and it must not professedly preach, but it must do both if it would live forever. By forever, I mean thirty years. With all its preaching it is not likely to outlive so long a term as that. The very things it preaches about, and which are novelties when it preaches about them, can cease to be novelties and become commonplaces in thirty years. Then that sermon can thenceforth interest no one.

I have always preached. That is the reason that I have lasted thirty years. If the humor came of its own accord and uninvited, I have allowed it a place in my sermon, but I was not writing the sermon for the sake of the humor. I should have written the sermon just the same, whether any humor applied for admission or not. I am saying these vain things in this frank way because I am a dead person speaking from the grave. Even I would be too modest to say them in life. I think we never become really and genuinely our entire and honest selves until we are dead—and not then until we have been dead years and years. People ought to start dead and then they would be honest so much earlier.

The humorous story is American, the comic story is English, the witty story is French. The humorous story depends for its effect upon the manner of the telling, the comic story and the witty story upon the matter. The humorous story may be spun out to great lengths and may wander around as much as it pleases and arrive nowhere in particular, but the comic and witty stories must be brief and end with a point. The humorous story bubbles gently along, the others burst.

The humorous story is told gravely; the teller does his best to conceal the fact that he even dimly suspects that there is anything funny about it; but the teller of the comic story tells you beforehand that it is one of the funniest things he has ever heard, then tells it with eager delight and is the first person to laugh when he gets through. And sometimes, if he has had good success, he is so glad and happy that he will repeat the "nub" of it and glance around from face to face, collecting applause, and then repeat it again. It is a pathetic thing to see.

Very often, of course, the rambling and disjointed humorous story finishes with a nub, point, snapper, or whatever you like to call it. Then the listener must be alert, for in many cases the teller will divert attention from that nub by dropping it in a carefully casual and indifferent way, with the pretense that he does not know it is a nub.

But the teller of the comic story does not slur the nub; he shouts it at you every time. And when he prints it, in England, France, Germany, and Italy, he italicizes it, puts some whooping exclamation points after it, and sometimes explains it in parentheses. All of which is very depressing and makes one want to renounce joking and lead a better life.

Humor is the great thing, the saving thing, after all. The minute it crops up all our hardnesses yield, all our irritations and resentments slip away, and a sunny spirit takes their place. Humor is mankind's greatest blessing.

I value humor highly and am constitutionally fond of it, but I should not like it as a steady diet. For its own best interests, humor should take its outings in grave company; its cheerful dress gets heightened color from the proximity of sober hues.

I think I have seldom deliberately set out to be humorous, but have nearly always allowed the humor to drop in or stay out according to its fancy. I have never tried to write a humorous lecture; I have only tried to write serious ones—it is the only way not to succeed.

There is no lasting quality to humor unless it's based on real substance. Being funny doesn't mean anything unless there is an underlying human note. People don't realize that this requires the same powers of observation, analysis, and understanding as in serious writing. I am never more tickled than when I laugh at myself.

[The human race] in its poverty has unquestionably one really effective weapon—laughter. Power, money, persuasion, supplication, persecution—these can lift at a colossal humbug—push it a little, weaken it a little, century by century; but only laughter can blow it to rags and atoms at a blast. Against the assault of laughter nothing can stand. ■

THE BEST OF
NEW ENGLAND HUMOR

EARLY DAYS

PART THREE

History of the New England States

WILL M. CRESSEY Actor, entertainer, and musician, the multi-talented Will M. Cressey was probably America's most prolific writer of vaudeville sketches in the early part of this century.

Born in 1863 in Bradford, New Hampshire, he began his career in show business touring the Northeast with his brother Harry in a skit entitled "The Musical Drummers." Later, after the brothers broke up their act, Cressey turned to writing skits for a living. In twenty-five years on the Keith and Orpheum circuits, he produced hundreds of sketches and amusing one-act plays. Although he sometimes appeared in them himself—along with his wife and stage partner, Blanche Dayne—most of the work Cressey produced was for other performers.

The vaudevillian in him is clearly evident in the following humorous histories of the New England states, which Cressey turned out for a Providence publisher in the early 1920s. The reader can almost hear a phantom pit drummer firing off rim-shots as the one-liners pile up in the comic historian's narrative.

The History of Massachusetts

The first white man to ever set eyes on what is now the state of Massachusetts was Leif Ericson, a Norwegian Swede who, according to his pictures, must have been some relation to the Smith Brothers, cough-drop growers. Leif came over from Sweden and collided with the United States at Fall River in the year 1001. (This is a date that you play forwards or backwards with equal results.) He called it Vinland. But it has been called much worse since then.

Leif didn't think much of the town and thought less of the name; he wanted to know what else they expected a river to do The following year his brother, Thorwald, came over. And he liked the town still less than his brother did. For he died there. And is there yet. In the cemetery.

The business of Discovering America seemed to sort of sag down for the next few hundred years. For the next we hear of it was in 1492, when Christopher Columbus got his name in the papers as a Discoverer. Chris was an Eye-talian sleight-of-hand performer over in Spain, whose big stunt was standing an egg on end. Finally Queen Isabella or her husband got tired of keeping him supplied with eggs, at sixty cents a dozen, so she gave him a ship and a string of fake pearls and told him to go over and discover America.

And so as soon as he could hock the pearls he set sail in "The Ark." And it rained for forty days and forty nights. In fact it was quite damp. And the excursion was all wet. Then, on the forty-first day Chris sent out a dove. And in a little while it came back carrying a sprig of hops, a head of barley, and a hunk of malt. And Chris shouted gleefully, "It is America!"

And he landed on Mount Ararat, renamed it Mount Tom, and called the land "Columbia, the Jim-Jam-Jem of the Ocean."

And that was the name of it on all of the timetables until 1499, when another Eye-talian discoverer, by the name of Amerigo Vespucci, discovered it again and renamed it America, in honor of himself.

But the real facts of the case are that neither one of them discovered America. For in 1496 an Englishman by the unique name of John Smith came over and spent a summer pestering around South Boston, Chelsea, and Revere Beach. And this was three years before Amerigo got here, and Christopher had not yet got past the Panama Canal. And it was this J. Smith gent who first gave it the name New England.

But it was not until the sixteenth century that New England really got started. Things over in England at that time were very much Knights-of-Columbus. And a lot of followers of Alexander Dowie decided to emigrate to Holland. And they did. And they were just as popular there as they had been in England. So the Dutchmen worked a "recall" on them and sent them back to England. Not to be outdone in politeness, England sent them back to Holland. And the Dutch interned them for ten years—at hard labor.

Right along in about here still another English member of The Discoverer's Union sailed over and discovered America again. He had a great name for an Englishman, Bartholemew Gosnol. He landed somewhere down on Cape Cod, collected a shipload of "Sassafras," and sailed back to London smelling very sassafras. This was in 1602.

By the time those Dowie-ites got out of the Holland Sing Sing they began to suspect that they were not wanted there. So they said, "Let' go over and discover America again, settle down there, and be Puritans."

And the rest of them said, "Let's." And the let'ted.

They bought a ship and, as it was October, called it the *Mayflower*. And they loaded it with Puritans and furniture and set sail. Judging from the time they made, sixty-three days, they must have got hold of an old U.S. Transport. The exact dimensions of this ship have been lost. But statisticians have figured it out, judging from the amount of furniture that "came over in the Mayflower," that it must have been slightly over three miles long, eighty-eight yards wide and fifteen hundred feet deep.

On the eleventh day of December 1620, they landed on Plymouth Rock, down at Plymouth, Massachusetts, had their pictures taken, and moved in. They must have come in on a tidal wave, for the rock is way up on the side of a hill, with an iron fence around it. But this rock has since become famous as the home of Plymouth Rock Pants, Plymouth Rock Hens, and Plymouth Gin.

From the eleventh of December to the ninth of January all they did was to unload furniture and attend Thanksgiving services, for it was not until this latter date that they started in to build the first house. There were just exactly seven workmen. The rest were bosses.

Then Miles Standish formed the first American Army. Six men. England trembled.

The Puritans got along pretty well for two years and then split on the liquor question. One section favored Plymouth Gin and the other Medford Rum. So the Medford crowd pulled out and started a second town over at Weymouth. They tried to reform the Indians and switch them off onto near beer, and the Indians went on the warpath. Something less than eight million of them gathered to wipe out the town. But General Miles Standish marched over from Plymouth with his army, now increased to eight men, attacked in force, and "repulsed the Indians with great loss." Some army.

Meanwhile the population was increasing by leaps and bounds. In 1624 there were 180 people in New England. Charlestown was started, and by 1630 was so crowded that John Winthrop moved over and started a new suburb, Boston. And he, being the only voter that way, elected himself governor.

In 1638 a Charlestown minister, Professor John Harvard, died and left five thousand dollars to start a college, to be called after him. (The history does not tell where, or how, a minister in those days ever accumulated five thousand dollars.)

It was in this same year that Stephen Daye brought over a printing press and one font of type and started an almanac. It had the Signs of the Zodiac and jokes in it. Sample joke:

"Why does a hen cross Washington Street?"

"To get from Winter to Summer."

Later on he started the *Boston Transcript*. They have more type now and a new press, but the general makeup of the paper is about the same.

By this time a lot of lawyers had graduated from Harvard, but as there were no laws yet business was poor. So they started in making laws. And they were good laws—for the lawyers. They are yet.

Salem broke out in an epidemic of witches. Historians disagree on the burning of witches, but agree that thirty-nine of them were executed one way or another. The first lady to appear in the title role in this production was a Mistress Hazel Peabody. Witch Hazel was named in her honor, but too late to do her any good.

The name "Cape Cod" attracted the codfish in such great numbers that cod fishing became one of the principal industries, cod liver oil the national drink, and codfish the principal article of food. No store was considered properly dressed unless it had a string of these open-faced fish hung across the front with their vests unbuttoned. A store so decorated could, like a Mason, be found in the darkness as well as in the light.

The smelt was another denizen of the deep which arose to headline honor. As a smelt, a smelt did not amount to much; but under the expert manipulation of the Cape Cod Fisheries Label Printers and the publicity bureaus, the lowly smelt became the highly prized, and higher priced, "Russian sardine" of commerce.

By 1635 Boston had become so crowded that Simon Willard took his own and twelve other families and moved out West—to Concord.

Concord later became famous as the home of the Concord Grape, Louisa M. Alcott, the Concord Bridge, and the birthplace of Paul Revere's horse.

It was at Lexington, a few miles east of here, that Paul got pinched for speeding.

Boston was made the capital. The Statehouse was built. And the dome, representing a bean-pot turned bottom side up, was gold plated.

Bostonians are conservative. Many people think that they are cold. They are not. They are just numb.

I know a lot more about Massachusetts, but have not got room to tell it.

The History of Connecticut

The original Indian name for Connecticut was QUANEH-TA-CUT. The whites have changed the spelling, but it still sounds just as much like a hen's peon of victory after having laid an egg as it ever did.

The first white man to try and introduce this spelling reform to the Indians was Herr Adrian Blok, from Holland, in 1614. But the Indians did not take kindly to The Dutch Farmer's Bloc, and Herr Blok's funeral was attended by all the First Indian Families.

It was not until 1633 that the first permanent settlement was made, also by the Dutch, at Hartford. They built a fort and called it the "House of

Hope." With some additions and alterations, the "House of Hope" is still there, only now they call it the Statehouse.

The original grant from Charles II of England for this territory gave the boundaries of Connecticut as extending "from Narraganset Bay to the Pacific Ocean." But it has shrunk in size and gained in importance since then. Connecticut was one of the first four United States. In 1643 the Colonies of Massachusetts, Plymouth, New Haven, and Connecticut formed this union. Two hundred and sixty-five years later, 1918, Connecticut was one of the three states that preached as they intended to practice, and voted against the Eighteenth Amendment. They showed their originality again by buying and paying for their land instead of just taking it. The township of Saybrook was secured on condition that one-fifth of all the gold and silver "oar" ever found in it should go to the Indians. And, as usual, the Indians got the worst of it, for there was never any found. The township of Quinnipiac came higher: twelve coats, twelve brass spoons, twelve hatchets, twelve porringers, twenty-four knives, and four cases of scissors. (What would an Indian do with a pair of scissors?) I forgot to say that later on they laughingly changed the name to Hartford. Rippowams cost twelve coats and a copper kettle. Later on, in honor of Mr. Stam, who bought the first Ford in town, they changed the name to Stamford.

Milford was evidently not bought, for in the town records of 1640 it states that "It was voted that the earth is given to The Saints. And voted that we are The Saints." This may have been true at the time, but if so then the stock has petered out considerably since. It was a land of religious liberty (if you had the same religion they did). But up to 1800 these wise old boys would only permit eleven lawyers in the state at any one time.

Sunday was strictly a day of rest. And it began at sunset Saturday and lasted until sunrise Monday. It was forbidden to cross a river, build a fire, harness a horse, cook food, or "to tell stories other than of a religious nature." No man could kiss his wife on a Sunday. (Hired girl, all right.) And no young, unmarried man could keep house.

There was a fine for "taking in boarders." (I know hotels in Connecticut that ought to be fined for it right now.) It was forbidden to "remain in any one building over half an hour at a time drinking wyne (wine), bear (beer), or hotte water." (How did Mister Volstead overlook that "hotte water"?)

Smoking was a pretty serious operation in those days: "No person under the age of twenty years, or any other, (then why mention the twenty years?) that shall not have accustomed himself to the use thereof, shall take any tobacco until he shall have brought a certificate under the hand of someone approved for knowledge and skill in physick, that it is useful to him, and shall also have a license from the courte for the same."

And no one could carry any tobacco with him, unless he was going at least ten miles away from home. And then he must go out in the fields or woods alone to smoke. (The wife says they should never have repealed that law.)

Even up until 1912 no trains could pass through Connecticut—and this is on the main and only line between New York and Boston—"during church hours."

At Hartford we find the site of the Charter Oak. This was undoubtedly the biggest tree in the world, for at least five-eighths of all the furniture in Connecticut today is "made from the Charter Oak."

Hartford is the home of insurance business. Life insurance consists in the company betting you will live and you betting you will not. And they win, either way. In fire insurance they bet your house will not burn down and you bet it will, and the law says if it does you go to jail.

The motto of New London, is "Mare Liberrum." A mare is a lady horse. "Liber" is German for "love." And if you don't know what "rum" means, ask your father. New London offers Nathan Hale, who had the best exit speech ever made by any American soldier.

Just across the river from New London is Groton. The present town clerk is the ninth generation in direct line to hold that position. In 1718 a Groton sea captain brought to his wife the first tea ever seen or heard of in the new country. Nobody knew how to serve it. So they boiled it, like greens, and served it with boiled pork. And none of the guests could spit for a week.

New Haven is best known as the home of Yale College, started 159 years ago. But it has changed considerably since then. Because one of the newspapers of those early days states: "Last night som of the College Freshmen got six quarts of rhum and two payles fool (pails full) of Sydar (cider) and made such prodidgius rough that they raised the tuter." And anybody knows they could not do that now. In the first place they could not get the "rhum" because the country is "dry," and if they could it would take more than six quarts to "raise a tuter" now.

Eli Whitney, a Hartford man, invented the cotton gin. And if Mister Volstead had been alive then he would have had Eli arrested for bootlegging. In 1771 David Bushnell built the first submarine boat. To be sure, it did not work, but the ones we are building *now* don't work so darned good. But after all is said and done, Connecticut's greatest claim to fame and the one by which she will be remembered is in her invention, perfection, and distribution of her wooden nutmegs, made from pine knots, thereby furnishing the inspiration for that well-known term—a "Conn Man."

The History of Rhode Island

Rhode Island either is or is not an island according to whether you refer to the island or the state. For the island of Rhode is only a part of the state of Rhode Island.

The first record of Rhode Island is in 1524 when a Frenchman by the name of Vezzerano landed at what is now Newport, stayed two weeks, accumulated all the wealth in the community, and used up the rest of his round-trip ticket to France.

For the next 211 years Rhode Island's social activities were confined entirely to the Indian tribes, until 1736 when Roger Williams came over from Seekonk—wherever that was—paddled up the river Moshassuck, landed, said, "Thank Providence I am in Providence," went up to the city hall, registered, asked for his mail, reserved a room for Anne Hutchinson, remarked that the marble in the building looked like preserved oysters, and went out and set up his camp in Roger Williams Park, which he named for himself.

The next day he met the mayor, Chief Canonicus, and the town treasurer, Chief Niantinomi, and bought the whole town for thirteen coats and thirteen hoes. (They evidently already had trousers or else did not wear any.) The boundaries were a little hazy, which resulted in trouble for the next hundred and thirty-two years, reading, "All the land on the rivers Moshassuck, Seekonk and Woonasquetucket." And the Indians "threw in two torkepes" at that. (A torkepe is an Indian toupee.)

The next year, 1737, another settlement was made at Pocasset. They did so well they got all swelled up and changed the name to Portsmouth.

The geographies state that "the rivers of Rhode Island are all short." Taking into consideration the fact that the state is only 48 miles long and 37 wide, this sounds like a reasonable statement.

This shortness of the rivers brings about a confusing condition to the stranger, as they flow one way at low tide and the opposite way at high tide.

The total area of the state is 1,248 square miles. But 181 miles of this is water, reducing the land area to 1,067 square miles.

There are 5,498 farms in the state and 10,986 farmers. This gives each farmer half a farm.

Ninety-one percent of the population live in towns or cities. So that every farmer off his half a farm has got to feed ten city folks in addition to his own family. No wonder Rhode Islanders live mostly on fish. For the state records of 1905 state that in that year the state produced: $875,000 worth of Oysters, $138,000 worth of Sculpins, $65,000 worth of Lobsters, and $86,000 worth of Squeteague. (Wouldn't you like to see a native of Keokuk, Iowa, trying to order a side order of Squeteague?)

In 1638 William Coddington (for whom the New England codfish was named), John Clark, and Anne Hutchinson came over from Massachusetts, at the special invitation of the state of Massachusetts, and started a settlement on the island of Aquidneck, where Providence now stands. The Roger Williams outfit were Baptists. They came here for "religious liberty." Any creed was welcome—as long as they were Baptists. The Coddington-Clark-Hutchinsons were Antinomians (whatever that was). And for the next few years the principal occupation of the two outfits consisted of quarreling, making up, combining, and separating at Providence, Newport, and Portsmouth.

They had laws and everything. One interesting one was that no one could drink on the Sabbath "more than necessity requireth."

They adopted a state seal consisting of a bunch of arrows and labeled "Amor Vicet Omnia," signifying that with love, and enough bows and arrows, you could conquer anything.

By 1760 Newport was humming with industry. As one old history states, "Newport was now the headquarters for piracy, sugar, smuggling, rum, molasses, and slaves." But time has worked wonders. There is very little molasses or sugar used there now.

Slavery was evidently a double-edged blessing, for one devout old preacher stated that it was a "wonderful blessing to bring to this Land of Freedom these poor benighted heathen to enjoy the blessings of gospel dispensation." That "land of freedom" for slaves sounds a little complicated, but of course that "gospel dispensation" made up for a lot of things. The town also had at this time twenty-two "still-houses," probably also under "gospel dispensation."

Rhode Island has a mean elevation of 200 feet, the meanest being Durfee Hill, towering aloft 800 feet. Mountain climbing is not an important Rhode Island industry. According to the government weather reports, Providence has a very equitable climate, ranging from 9 below to 103 above, which ought to suit most anybody at some time of the year.

Narragansett Bay, which is built around Narragansett Pier, contains the three islands, Conanicut (which is a dead steal from Connecticut), Prudence, and Rhode Island, with a fourth one, Block Island, which was washed out ten miles offshore during the spring freshets the year Mr. Noah built the ark.

Up until 1731 whaling was one of the principal industries. The state paid a bounty of five shillings a barrel on whale oil and a penny a pound on whalebone. But Mr. Rockefeller ruined the whale-oil business, and the corset went out of vogue, and the state was only big enough to haul out a couple of whales at a time, and the whales stopped biting, and the whale fishermen changed their tackle and went in for sardines.

On the fourth day of May, 1776, the state of Rhode Island beat the United States by two months and issued their own private Declaration of Independence. And on the following 25th of July held the first "Fourth-of-July" celebration ever observed in America. Beginning in 1803, for twenty-five years there were no public schools in the state. Some of the inhabitants do not know that the law has been repealed yet.

The first patent ever issued in America was granted to a Mr. Samuels for a water wheel. He also invented the scythe. And his wife invented cotton thread. But it is a safe bet that Sam had to keep right on sewing on his own buttons as before. Another Rhode Island man, Oziel Wilkinson, invented cut-iron nails, which made pounding your thumb much easier.

Where the city hall now stands used to stand the Old Market Place. It was here that the Providencers held their little Tea Party one afternoon and burned up three hundred pounds of the "needless herb which is highly detrimental to Liberty, Interest, and Health," in order to show their opinion of Uncle King George's tea tax.

Another morning there was a notice pasted up on the door of this building offering a big reward for the names of the capturers of the Gaspee. There were only about eighty men in the town, and there were seventy-nine men in the attacking party; but somehow nobody could remember who they were, so nobody claimed the reward.

The first long-distance telephone message ever sent over a wire was sent from Providence to Boston. And they got the right number the first time.

Most anybody could afford to keep a cow in those days. Corn was only five cents a bushel. All the trouble was to get the cow, as they cost $106 apiece.

But today Rhode Island is a wonderful state—what there is of it—and there is enough of it such as it is. It is governed—or misgoverned, according to whether your own party is in or out—by a governor, a lieutenant governor, and a House of Representatives, in which the minority, any time they cannot have their own way, move over into another state until after the next election.

George M. Cohan came from Providence (as soon as he could). Next to Roger Williams, Ann Hathaway, and George M. Cohan, Rhode Island's greatest contribution to the world has been the "Rhode Island Clam Bake."

Rhode Island was settled by the English. That is why the letter *h* in "Rhode" is silent. (To get the Irish pronunciation, sound the *h*.)

One of the definitions of the word "providence" is "prudent economy." Probably referring in this case to the width of the downtown streets.

Up to 1886, Rhode Island was "wet." The next three years were "dry," and then they went back to the "wet" column until 1918, when they ratified the Eighteenth Amendment; and since that time no Rhode Island man has ever taken a drink.

Which statement is strong enough to close any history.

The History of Vermont

Vermont was originally spelled "Vert Mont," the French words for "Green Mountains." And while I have no official records to offer in proof, I feel safe in saying that the reason they called the mountains "Green" was because they were colored green, at that time of the year at least.

The first of these French real estate agents to cast eyes on this ter-ritory was a Monsignor Champlain, in 1609. And the minute he stepped out of his airplane, down back of the freight depot at Burlington, he looked around and said, "Why, this is Vermont!" And it was. And has been ever since.

I don't know whether it was the climate, or the water, or what it was, but these Vermonters have always been the most cantankerous, independent, stubborn folks in America. They just never would belong to *anybody*. England, France, New York, Massachusetts, New Hampshire would bargain and traffic and trade Vermont around; and then, just as they had got everything settled to everybody's satisfaction, Vermont would gum up the whole trade by refusing to be traded.

You see, just as soon as Vermont began to amount to anything—to realize that in Lake Champlain they had the largest body of fresh water on the continent, outside of the Great Lakes—to realize that they were producing and raising most of the admirals for the U.S. Navy—to learn that their Republican majorities were setting the styles for the rest of the states—just as soon as all these things began to happen all these other states began trying to ring in on them.

First, England made a trade with New Hampshire whereby Vermont was to be assigned to New Hampshire under the name of "The New Hampshire Grants." Then New York bobbed up and said that under some former grant she had a claim on about half of the state.

But these ramtankerous Vermonters just reared right back in the breeching, said they never did like that Grant family anyway, and Vermont was theirs and they would be tetotally jiggered if they would belong to *anybody*. And to show that they meant it, they formed a young army of their own, called themselves the "Green Mountain Boys," and said: "East is East and West is West, and if you don't like it, pull down your vest."

Why, even when the United States of America was formed, they did not come in for ten years. Not until they got their boundaries bulged out where they wanted them.

Then all through the various French, Indian, and English invasions they formed their own armies and fought their own individual battles without asking or receiving any help from anybody.

And each and all of these invaders took a wallop at them, too. They even had an invasion by the Confederates during the Rebellion. For on the nineteenth of October 1865, a band of young Confederates came over from Canada—making one wonder what a band of patriotic young Southerners was doing up in Canada at that time—and raided St. Albans, killing one man and stealing $200,000 from the banks.

The first settlement in Vermont was made in Massachusetts. In 1724 the first permanent settlement in what is now Vermont was made at Fort Dummer, near Brattleboro, which was then in Massachusetts.

Previous to this the French had tried to establish themselves at Isle la Mott, and the English at Chimney Point; but owing to lack of advertising and the refusal of the Vermont Central Railroad to make summer excursion rates, they petered out.

From 1791 to 1808 Vermont had no state capital. The legislature used to visit around at different towns each year, thereby increasing their mileage allowance and avoiding the payment of bills they had contracted the previous year. In 1808 Montpelier was made the capital.

In 1852 they decided to follow Maine's example, and they voted the state "dry." In 1902 they fell off the wagon again, under the guise of "local option," and stayed that way until 1918, when, with the rest of the country, they adopted Saint Volstead as their patron saint. And no Vermont man has ever taken a drink since. *Meb-be*.

The rest of the New England states drew on French, Swedish, Norwegian, Spanish, English, and Indian for their names. But with the exception of a few rivers and lakes, like Mississquoi, Memphremagog, and Ottauqueechee, Vermont stuck to good, plain old Yankee names, usually naming the town for somebody who had been instrumental in establishing it.

Then, just to make sure that Mister Jones, who started Jonesville, would not be forgotten, they would have North Jonesville, South Jonesville, East Jonesville, and West Jonesville, with probably a Jonesville Upper Falls or a Jonesville Corners.

THE BATTLE OF BENNINGTON

While the Vermont boys fought in many Revolutionary battles, this was probably the best known.

There was a little fort and a little American army here at Bennington under the command of Mrs. Mollie Stark's husband, John.

General Burgoyne, British Commander, was down at Boston with an imported Hessian (German) army. Well, the Yankee-hunting down around Boston was not so good. There were Yankees enough, but he couldn't find them. And so, as it was nice weather and he had a new car, he decided to take a run up to Bennington, see the monument, wipe out the little American force, have dinner at the Walloonsack Inn, and motor back by moonlight.

And it was a real good plan. But something slipped. It seems that Mr. and Mrs. Stark had just got moved into their rooms at the hotel; and the girls were going to school; and a lot of the officers and men had joined the golf club and were getting acquainted with the village girls, and they did not want to be wiped out; and they said they'd be darned if they *would be* wiped out. In fact, General John said to his wife only that morning that if the

British won she would never have to go to Reno to arrange for a second husband.

And so when the Burgoyne Excursion arrived, instead of welcoming them to the city, General John and his Green Mountain Boys were real rough. So much so that Mr. Burgoyne and his German army had about the same luck that the German armies have been having with American boys ever since. In fact, Mr. Burgoyne was about the sole remnant of his army that got back at all. And he vowed he would never visit those Vermont boys again. They played too rough. And he never did.

Just at present Vermont is putting on considerable dog because of the fact that they are furnishing the country with a president. Calvin Coolidge, a Green Mountain Boy, who has refrained from saying more foolish things than any president we ever had.

And then there was Admiral George Dewey, born at Montpelier, who just ruined the whole Spanish navy down in Manila Bay without the loss of a single American boy and had Dewey Arches and Dewey Monuments and Dewey Memorials stuck up everywhere—until he gave his wife a house.

And then there was Joseph Smith, another Vermonter, who commenced "seeing things" when he was fourteen and finally had a personal call from the Lord (the only occasion upon which Vermont has been so honored), who told him to go out back of the icehouse at the Manchester Hotel and dig—and he did—and dug up a book that told him he was a Mormon and a natural-born sheik—and he believed it—and went out to Carthage, Illinois, where he did real well, until the former husbands of his numerous wives took him out one night and sent him to a place where he could have all the wives he wanted to.

A Vermont Boy will tackle anything—and succeed. But this is enough information for ten cents.

The History of New Hampshire

Mount Washington was the highest point in the Garden of Eden.

When the Ark finally landed, Noah stepped out, looked around and said, "Who said this was Ararat? This is Mount Washington, in New Hampshire."

And Ham took his family and went down through Dixville Notch and started Portsmouth.

And Shem went down Crawford Notch route and started Nashua.

And Jephet took the Franconia Notch route and settled at Concord.

Noah went over to Bethlehem and started a hay fever sanatorium, and as business was a little light the first two years, he spent his leisure time chiseling a big stone face way up on top of the mountain, over Echo

Lake. And you don't have to take my word for it, either. Go up and look at it—it is there yet.

The present era of New Hampshire's history starts in the year 1621, when a little fur-trading post was started at Rye. But Rye was on a rough, exposed, rocky shore, and the combination of the rock and the rye was too much, and the camp was abandoned.

The first permanent one was at Portsmouth in 1629. And that was not so darned permanent for a while.

In January 1776, six months before the Declaration of Independence, New Hampshire established the first independent state government in America. (It did not last long, but it was a good offer.)

At this time the first state seal was adopted. It consisted of a fish, a bundle of arrows, and a tree, signifying, "It Is A Poor Fish Who Won't Get Behind A Tree When The Indians Are After Him." Later on, the present one was adopted, showing a seashore, a ship, and a sunrise. As New Hampshire has only eighteen miles of seacoast, they had to pull the ship up on the shore in order to have ocean enough left for the sun to rise from.

It was the state of New Hampshire that made the United States of America a nation. It required the votes of nine states. New Hampshire cast the ninth vote. (But to offset this, they were the first to ratify the Eighteenth Amendment to its Constitution.)

PORTSMOUTH—the original name of which was Strawberry Banks, was the first permanent settlement, the first state capital, and where the peace treaty between Russia and Japan was signed. (And Russia and Japan are fighting over it yet.)

Portsmouth's greatest pride is the Portsmouth Navy Yard—situated across the river at Kittery, Maine.

NASHUA—celebrated for its historical buildings: the Nashua Opera House, erected by Julius Caesar in 903, and the American House, built by Napoleon Bonaparte's uncle, on his mother's side, in 1106.

MANCHESTER—established in 1722 by a party of Scotch, Irish, and two Englishmen, from South Boston. The Scotch built a Caledonian Hall, the Irish organized a police force, and two years later the two Englishmen had not spoken, as they had not been introduced.

CONCORD—established in 1729 under the name of Pennecook. Later changed to Rumford in honor of the Countess Rumford who lived here while perfecting her Rumford Baking Powder. And still later, in honor of her success at it, changed to Conquored. The spelling was later changed to Concord, but the pronunciation was retained in order to distinguish it from Concord, Massachusetts. The state prison at Concord stands high among our highest criminal circles, always does a capacity business, and frequently has a waiting list. In the grounds surrounding the Statehouse are many fine works of art, including the town pump.

BATH—cleanliness is next to Holderness.

EPSUM—where the Epsum Salt mines are.

HENNIKER—only place on earth of that name.

NEWPORT—a "port" fifty miles from water.

HANOVER—sometimes the letter G is inserted between the letters N and O for the benefit of the Dartmouth students.

THE WEIRS—the man that named it is dead and he never told anybody what it meant and now it is too late.

New Hampshire also specializes in Distinguished Sons and Daughters.

FRANKLIN PIERCE—born at Hillsboro; studied law; invented Dr. Pierce's Medical Discovery; got into debt, politics, and the White House.

DANIEL WEBSTER—lived in, died in, or did something in every other house within fifteen miles of Concord. (For particulars see tablets on houses.) Had upright red hair, looked like William Hearst, had a town named for him, wrote a dictionary, and made speeches.

HORACE GREELEY—invented "ringworm" whiskers, said "go West, young man," and founded the greatest bound copy of advertisements in America, the *Saturday Evening Post*.

SALMON P. CHASE—(state runs strongly to fish. Had a governor named "Bass.") Secretary of the treasury under Lincoln. Got his face on a lot of money.

CHARLES A. PILLSBURY—invented Pillsbury's Flour. Made a lot of money for himself and a lot of dough for others.

GENERAL JOHN STARK—Mollie Stark's husband.

MARY BAKER EDDY—discoverer of Christian Science, founder of the *Christian Science Monitor*, author of best-selling book since the Bible, and furnisher of more employment to builders of churches than anyone who has lived for nineteen hundred years.

New Hampshire is called the Granite State, because it is built entirely of granite, covered with a couple of inches of dirt. The New Hampshire farmer does not "till the soil," he blasts it. For nine months of the year he brings in wood, shovels snow, thaws out the pump, and wonders why Peary wanted to discover the North Pole. The other three months he blasts, plants, and hopes.

He is industrious, thrifty, and honest. Industrious because he has to be, thrifty because he has nothing to be any other way with, and honest because he was born that way.

The author of this history came from New Hampshire.

The History of Maine

Maine was named for a battleship. Although some authorities claim that it was named for a town in France where Henrietta Maria, the wife of King Charles, The One I, of England, came from. Take your choice.

The coast of Maine was the first spot on the North American continent to be seen by a white man. For in the year 986 a Norwegian fisherman got blown out to sea, got one look at this rock-bound coast, begged pardon for intruding, and went back. The name of this intrepid discoverer was Bjarne (the Norwegian way of spelling "John") Herjulfsun (Norwegian for "Johnson").

Five years later another member of the Norwegian Yacht Club decided to take a run over to America and see if this "B-Jay-B-Clothes-Jigger-B-Johnson" had told the truth about the "bluffs" they were putting up against immigration. So he did. And he landed. So it is to Leif Ericson that the honor goes of being the first white man to set foot on American soil in 1001, and he landed in Maine. And this was 491 years before Christopher Columbus, that Spanish egg-balancer, even saw the island of San Salvadore. (He has not seen North America *yet*.)

To Maine also goes the credit of the first settlement. For in the year 1500 a party of French fishermen came over and wintered at the mouth of the Kennebec River. (And even this was fifteen years before Uncle Monkeygland Ponce de Leon built the Ponce de Leon Hotel at St. Augustine, Florida.)

In 1607 Mr. George Popham came over from England and tried to start a permanent settlement at this same place. But he kept fussing around with the Indians until he did not have anything left to fuss with, and finally appeared as "the piece-de-resistance" of an Indian banquet, and that was the end of him, and the settlement.

Then on September 6, 1620, the Pilgrim Fathers made their celebrated dash from Holland to America in sixty-three days, ran onto a rock down at Plymouth, Massachusetts, landed, held a prayer meeting, and went into the antique furniture business.

There! Now you are discovered!

The coast of Maine is 250 miles long, as the crow flies. But as the fish swims, following the shoreline, it is 2500 miles.

While Maine is situated at the upper right-hand corner of the United States map, it is always spoken of as Down East.

Maine is called the "Pine Tree State," because eight-tenths of it is pine trees, one-tenth rivers and lakes. And the other tenth towns.

Maine is the only place in the world which can make "Sa" spell "Sock." For they spell it "Saco" and pronounce it "Sock-o."

Right up against this Saco they have got another town, Biddeford (named for Henry Ford's great aunt), and the two of them are so near together that only the traffic cops can tell which one is going to "sock" you with the fine.

Maine is the summer headquarters for St. Petersburg, Florida. In the fall the whole state moves back to St. Petersburg.

Probably Maine's most distinguished and most widely known son is Neal Dow, Senator Volstead's grandfather and the inventor of Prohibition, the Water Wagon, the Side Door, the Three-Mile-limit, and the Patron Saint of Bimini and Cuba.

Maine was made the first "dry" state in 1850. And it has voted "dry" ever since. And the drier it voted the wetter it got. Two of the settlements of the state are "Brewer" and "Bar Harbor"; but neither of them mean now what they were evidently originally intended to mean.

Maine has 3,145 square miles of lakes and rivers, most of them with unpronounceable names. Aroostook County potatoes are in great demand for seeding. And potato seeds come very high. Right between seedless oranges and seed pearls. Another big industry in Maine is lime. Limes are used to make limeade, gin fizzes, gin rickies, and Bacardi cocktails—if you can get the gin and the Bacardi.

Whaling used to be another leading industry. But owing to the large numbers of tourists and fishermen who have invaded the state in late years, the whales are not biting as they used to.

Among Maine's various other crops and industries are ice, spruce gum, Christmas trees, canoes, boneless codfish, Poland Water, alleged sardines, Republican majorities, country fiddlers, and tourists.

Maine has two seasons. Winter and August.

The First City of Importance in Maine as you come up from Nova Scotia is:

BAR HARBOR—it is a wild town. In addition to the prevailing arid condition of the state, there is hanging over its portals the inscription: "Abandon Autos All Ye Who Enter Here." The speed limit on the island is four miles on straightaways and two miles on corners.

KENNEBUNKPORT—the loveliest bunch of rocks on the Atlantic coast. It is here that Rupert Hughes comes to write his stories of the Wild West.

BANGOR—great lumber town. Streets full of chips. The National Republican Party always comes here for the prohibition plank in their platforms.

LEWISTON—(named for Lewis Stone, the moving picture star). Located on Mr. Andrew Scoggin's river, where it takes a sixty-foot drop. Large cotton and woolen mills. Prospectus says they have "seventy-five hundred hands" working in these mills. Allowing two hands to each person, this would make 3,750 workmen.

AUGUSTA—the state capital. Two insane asylums, including the state legislature.

BATH—and the only one in the state. But then it is too cold for bathing in Maine most of the time. In addition to bathing, they also build ships here. Good ones, too.

BRUNSWICK—Bowdoin College and Maine Medical College here. And nine miles from the only bath in the state.

CALAIS—on the St. Croix river. Named for the place in France that, fifteen minutes after you leave Dover, England, you hope you will live to reach.

CARIBOU—principal industries raising corn and making starch. Sounds like a pudding.

EASTPORT—most eastern town in America. Eighteen sardine factories. A sardine is an educated smelt. Education pays. As a lowdown ignorant smelt it is worth ten cents a bushel. As an educated, well-dressed sardine it fetches thirty cents a can.

POLAND SPRINGS—best hotel in New England. Run by the three Ricker brothers. They are Quakers. Quakers never shave. A meeting of the firm looks like an explosion in the Ostermore Mattress factory. This spring is the only thing in the state which has never gone dry. In addition to the water drunk upon the premises, enough is shipped every day to float the national debt.

PORTLAND—where the cement comes from. Portland is surrounded by islands-the islands are surrounded by forts—the forts are surrounded by the latest things in armament. If you don't believe it, try to come in, when they don't want you to. Portland has produced some real good writers. Messrs. Longfellow and Wadsworth turned out some stuff that was just as good as Ring Lardner and Octavius Roy Cohen are doing today.

OLD ORCHARD—more water. If there ever was an orchard on this beach it must have been a "pair" orchard, where the "peaches" made "dates" with the "prunes." In former years Old Orchard merchants did quite a business in bathing suits. But they say there is no money in bathing suits now. Nor much of anything else—except girls—and they are more out than in. It is claimed that more Portland marriages—and divorces—start at Old Orchard Beach than in all the rest of Maine put together.

YORK BEACH—Maine's best-known watering place. And here during July and August can be found the most interesting collection of wild, and partly wild, life indigenous to New England: Bares, Calves, Diving Venuses and Floating Flappers, Wild Women and Tame Chickens, Night Hawks, Poker Sharks, Diamond-Back Widows, Eyeless Tigers and Sightless Pigs, Oyster Pirates and Human Pelicans, and camp after camp of Wild Indians.

And these are the main things about Maine. ■

The Silence Dogood Papers

BENJAMIN FRANKLIN Although Benjamin Franklin is most readily identified with the city of Philadelphia, he was a true Bostonian, born and bred. It was there, as a teenage apprentice in his brother James's printing shop, that Franklin's literary genius— and exquisite sense of humor—first surfaced.

James Franklin published the *New-England Courant*, which printed contributions from local academics and others with a talent for pungent expression. Sixteen-year-old Benjamin decided to try his hand at writing for the newspaper. But, as he later recounted, "Being still a boy and suspecting that my brother would object to printing anything of mine in his paper if he knew it to be mine, I contrived to disguise my hand, and writing an anonymous paper I put it in at night under the door of the printing house."

Between April and October of 1722, when he was finally unmasked, Franklin had fourteen letters printed in the *Courant* under the pseudonym of Silence Dogood, who described herself as a country minister's widow with "a natural inclination to observe and reprove the faults of others, at which I have an excellent faculty."

It was not an idle boast, as can be seen from the following examples. In the first, the young Franklin takes his revenge upon an already famous Massachusetts "temple of learning" for having been denied a college education. In the second, Silence Dogood comments bitingly upon the literary shortcomings of New England's provincial prose.

Mrs. Silence Dogood
Dreams About A College

Dogood Papers, No. IV
From Monday, May 7, to Monday, May 14, 1722
An sum etiam nunc vel Græcè loqui vel Latinè docendus?
CICERO

To the Author of *The New-England Courant.*
Sir,

Discoursing the other day at dinner with my reverend boarder, for-merly mentioned (whom for distinction's sake we will call by the name of *Clericus*), concerning the education of children, I asked his advice about my young son William, whether or no I had best bestow upon him academical learning, or (as our phrase is) *bring him up at our college.* He persuaded me to do it by all means, using many weighty arguments with me and answering all the objections that I could form against it, telling me, withal, that he did not doubt but that the lad would take his learning very well and not idle away his time as too many there nowadays do. These words of Clericus gave me a curiosity to inquire a little more strictly into the present circum-stances of that famous seminary of learning, but the information which he gave me was neither pleasant nor such as I expected.

As soon as dinner was over, I took a solitary walk into my orchard, still ruminating on Clericus's discourse with much consideration, until I came to my usual place of retirement under the great apple tree, where, having seated myself and carelessly laid my head on a verdant bank, I fell by degrees into a soft and undisturbed slumber. My waking thoughts remained with me in my sleep, and before I awakened again, I dreamt the following dream.

I fancied I was traveling over pleasant and delightful fields and mead-ows and through many small country towns and villages, and as I passed along, all places resounded with the fame of the Temple of Learning. Every peasant who had wherewithal was preparing to send one of his children at least to this famous place, and in this case most of them consulted their own purses instead of their children's capacities; so that I observed a great many, yea, the most part of those who were traveling thither, were little better than dunces and blockheads. Alas! Alas!

At length I entered upon a spacious plain, in the midst of which was erected a large and stately edifice. It was to this that a great company of youths from all parts of the country were going; so, stepping in among the crowd, I passed on with them and presently arrived at the gate.

The passage was kept by two sturdy porters named *Riches* and *Poverty*, and the latter obstinately refused to give entrance to any who had not first gained the favor of the former; so that, I observed, many who came even to the very gate were obliged to travel back again as ignorant as they came, for want of this necessary qualification. However, as a spectator I gained admittance and with the rest entered directly into the temple.

In the middle of the great hall stood a stately and magnificent throne, which was ascended to by two high and difficult steps. On the top of it sat *Learning* in awful state; she was appareled wholly in black and surrounded almost on every side with innumerable volumes in all languages. She seemed very busily employed in writing something on half a sheet of paper, and upon enquiry I understood she was preparing a paper called, *The New-England Courant*. On her right hand sat *English*, with a pleasant smiling countenance and handsomely attired, and on her left were seated several antique figures with their faces veiled. I was considerably puzzled to guess who they were, until one informed me (who stood beside me) that those figures on her left hand were *Latin*, *Greek*, *Hebrew*, etc., and that they were very much reserved and seldom or never unveiled their faces here, and then to few or none, though most of those who have in this place acquired so much learning as to distinguish them from *English* pretended to an intimate acquaintance with them. I then inquired of him what could be the reason why they continued veiled, in this place especially. He pointed to the foot of the throne, where I saw *Idleness*, attended with *Ignorance*, and these (he informed me) were they who first veiled them and still kept them so.

Now I observed that the whole tribe who entered into the temple with me began to climb the throne, but the work proving troublesome and difficult to most of them, they withdrew their hands from the plow and contented themselves to sit at the foot, with Madam *Idleness* and her maid *Ignorance*, until those who were assisted by diligence and a docible temper had well-nigh got up the first step. But the time drawing nigh in which they could no way avoid ascending, they were fain to crave the assistance of those who had got up before them, and who, for the reward perhaps of a pint of milk or a piece of plum-cake, lent the lubbers a helping hand and sat them in the eye of the world upon a level with themselves.

The other step being in the same manner ascended and the usual ceremonies at an end, every beetle-scull seemed well satisfied with his own portion of learning, though perhaps he was e'en just as ignorant as ever. And now the time of their departure being come, they marched out of doors to make room for another company who waited for entrance. And I, having seen all that was to be seen, quitted the hall likewise and went to make my observations on those who were just gone out before me.

Some I perceived took to merchandising, others to traveling, some to one thing, some to another, and some to nothing; and many of them from henceforth, for want of patrimony, lived as poor as churchmice, being unable to dig and ashamed to beg, and to live by their wits it was impossible. But the most part of the crowd went along a large beaten path, which led to a temple at the further end of the plain called the *Temple of Theology*. The business of those who were employed in this temple being laborious and painful, I wondered exceedingly to see so many go toward it; but while I was pondering this matter in my mind, I spied *Pecunia* behind a curtain beckoning to them with her hand, which sight immediately satisfied me for whose sake it was that a great part of them (I will not say all) traveled that road. In this temple I saw nothing worth mentioning, except the ambitious and fraudulent contrivances of *Plagius*, who (notwithstanding he had been severely reprehended for such practices before) was diligently transcribing some eloquent paragraphs out of Tillotson's works, etc., to embellish his own.

Now I bethought myself in my sleep that it was time to be at home, and as I fancied I was traveling back thither, I reflected in my mind on the extreme folly of those parents who, blind to their children's dullness and insensible of the solidity of their skulls, because they think their purses can afford it, will needs send them to the Temple of Learning, where, for want of a suitable genius, they learn little more than how to carry themselves handsomely and enter a room genteelly (which might as well be acquired at a dancing school), and from whence they return, after abundance of trouble and charge, as great blockheads as ever, only more proud and self-conceited.

While I was in the midst of these unpleasant reflections, Clericus (who with a book in his hand was walking under the trees) accidentally awakened me; to him I related my dream with all its particulars, and he, without much study, presently interpreted it, assuring me that it was a lively representation of Harvard College, Etc.

I remain, Sir, Your humble Servant,

Silence Dogood

Excerpt from Dogood Papers, No. VII

A RECEIPT TO MAKE A
NEW ENGLAND FUNERAL ELEGY

For the Title of your Elegy: Of these you may have enough ready made to your hands, but if you should choose to make it yourself, you must be sure not to omit the words AEtatis Suae, which will beautify it exceedingly.

For the Subject of your Elegy: Take one of your neighbors who has lately departed this life; it is no great matter at what age the party died, but it will be best if he went away suddenly, being killed, drowned, or frozen to death.

Having chosen the person, take all his virtues, excellencies, etc., and if he have not enough, you may borrow some to make up a sufficient quantity. To these add his last words, dying expressions, etc., if they are to be had; mix all these together, and be sure you strain them well. Then season all with a handful or two of melancholy expressions, such as, "dreadful, deadly, cruel cold death, unhappy fate, weeping eyes, etc." Having mixed all these ingredients well, put them into the empty skull of some young Harvard (but in case you have ne'er one at hand, you may use your own); there let them ferment for the space of a fortnight, and by that time they will be incorporated into a body, which take out, and having prepared a sufficient quantity of double rhymes, such as power, flower; quiver, shiver; grieve us, leave us; tell you, excel you; expeditions, physicians; fatigue him, intrigue him; etc., you must spread all upon paper, and if you can procure a scrap of Latin to put at the end, it will garnish it mightily. Then having affixed your name at the bottom, with a Moestus Composuit, you will have an excellent elegy.

N. B. This receipt will serve when a female is the subject of your elegy, provided you borrow a greater quantity of virtues, excellencies, etc.

Sir,

Your Servant,

Silence Dogood

The Adventures of Jonathan Corncob

JONATHAN CORNCOB The author of *The Adventures of Jonathan Corncob*, first published in London in 1787, is unknown. Noel Perrin, a Dartmouth College professor of English who rediscovered the book nearly two centuries after its first appearance, theorizes that it was the work of a British naval officer stationed in New England during the American Revolution. Others have suggested it was an exiled American Loyalist.

Either way, the mocking tone of the book suggests the author was not altogether smitten with the new nation or its people. "Jonathan" was a common term of derision used by the British for rustic Americans, and "Corncob" clearly served as a scornful reinforcement of the sentiment. Still, the lusty rapscallion who is the hero of these tales—or anti-hero, really—possesses a winsomeness that may have been unintended by the author.

■ Some great men have been suckled in a wood, as was the immortal founder of Rome, and others in a stable, but as I was neither destined for the founder of an empire nor of a religion, I opened my eyes on this wicked world in as snug a farmhouse as any in Massachusetts Bay. My honored mother, Mrs. Charity Corncob, was an excellent woman: she bred like a rabbit, scolded all day like a cat in love, and snored all night as loud as the foreman of a jury on a tedious trial. During her pregnancy, she dreamed that she was brought to bed of a screech owl, and went to consult an old woman in the neighborhood who passed for a witch. The old woman assured her that her dream was an unlucky prognostic and told her that if I was not cut off in my youth, I should certainly die at a more advanced age, either by some unforeseen accident or of some violent disease. My poor mother burst into tears and asked her if there was no way of averting so cruel a destiny. The old woman answered in the negative, and Mrs. Corncob returned home much distressed at what she had heard. No sooner was I born than I began to cry, and this circumstance tended not a little to fortify my mother's faith in the prediction of the ancient sibyl.

"Poor dear boy," said Mrs. Corncob, sighing. "Oh! that ever I should be doomed to be the mother of so unlucky a child. However, one comfort is that he cannot be drowned while he carries about him the caul that covered his face when he was born."

But when I was a year and a half old, and she saw me frequently fall and pull the chairs upon my back, she had no longer any doubt of the fatal prophecy. Wretched as she was made by these gloomy omens, she did not communicate her fears to my honored father, Mr. Habakkuk Corncob, as she was apprehensive of hurting his health, already in a weakly state, for he had been troubled with the green sickness ever since a disappointment in love he met with at the age of two and twenty.

Mr. Habakkuk Corncob was a rigid Presbyterian; he considered any man who played at cards as irrevocably d——n'd, as well as anyone who walked out on a Sunday. He employed every part of that day that was not spent at the meetinghouse in reading the book of Leviticus for the instruction of his family, and thought himself peculiarly indulgent when, by way of amusement, he favored us with the history of Shadrach, Meshach, and Abednego, or a few pages of the *Pilgrim's Progress*. These were the only two books he considered as worthy his attention, except indeed that kind of almanac in which the different parts of the body are placed opposite the days of the month. This almanac was his oracle and directed all his operations: He never cut his nails but on the day marked Hands, so that by the time the month came round, his claws were as long as those of a mandarin. The only day on which he profited by the privileges of a husband was that indicated by Secrets, and this perhaps was the reason why my mother, Mrs. Charity Corncob, poor woman, sometimes advised him to take an almanac of another kind.

Though my father's state of health was infirm, it was much superior to that of my aunt, Lord have mercy on her soul! She had been thirty years troubled with an asthma, which unluckily turned to a consumption just when she had hopes of getting rid of it. Whether it was owing to her ill health, or natural disposition, I know not, but she was a plague to everybody in the house, from Mr. Habakkuk, my father, to our black cur dog.

One day, after quarreling with my father and mother and boxing the ears of every child in the house, finding herself left without any person to scold, she jumped up and kicked the cat round the room. The cat escaped out of the window, and my poor aunt was obliged to take up the poker and poke the fire out. She might perhaps have lived somewhat longer if she had not fallen into a dispute with my father about her age. My father asserted strenuously that she was fifty-two years old; my aunt said she was only forty-eight.

"Fifty-two," said my father.

"Forty-eight," said my aunt.

"Fifty-two," said my father again.

At length my aunt, finding herself out of breath, mustered up all her strength, with a determination of having the *last word*, called out forty-eight and expired. At this time I was only seven years old, and when I heard the news, I came jumping and laughing into the room. "Old Bathsheba is dead," said I, "*ha! ha! ha!*"

My mother, who was making a violent lamentation, ran up to me and, letting down my breeches, laid me across her knee and flogged me till I joined my tears to those of the rest of the family, though I did not very well understand why I was obliged to cry at the death of a person whom everybody in the house had wished dead a thousand times a day.

All the neighbors crowded to our house to condole with us, and as they unanimously said my aunt was in heaven, the whole family was soon consoled, and the next day we were all as merry as ever.

Providence had certainly ordained that my aunt Bathsheba should be as great a plague to us when dead as she was when living. A few days after she was buried, my father took his gun down from the hooks over the chimney, with the intention of shooting a few squirrels for our supper. About half an hour after, he rushed pale and breathless into the room, threw himself into a chair, and called for a glass of New England rum. My mother and the rest of us, alarmed at his situation, asked all together what was the matter. As soon as he recovered a little from his fright, he told us that he had seen the spirit of Bathsheba. My mother started; my four brothers, my two sisters and myself all opened our mouths.

"Yes," continued he, "I have seen the spirit of Bathsheba; I am sure of it. I was scarcely in the wood before I met with a large black wild turkey; I immediately cocked my gun, put it to my shoulder, and was going to *blaze away*, when the turkey called out 'forty-eight' as plain as it could speak, and ran off towards the churchyard. I swear it could be nobody but Bathsheba, for it had just her waddling way of walking."

My father and mother were so afraid of a visit from the wild turkey that for a long time after they kept a light all night in their bedroom, which, as far as it related to the bedroom, had the desired effect, but did not prevent my mother from seeing Bathsheba in the dairy. Mrs. Corncob was found there in a swoon by my eldest sister, and as soon as she recovered her speech, told us that she had seen Bathsheba, in the shape of a black cat, stealing cream.

"What made me sure of it," said my mother, "was her having only one eye like my poor dear cousin, and her coming to the dairy exactly at the time Bathsheba used to drink her bowl of milk in the afternoon." In a short time there was not one of us that had not seen our aunt in the shape of something black, and we no longer dared to go to bed till we had visited every room in the house and made a very scrupulous search after my aunt Bathsheba.

My father, who had never learned to write, often regretted that he was not scholar enough to lay Bathsheba's ghost and determined that my education should not be neglected, especially as he destined me to super-intend his shop, or as it is called in New England, his *store*, for he was not only farmer, but merchant, and sold butter, cheese, spike-nails, rye meal, shuttlecocks, New England rum, hartshorn shavings, broadcloth, gunpow-der, and yellow basilicon. Besides the inferior parts of education, such as reading, writing, and arithmetic, I studied Latin, and at the end of seven years made very tolerable nonsense verses. I was considered, in Massachu-setts Bay, as a prodigy of learning and was not less distinguished for my address in all the fashionable exercises and amusements of that country. I excelled in walking in snowshoes, driving a sled, shooting squirrels, and bobbing for eels; but of all my amusements, none had such charms for me as *bundling*.

I had already bundled with half the girls in the neighborhood when my evil genius led me to pay a visit to Miss Desire Slawbunk one evening when her father and mother were gone out. Miss Slawbunk was an Ameri-can beauty; her complexion was a little dusky, her features regular, and she had a certain languor in her look that was not unpleasing. Unfortu-nately, she preferred molasses to all other sauces: whether she ate pickled pork or kidney beans, she never failed to call for molasses, and owing to this immoderate use of it had lost six of her front teeth above, and six below.

"I swear now, Miss Desire," said I, "I am come to *tarry* a little with you."

"I guess you *be* very welcome, Mr. Jonathan."

"It is a *considerable* of a cold night."

"Yes," answered Desire, "*some cold.*"

This remark of the coldness of the weather made the lady observe that her fire was by no means brilliant. After in vain arranging the green wood, she stooped down before the fire in a sitting posture, and began puffing with her apron. It would not do, and Miss Slawbunk, wishing to produce more wind, had recourse to her petticoats. The inexorable logs still refused to burn. Miss Slawbunk grew angry, and the undulations of her petticoats grew proportionately wider and more violent. It was then that, sitting in the chimney corner, my discoveries became every moment more interesting, every faint gleam of the languid fire presenting to my eyes a soft assem-blage of light and shade that vied with all the snow and forests of the continent. Without improving the fire, she had produced an equal effect: her exertions had warmed herself, and what I had seen had changed my aguish shivering to a high fever. Though I had not come with any such intention, I could not help proposing to bundle. Miss Slawbunk consented, smiling very kindly but, as you will suppose, without shewing her teeth.

We undressed according to the rules of bundling, scrupulously reserving the breeches and underpetticoat. Soon after we were in bed, my hand happening to touch Desire, she started from me.

"Miss Slawbunk," said I, "it seems to me that you be *considerable* ticklish."

Miss Slawbunk denied it.

To prove my assertion, I began to tickle her under the fifth rib. She tickled me in her turn, and by degrees we carried the pleasantry so far that, without being aware of the consequences, we exceeded all the bounds of bundling. Heaven only can tell what became of the petticoat during the night, but in the morning we found it kicked out of the foot of the bed. A few months after, it grew too short for Miss Slawbunk; a committee was assembled, and I was sentenced, for this breach of the laws of bundling, to marry the lady, or pay a fine of 50& currency.

Not being inclined to comply with the first proposal, and being unable to pay the fine, I sold to some British officers, prisoners on parole in the neighborhood, a quantity of my father's New England spirits and exchanged with them all the brown paper money of the Congress I could collect, for twenty hard dollars, which, as they were a rarity in that country, I secured in the waistband of my breeches, and with this small fortune determined to set off for New York, then in the possession of the British troops. ■

NEW ENGLAND IN THE REVOLUTION

The Revolutionary War

BILL NYE Edgar Wilson ("Bill") Nye, born in Maine in 1850, redefined written American humor in the latter half of the nineteenth century. Until Nye came along, much of the popular comic literature of the day depended upon a self-mocking mixture of mangled grammar and semiphonetic spelling. Nye changed all that by showing that American humorous writing could be both funny and literate.

Nye began his writing career in Wyoming as editor and publisher of the *Laramie Boomerang*, a newspaper named after his mule. His comic pieces were eventually picked up by other papers, and he returned East to become an enormously popular—and wealthy—syndicated columnist.

Nye also appeared on the lecture circuit and produced several best-sellers, mostly collections of his columns. But his two most successful books were original comic histories of Europe and the United States. He had barely completed work on the latter, from which the following piece is taken, when he died at age forty-five.

■ William Pitt was partly to blame for the Revolutionary War. He claimed that the Colonists ought not to manufacture so much as a horseshoe nail except by permission of Parliament.

It was already hard enough to be a Colonist, without the privilege of expressing one's self even to an Indian without being fined. But when we pause to think that England seemed to demand that the Colonist should take the long wet walk to Liverpool during a busy season of the year to get his horse shod, we say at once that P. Henry was right when he exclaimed that the war was inevitable and moved that permission be granted for it to come.

Then came the Stamp Act, making almost everything illegal that was not written on stamp paper furnished by the maternal country.

John Adams, Patrick Henry, and John Otis made speeches regarding the situation. Bells were tolled, and fasting and prayer marked the first of November, the day for the law to go into effect.

These things alarmed England for the time, and the Stamp Act was repealed; but the king, who had been pretty free with his money and had entertained a good deal, began to look out for a chance to tax the Colonists and ordered his Exchequer Board to attend to it.

Patrick Henry got excited and said in an early speech, "Caesar had his Brutus, Charles the First his Cromwell, and George the Third ————." Here he paused and took a long swig of pure water and added, looking at the newspaper reporters, "If this be treason, make the most of it." He also said that George the Third might profit by their example. A good many would like to know what he started out to say, but it is too hard to determine.

Boston ladies gave up tea and used the dried leaves of the raspberry, and the girls of 1777 graduated in homespun. Could the iron heel of despotism crunch such a spirit of liberty as that? Scarcely. In one family at Newport 487 yards of cloth and thirty-six pairs of stockings were spun and made in eighteen months.

When the war broke out, it is estimated that each Colonial soldier had twenty-seven pairs of blue woolen socks with white double heels and toes. Does the intelligent reader believe that "Tommy Atkins," with two pairs of socks "and hit a-rainin'," could whip men with twenty-seven pairs each? Not without restoratives.

Troops were now sent to restore order. They were clothed by the British government but boarded around with the Colonists. This was irritating to the people, because they had never met or called on the British troops. Again, they did not know the troops were coming and had made no provision for them.

Boston was considered the hotbed of the rebellion, and General Gage was ordered to send two regiments of troops there. He did so, and a fight ensued in which three citizens were killed.

In looking over this incident, we must not forget that in those days three citizens went a good deal farther than they do now.

The fight, however, was brief. General Gage, getting into a side street, separated from his command, and, coming out on the Common abruptly, he tried eight or nine more streets, but he came out each time on the Common, until, torn with conflicting emotions, he hired a Herdic, which took him around the corner to his quarters.

On December 16, 1773, occurred the tea party at Boston, which must have been a good deal livelier than those of today. The historian regrets that he was not there; he would have tried to be the life of the party.

England had finally so arranged the price of tea that, including the tax, it was cheaper in America than in the old country. This exasperated the patriots, who claimed that they were confronted by a theory and not a condition. At Charleston this tea was stored in damp cellars, where it spoiled. New York and Philadelphia returned their ships, but the British would not allow any shenanegin', as George III so tersely termed it, in Boston.

Therefore a large party met in Faneuil Hall and decided that the tea should not be landed. A party made up as Indians and, going on board, threw the tea overboard. Boston Harbor, as far out as the Bug Light, even today is said to be carpeted with tea grounds.

George III now closed Boston harbor and made General Gage governor of Massachusetts. The Virginia Assembly murmured at this and was dissolved and sent home without its mileage.

Those opposed to royalty were termed Whigs, those in favor were called Tories. Now they are called Chappies or Authors.

On the fifth of September 1774, the first Continental Congress assembled at Philadelphia and was entertained by the Clover Club. Congress acted slowly even then, and after considerable delay resolved that the conduct of Great Britain was, under the circumstances, uncalled for. It also voted to hold no intercourse with Great Britain and decided not to visit Shakespeare's grave unless the mother-country should apologize.

In 1775, on the nineteenth of April, General Gage sent out troops to see about some military stores at Concord, but at Lexington he met with a company of minutemen gathering on the village green. Major Pitcairn, who was in command of the Tommies, rode up to the minutemen and, drawing his bright new Sheffield sword, exclaimed, "Disperse, you rebels! Throw down your arms and disperse!" or some such remark as that.

The Americans hated to do that, so they did not. In the skirmish that ensued, seven of their number were killed.

Thus opened the Revolutionary War—a contest which but for the earnestness and irritability of the Americans would have been extremely brief. It showed the relative difference between the fighting qualities of soldiers who fight for two pounds ten shillings per month and those who fight because they have lost their temper.

The regulars destroyed the stores, but on the way home they found every rock pile hid an old-fashioned gun and a minuteman. This shows that there must have been an enormous number of minutemen then. All the English who got back to Boston were those who went out to reinforce the original command.

The news went over the country like wildfire. These are the words of the historian. Really, that is a poor comparison, for wildfire doesn't jump rivers and bays, or get up and eat breakfast by candlelight in order to be on the road and spread the news.

General Putnam left a pair of tired steers standing in the furrow and rode 100 miles without feed or water to Boston.

Twenty thousand men were soon at work building entrenchments around Boston so that the English troops could not get out to the suburbs where many of them resided.

I will now speak of the battle of Bunker Hill.

This battle occurred June 17. The Americans heard that their enemy intended to fortify Bunker Hill, and so they determined to do it themselves, in order to have it done in a way that would be a credit to the town.

A body of men under Colonel Prescott, after prayer by the president of Harvard University, marched to Charlestown Neck. They decided to fortify Breed's Hill, as it was more commanding, and all night long they kept on fortifying. The surprise of the English at daylight was well worth going from Lowell to witness.

Howe sent three thousand men across and formed them on the landing. He marched them up the hill to within ten rods of the earthworks, when it occurred to Prescott that it would now be the appropriate thing to fire. He made a statement of that kind to his troops, and those of the enemy who were alive went back to Charlestown. But that was no place for them, as they had previously set it afire, so they came back up the hill, where they were once more well received and tendered the freedom of a future state.

Three times the English did this, when the ammunition in the fortifications gave out, and they charged with fixed bayonets and reinforcements.

The Americans were driven from the field, but it was a victory after all. It united the Colonies and made them so vexed at the English that it took some time to bring on an era of good feeling.

Lord Howe, referring afterwards to this battle, said that the Americans did not stand up and fight like the regulars, suggesting that thereafter the Colonial army should arrange itself in the following manner before a battle!

However, the suggestion was not acted on. The Colonial soldiers declined to put on a bright red coat and a pillbox cap that kept falling off in battle, thus delaying the carnage, but preferred to wear homespun which was of a neutral shade and shoot their enemy from behind stumps. They said it was all right to dress up for a muster, but they preferred their working clothes for fighting. After the war a statistician made the estimate that nine percent of the British troops were shot while ascertaining if their caps were on straight.*

General Israel Putnam was known as the champion roughrider of his day, and once when hotly pursued rode down three flights of steps, which, added to the flight he made from the English soldiers, made four flights. Putnam knew not fear or cowardice, and his name even today is the synonym for valor and heroism. ■

*The authority given for this statement, I admit, is meager, but it is as accurate as many of the figures by means of which people prove things.—B. N.

Paul Revere's Ride

ROBERT C. BENCHLEY Although we associate Robert Benchley (1889–1945) with New York and Hollywood, his roots were in
New England. This prolific essayist, humorist, columnist, drama
critic, actor, and screenwriter was born in Worcester, Massachusetts, and schooled at Harvard.

Benchley is best known today for his collections of comic
essays, drawn from newspaper and magazine pieces written in the
1920s and 1930s—publications ranging from the popular *New York
World* to the old pre-Luce humorous magazine *Life* to the sophisticated and literary *The New Yorker*. He achieved popular success
with a series of absurd movie shorts that he wrote and starred in,
including the 1935 Oscar-winning *How to Sleep*.

Moviemaking bored and depressed him, however, and he
was really only happy writing for the print media. He was at his
funniest when depicting himself as the classic victim of life's most
ordinary frustrations and humiliations. One critic described his
tragicomic approach this way: "King Lear loses a throne; Benchley
loses a filling."

How a Modest Go-Getter Did His
Bit for the Juno Acid Bath Corporation

Following are the salesman's report sheets sent into the home office in
New York by Thaddeus Olin, agent for the Juno Acid Bath Corporation. Mr.
Olin had the New England territory during the spring of 1775, and these
report sheets are dated April 16, 17, 18, and 19 of that year.

April 16, 1775
Boston

Called on the following engravers this a.m.: Boston Engraving Co.,
E.H. Hosstetter, Theodore Platney, Paul Revere, Benjamin B. Ashley, and
Roger Durgin.

Boston Engraving Co. are all taken care of for their acid.

E. H. Hosstetter took three tins of acid No. 4 on trial and renewed his old order of 7 Queen-Biters.

Theodore Platney has gone out of business since my last trip.

Paul Revere was not in. The man in his shop said that he was busy with some sort of local shindig. Said I might catch him in tomorrow morning.

The Benjamin Ashley people said they were satisfied with their present product and contemplated no change.

Roger Durgin died last March.

Things are pretty quiet in Boston right now.

April 17

Called on Boston Engraving people again to see if they might not want to try some Daisy No. 3. Mr. Lithgo was interested and said to come in tomorrow when Mr. Lithgo, Senior, would be there.

Paul Revere was not in. He had been in for a few minutes before the shop opened and had left word that he would be up at Sam Adams's in case anyone wanted him. Went up to the Adams place, but the girl there said that Mr. Revere and Mr. Adams had gone over to Mr. Dawes's place on Milk Street. Went to Dawes's place, but the man there said Dawes and Adams and Revere were in conference. There seems to be some sort of parade or something they are getting up, something to do with the opening of the new footbridge to Cambridge, I believe.

Things are pretty quiet here in Boston, except for the trade from the British fleet, which is out in the harbor.

Spent the evening looking around in the coffee houses. Everyone here is cribbage-crazy. All they seem to think of is cribbage, cribbage, cribbage.

April 18

To the Boston Engraving Company and saw Mr. Lithgo, Senior. He seemed interested in the Daisy No. 3 acid and said to drop in again later in the week.

Paul Revere was out. His assistant said that he knew that Mr. Revere was in need of a new batch of acid and had spoken to him about our Vulcan No. 2 and said he might try some. I would have to see Mr. Revere personally, he said, as Mr. Revere makes all purchases himself. He said that he thought I could catch him over at the Dawes place.

Tried the Dawes place, but they said that he and Mr. Revere had gone over to the livery stable on State Street.

Went to the livery stable but Revere had gone. They said he had engaged a horse for tonight for some sort of entertainment he was taking part in. The hostler said he heard Mr. Revere say to Mr. Dawes that they might as well go up to the North Church and see if everything was all set; so I gather it is a church entertainment.

Followed them up to the North Church, but there was nobody there except the caretaker, who said that he thought I could catch Mr. Revere over at Charlestown late that night. He described him to me so that I would know him and said that he probably would·be on horseback. As it seemed to me to be pretty important that we land the Revere order for Vulcan No. 2, I figured out that whatever inconvenience it might cause me to go over to Charlestown or whatever added expense to the firm would be justified.

Spent the afternoon visiting several printing establishments, but none of them do any engraving.

Things are pretty quiet here in Boston.

Went over to Charlestown after supper and hung around the "Bell in Hand" tavern looking for Mr. Revere. Met a man there who used to live in Peapack, New Jersey, and we got to talking about what a funny name for a town that was. Another man said that in Massachusetts there was actually a place called Podunk, up near Worcester. We had some very good cheese and talked over names of towns for a while. Then the second man, the one who knew about Podunk, said he had to go as he had a date with a man. After he had left I happened to bring the conversation around to the fact that I was waiting for a Mr. Paul Revere, and the first man told me that I had been talking to him for half an hour and that he had just gone.

I rushed out to the corner, but the man who keeps the watering-trough there said that someone answering Mr. Revere's description had just galloped off on a horse in the direction of Medford. Well, this just made me determined to land that order for Juno Acid Bath Corporation or die in the attempt. So I hired a horse at the tavern stable and started off toward Medford.

Just before I hit Medford I saw a man standing out in his nightshirt in front of his house, looking up the road. I asked him if he had seen anybody who looked like Mr. Revere. He seemed pretty sore and said some crazy coot had just ridden by and knocked at his door and yelled something that he couldn't understand and that if he caught him he'd break his back. From his description of the horse I gathered that Mr. Revere was the man, so I galloped on.

A lot of people in Medford Town were up and standing in front of their houses, cursing like the one I had just seen. It seems that Mr. Revere had gone along the roadside, knocking on doors and yelling something which nobody understood, and then galloping on again.

"Some goddam drunk," said one of the Medfordites, and they all went back to bed.

I wasn't going to be cheated out of my order now, no matter what happened, and I don't think that Mr. Revere could have been drunk, because while he was with us at the "Bell in Hand," he had only four short ales. He had a lot of cheese, though.

Something seemed to have been the matter with him, however, because in every town that I rode through I found people just going back to bed after having been aroused up out of their sleep by a mysterious rider. I didn't tell them that it was Mr. Revere, or that it was probably some stunt to do with the shindig that he and Mr. Dawes were putting on for the North Church. I figured out that it was a little publicity stunt.

Finally, just as I got into Lexington, I saw my man getting off his horse at a house right alongside the Green. I rushed up and caught him just as he was going in. I introduced myself and told him that I represented the Juno Acid Bath Corporation of New York and asked him if he could give me a few minutes, as I had been following him all the way from Charlestown and had been to his office three days in succession. He said that he was busy right at that minute, but that if I wanted to come along with him upstairs he would talk business on the way. He asked me if I wasn't the man he had been talking to at the "Bell in Hand," and I said yes and asked him how Podunk was. This got him in good humour, and he said that we might as well sit right down then and that he would get someone else to do what he had to do. So he called a manservant and told him to go right upstairs, wake up Mr. Hancock and Mr. Adams, and tell them to get up, and no fooling. "Keep after them, Sambo," he said, "and don't let them roll over and go to sleep again. It's very important."

So we sat down in the living room, and I got out our statement of sales for 1774 and showed him that, in face of increased competition, Juno had practically doubled its output. "There must be some reason for an acid outselling its competitors three to one," I said, "and that reason, Mr. Revere, is that a Juno product is a guaranteed product." He asked me about the extra sixpence a tin, and I asked him if he would rather pay a sixpence less and get an inferior grade of acid, and he said "no." So I finally landed an order of three dozen tins of Vulcan No. 2 and a dozen jars of Acme Silver Polish, as Mr. Revere is a silversmith, also, on the side.

Took a look around Lexington before I went back to Boston, but didn't see any engraving plants. Lexington is pretty quiet right now.

Respectfully submitted,
THADDEUS OLIN

Attached
Expense Voucher
Juno Acid Bath Corporation, New York

Thaddeus Olin, Agent

Hotel in Boston		15S.
Stage fare		30S.
Meals (4 days)		28S.
Entertaining prospects	£3	4S.
Horse rent, Charlestown to Lexington and		
return	£2	6S.
Total Expense	£9	3S.
To Profit on three dozen tins of Vulcan No. 2 and		18S.
One dozen jars Acme Silver Polish		4S.
	£1	2S.
Net Loss	£8	1S.

The Spirit of '75
Letters of a Minuteman

DONALD OGDEN STEWART The versatile Donald Ogden
Stewart was a successful author, actor, and playwright whose most
conspicuous talent was in the specialized field of adapting books
and stage plays for the movies. His script for The Philadelphia Story
earned him an Academy Award for best screenplay of 1940.

One of Stewart's many books was A Parody Outline of History,
published in 1921, in which he rendered accounts of several American historical events in the styles of different popular contemporary authors.

In the Manner of Ring Lardner

Friend Ethen—

Well Ethen you will be surprised O. K. to hear I & the wife took a little
trip down to Boston last wk. to a T. party & I guess you are thinking we will
be getting the swelt hed over being ast to a T. party. In Boston.

Well Ethen if you think that why you will be a 100 mi. offen the track
because Ethen I and Prudence aint the kind that gets a swelt hed over being
ast any wares like some of are naybers up here when they are ast any wares
so you see Ethen even if we had been ast any wares we wouldnt of had no
swelt hed. On acct of being ast any wares.

Well last Thurs. I and Prudence drove old Bessy down to Boston Bessy
is are horse see Ethen which is about 13 mi. from here Boston I mean Ethen
as the crow flys only no crow would ever fly to Boston if he could help it
because all the crows that ever flew to Boston was shot by them lousie
taverin keepers to make meals out of Ethen I never tast it nothing so rotten
in my life as the meals they give us there & the priceis would knock your I
out. 3 shillings for a peace of stake about as big as your I, and 4 pence for
a cup of coffy. The streets aint the only thing about Boston thats crook it.
Them taverin keepers is crook it to I mean see Ethen.

After supper I & her was walking a round giving the town the double O when we seen that Fanny Ewell Hall was all lit up like Charley Davis on Sat. night & I says to Prudence lets go inside I think its free and she says I bet you knowed it was free al right befor you ast me & sure enough it was free only I hadnt knowed it before only I guess that Prudence knows that when I say a thing it is generally O. K. Well Fanny Ewell Hall was pack jam full of people & we couldnt see nothing because there was a cockide stiff standing right in front of us & jumping up & down & yelling No T. No T. at the top of his lunges & Prudence says well why dont you take coffy or milk & for Gods sake stay offen my foot & he turns to her & says maddam do you want T. & slavery & she says no coffy & a hot dog just kidding him see Ethen & he says maddam no T. shall ever land & she says no but my husbend will in a bout 1 min. & I was just going to plank him 1 when the door behint us bust open & a lot of indyans come in yelling every body down to Grifins worf there is going to be a T. party only Ethen they wasnt indyans at all but jest wite men drest up to look like indyans & I says to a fello those aint indyans & he says no how did you guess it & I says because I have seen real indyans many a time & he says to a nother fello say Bill here is a man who says them aint real indyans & the other fello says gosh I dont believe it & they laffed only the laff was on them Ethen because they wasnt real indyans & that is only tipical of how you cant tell these Boston swelt heds nothing & I guess if they had ever seen a real indyan they would of known better than to laff. Well I and Prudence follered the crowd down to Grifins worf & them indyans which was only wite men drest up clumb onto a ship there & begun throwing the cargo into Boston harbor & I says to a fello what is in them boxes & he says T. & I says well why are they throwing it away & he says because they do not want to pay the tacks which is about as sensable Ethen if I was to rite a lot of letters & then as fast as I rote 1 I would tare it up because I did not want to pay for a stamp. Well I says somebody ought to catch h—ll for this & he says are you a torie & I seen he was trying to kid me & I says no I am a congregationalis & a loyal subject of king Geo. Rex & he says o I thought you was a torie & a lot of fellos who was with him give him the laff because he hadnt been abel to kid me. Well after a whiles he says the indyans seem to be about threw & I says yes only they aint indyans & the laff was on him again & he seen it wasnt no use to try & kid me & Prudence says come on lets beat it & on the way home I says I bet them Boston birds will feel small when they find out that those wasnt indyans at all & she act it like she was mad about something & says well they cant blame you for not trying to tell them & its a wonder you didnt hire Fanny Ewell Hall while you was about it & I says o is it & I might know youd get sore because I was the 1st to find out about the indyans being wite men in disgised & she says yes I suppose if somebody was to paint stripes on a cow you would make a speach about it & say that you had discovered that it wasnt no tiger & I wish I had been 1 of them indyans tonight because I would of loved to of beened you with a Tommy Hawk & I says o you would would you & she seen it wasnt no use to argue with me & anyway Ethen nobody would be fool enough to paint stripes on a cow unless maybe they was born in Boston. Well Ethen thats the way it goes & when you do put one over on the wife they want to hit you with a Tommy Hawk with best rgds.

Ed

Friend Ethen—

No matter what a married man does in this world he gets in wrong & I suppose if I was to die tonight Prudence would bawl me out for not having let her know I was going to do it & just because I joined the minit men the other eve. she has been acting like as if I had joined the Baptis Church & I bet you are saying what in the h—ll is a minit man. Well Ethen I will tell you. The other night I says to Prudence I think I will drive over to Lexington to get Bessy shodd. Bessy is are horse see Ethen. Well she says you will do nothing of the kind because all you want to do in Lexington is get a snoot ful & if you think I am going to wate up all night while you get boiled well you have got another guess coming. She says the last time you had Bessy shodd the naybers are talking about it yet & I says do you mean because I & Charley Davis was singing & having a little fun & she says no because nobody wouldnt call that singing & do you call it a little fun when you brought Bessy up stares with you to show me how well she had been shodd at 3 A.M. in the morning answer me that which is only her way of exagerating things Ethen because we didnt bring Bessy only as far as the stares & I only did it because Charley had been drinking a little to much & I didnt want to iritate him because the way to handel drunks is to not iritate them they are only worse only you cant tell a woman that & they think the way to handel drunks is to look him in the eye & say arent you ashamed of yourselves which only iritates him the moar. Well I says I am not going to half no horse of mine going a round 1/2 shodd al the time & Prudence says well I am not going to half no husband of mine going a round 1/2 shot al the time & I says I will not go near Charley Davis this time because I have lernt my lesson & she says al right if you will promise to not go near Charley Davis you can go & when I got to Lexington I thought I would stop in the taverin a min. just to say hulloh to the boys because if a fello doesnt stop in the taverin to say hulloh to the boys who are just as good as he is they are lible to say he has a swelt hed & is to proud to stop in the taverin to say hulloh to the boys. Who are just as good as he is. Well I didnt have any i dear that Charley Davis would be there because I had told Prudence I wasnt going to go near him & just because I said that I cant be expect it to sneek into toun like as if I was a convick can I Ethen. Well the taverin was crowd it & they had all got a good start & the long & the short of it was that the 1st person I seen was Charley Davis & he says hulloh there pink whiskers you are just in time to join the minit men which is only a nicked name he has for me because my whiskers are red brown. No I says I cannot join anything tonight fellos because I must go right back home & he says if you dont join the minit men now some day you wont have no home to go home to & I says what do you mean I wont have no home to go home to & he says because the Brittish are going to burn down all the homes of we farmers because we will not sell them any food but first you had better have a drink. Well Ethen a fello dont like to be a sissey about taking 1 drink does he & then I says now fellos I must go home & then a couple of more fellos come in & they said Ed you wont go home till we have brought you a drink & elect it you to the minit men will you & I said no but I must go home right after that. Well then we got to singing & we was going pretty good & after a while I said now fellos I must go home & Charley Davis says to me Ed before you go I want to have you shake hands with my friend Tom Duffy who is here from Boston & he will tell you all about the minit men & you can join tonight but look out or he will drink you under the tabel because he is the worst fish in Boston & I says sure only I have got to be going home soon because you remember what hapend last time & I would like to see any body from Boston drink me under the tabel & bet. you & I Ethen if that fellow is a fish then my grandmother is the prince of whales & let me tell you what hapend. After we had drank about 4 or 5 I seen he was getting sort of wite & I says well Boston lets settle down now to some good steddy drinking & he says listen & I says what & he says listen & I says what & he says do you know my wife & I says no & he says listen & I says what & he says shes the best little woman in the world & I says sure & he says what did you say & I says when & he says you have insult it my wife the best little woman in the world & he begun to cry & we had only had a bout 1 qt & wouldnt that knock you for a cockide gool Ethen, only I guess you arent surprised knowing how much I can holt without feeling any affects. Well I was feeling pretty good on acct. of drinking the pride of Boston under the tabel & not feeling any affects only I was feeling good like a fello naturely feels & the fellos kind of made a lot of fuss on acct. me drinking him under the tabel so I couldnt very well of gone home then & after a while Charley Davis made a speach & well comed me into the minit men & so I am a minit man Ethen but I cant exackly explain it to you until I see Charley again because he didnt make it very clear that night. Well after a while we woke the Boston fish up & we all went home & I was feeling pretty good on acct. it being such a nice night & all the stars being out & etc. & when I got home I said Prudence guess what hapend & she says I can guess & I says Prudence I have been elect it a minit man & she says well go on up stares & sleep it off & I says sleep what off & she says stop talking so loud do you want the naybers to wake up & I says whos talking loud & she says o go to bed & I says I am talking in conversational tones & she says well you must be conversing with somebody in Boston & I says o you mean that little blond on Beecon St. &

Ethen she went a 1,000,000 mi. up in the air & I seen it wasnt no use to try & tell her that the reason I was feeling good was on acct. having drank a Boston swelt hed to sleep without feeling any affects & I bet the next time I get a chanct I am going to get snooted right because a fello gets blamed just as much if he doesnt feel the affects as if he was brought home in a stuper & I was just kidding her about that blond on Beecon St. Some women dont know when they are well off Ethen & I bet that guy from Bostons Tom Duffy I mean wife wishes she was in Prudences shoes instead of her having married a man what cant holt no more than a qt. without being brought home in a stuper. Best rgds.

Ed

Friend Ethen—

Well Ethen this is a funny world & when I joined the minit men last mo. how was I to know that they called them minit men because they was lible to get shot any minit. & here I am riteing to you in a tent outside Boston & any minit a canon ball is lible to knock me for a continental loop & my house has been burnt & Prudence is up in Conk Cord with her sister the one who married that short skate dum bell Collins who has owed me 2 lbs. for a yr. & 1/2 well Ethen it never ranes but it pores & you can be glad you are liveing in a nice quiet place like Philly.

Well the other night I and Prudence was sound asleep when I heard some body banging at the frt. door & I stuck my head out the up stares window & I says who are you & he says I am Paul Revear & I says well this is a h—ll of a time to be wakeing a peaceful man out of their bed what do you want & he says the Brittish are comeing & I says o are they well this is the 19 of April not the 1st & I was going down stares to plank him I but he had rode away tow wards Lexington before I had a chanct & as it turned out after words the joke was on me OK Well who is it says Prudence Charley Davis again because you might as well come back to bed if it is & I says no it was some Boston smart alick trying to be funny & I guess they are soar down there on acct. what hapend to their prize fish up here last mo. & are trying to get even do you know a Paul Revear & she says yes there was a boy at school named Paul Revear who was crazy about me was he dark well Ethen if all the fellos she says has been crazy about her was layed end to end they would circum navygate the globe twicet & I says no he was yello & that had her stopt so we went back to sleep only I couldnt help laffing over the way I had slipt it across. About Revear being yello. Well along a bout a.m. there was a lot of gun firing tow wards Lexington & Prudence grabed me & says whats the shooting for & I says probably that fello Revear who was so crazy a bout you has got funny oncet to oft ten & it will teach them Boston doodes a lesson. Well Ethen I was wrong for oncet & the firing kept getting worse & I hitcht up old Bessy & drove over to Lexington Bessy is are horse & Ethen there was the h—ll to pay there because the g—d

═ 49 ═

d—m Brittish redcotes on had marcht up from Boston & had fired on the Lexington fellos & Charley Davis had been shot dead & a lot of the other fellos was wooned it & they said you had better get your wife to the h—ll out of your house because the g—d d—m Brittish redcotes are coming back & they will burn everything along the rode the ———— I guess you know what word goes there Ethen & I was so d—m mad at those g—d d—m Brittish redcotes an acct. shooting Charley Davis dead that I said give me a gun & show me the ———— who done it & they says no you had better get your wife to a safe place to go to & then you can come back because the ———— will be along this way again the ————. Well I drove as fast as I could back to the farm & somebody had already told Prudence what had hapend & as soon as I drove into the yd. she come out with my muskit & hand it it to me & says dont you worry about me but you kill every d—m redcote you can see & I says the ————s has killed Charley Davis & she says I know it & here is all the bullits I could find. Well when I got back to Lexington the redcotes was just coming along & Ethen I guess they wont forget that march back to Boston for a little whiles & I guess I wont either because the ————s burnt down my house & barn & Prudence is gone to stay with her sister in Conk Cord & here I am camping in a tent with a lot of other minit men on the out skirts of Boston & there is a roomer a round camp that to morrow we are going to move over to Bunker Hill which is a good name for a Boston Hill Ill say & Ethen if you was to of told me a mo. ago that I would be fighting to get Boston away from the Brittish I would of planked you I because they could of had Boston for all I cared. Well Ethen I must go out and drill some more now & probably we will half to listen to some Boston bird makeing a speach they are great fellos for speaches about down with Brittish tirrany & give me liberty or give me death but if you was to ast me Ethen I would say give me back that house & barn what those lousie redcotes burnt & when this excitement is all over what I want to know is Ethen where do I get off at.

Yrs
Ed

A Connecticut Yankee in the Revolution

JOSEPH PLUMB MARTIN Writers like Bill Nye, Robert Benchley, and Donald Ogden Stewart were hardly the first to find humorous inspiration in the American Revolution. Joseph Plumb Martin, who was actually there—he served for seven years during the war as an American foot soldier under Washington, Lafayette, and Steuben—later set down a good-humored account of his experiences.

As a teenage farm boy, Martin enlisted in the Eighth Connecticut Continental Regiment when the war broke out in earnest. He saw action in New York, Monmouth, and Yorktown and spent the agonizing winter of 1777–78 at Valley Forge.

His memoirs were published when he was seventy years old, but his memory of the events he recounts was remarkably true to the historical record, and his unfailing sense of humor remained fresh and youthful.

■ A simple affair happened while I was upon guard at a time while we were here, which made considerable disturbance amongst the guard and caused me some extra hours of fatigue at the time. As I was the cause of it at first, I will relate it. The guard consisted of nearly two hundred men, commanded by a field officer. We kept a long chain of sentinels placed almost within speaking distance of each other, and being in close neighborhood with the enemy we were necessitated to be pretty alert. I was upon my post as sentinel about the middle of the night. Thinking we had overgone the time in which we ought to have been relieved, I stepped a little off my post towards one of the next sentries, it being quite dark, and asked him in a low voice how long he had been on sentry. He started as if attacked by the enemy and roared out, "Who comes there?" I saw I had alarmed him and stole back to my post as quick as possible. He still kept up his cry, "Who comes there?" and receiving no answer, he discharged his piece, which alarmed the whole guard, who immediately formed and prepared for action and sent off a noncommissioned officer and file of men to ascertain the cause of alarm.

They came first to the man who had fired and asked him what was the matter. He said that someone had made an abrupt advance upon his premises and demanded, "How comes you on, sentry?" They next came to me, inquiring what I had seen. I told them that I had not seen or heard anything to alarm me but what the other sentinel had caused. The men returned to the guard, and we were soon relieved, which was all I had wanted.

Being pinched with hunger, I one day strolled to a place where sometime before some cattle had been slaughtered. Here I had the good luck (or rather bad luck, as it turned out in the end) to find an ox's milt, which had escaped the hogs and dogs. With this prize I steered off to my tent, threw it upon the fire and broiled it, and then sat down to eat it, without either bread or salt. I had not had it long in my stomach before it began to make strong remonstrances and to manifest a great inclination to be set at liberty again. I was very willing to listen to its requests, and with eyes overflowing with tears at parting with what I had thought to be a friend, I gave it a discharge. But the very thoughts of it would for some time after almost make me think that I had another milt in my stomach.

During these operations, we were encamped at a place called the Short Hills. While lying here, I came near taking another final discharge from the army in consequence of my indiscretion and levity. I was one day upon a camp guard. We kept our guard in the fields, and to defend us from the night dew we laid down under some trees which stood upon the brink of a very deep gully. The sides and tops of the banks of this gully were covered with walnut or hickory saplings three, four, or five inches diameter at their butts, and many of them were fifty or sixty feet in height. In the morning before the guard was relieved, some of the men (and I among the rest, to be sure; I was never far away when such kind of business was going forward) took it into our heads to divert ourselves by climbing these trees as high as they would bear us, and then swinging off our feet; the weight would bring us by a gentle flight to the ground, when the tree would resume its former position.

After exercising ourselves some time at this diversion, I thought I would have one capital swing. Accordingly, I climbed one of the tallest trees that stood directly on the verge of the gully, and swung off over the gully.

When the tree had bent to about a horizontal position, it snapped off as short as a pipestem. I suppose I was nearly or quite forty feet from the ground, from which distance I came, feet foremost, to the ground at quick time. The ground was soft, being loamy and entirely free from stones, so that it did me but little hurt, but I held the part of the tree I had broken off firmly in my grasp, and when I struck the ground with my feet I brought it with all the force of my weight and its own directly upon the top of my unthinking skull, which knocked me as stiff as a ringbolt. It was several minutes before I recovered recollection enough to know or remember what I had been about, but I weathered the point, although it gave me a severe headache for several days afterwards as a memento to keep upon the ground and not attempt to act the part of a flying squirrel.

The next morning we were joined by the French army from Rhode Island. Between us and the British redoubt there was a large deep gully. Our officers gave leave to as many as chose, of our men, to go over the gully and skirmish with the small parties of horsemen and footmen that kept patrolling from the redoubt to the gully, watching that none of us took shelter there to annoy them. Accordingly, a number of us kept disturbing their tranquillity all day. Sometimes only four or five of us, sometimes ten or twelve; sometimes we would drive them into the redoubt, when they would reinforce and sally out and drive us all over the gully. We kept up this sport till late in the afternoon, when myself and two others of our noncommissioned officers went down near the creek that makes the island upon which New York is situated. The two other men that were with me stopped under an apple tree that stood in a small gully. I saw four or five British horsemen on their horses a considerable distance from me, on the island. When they saw me they hallooed to me, calling me "a white-livered son of a b———h." (I was dressed in a white hunting shirt, or was without my coat—the latter, I think, as it was warm, and I wore a white underdress.) We then became quite sociable; they advised me to come over to their side and they would give me roast turkeys. I told them that they must wait till we left the coast clear, ere they could get into the country to steal them, as they used to do. They then said they would give me pork and 'lasses and then inquired what execution some cannon had done, just before fired from the island, if they had not killed and wounded some of our men, and if we did not want help, as our surgeons were a pack of ignoramuses. I told them, in reply, that they had done no other execution with their guns than wounding a dog (which was the case), and as they and their surgeons were of the same species of animals, I supposed the poor wounded dog would account it a particular favor to have some of his own kind to assist him.

While we were carrying on this very polite conversation, I observed at a house on the island, in a different direction from the horsemen, a large number of men; but as they appeared to be a motley group, I did not pay them much attention. Just as I was finishing the last sentence of my conversation with the horsemen, happening to cast my eyes toward the house (and very providentially, too), I saw the flash of a gun. I instinctively dropped, as quick as a loon could dive, when the ball passed directly over me and lodged in the tree under which my comrades were standing. They saw the upper part of my gun drop as I fell and said, "They have killed him." But they were mistaken. The people at the house set up a shouting, thinking they had done the job for one poor Yankee, but they were mistaken, too, for I immediately rose up and, slapping my backsides to them, slowly moved off.

We this forenoon passed through a pretty village called Maidenhead (don't stare, dear reader, I did not name it). An hour or two before we came to this place, I saw a pretty young lady standing in the door of a house just by the roadside. I very innocently inquired of her how far it was to Maidenhead. She answered, "Five miles." One of my men who, though young, did not stand in very imminent danger of being hanged for his beauty, observed to the young lady "that he thought the commodity scarce in the market, since he had to go so far to seek it." "Don't trouble yourself," said she, "about that, there is no danger of its being more scarce on your account." The fellow leered and, I believe, wished he had held his tongue. ■

FUNNY STUFF

You Can't Beat That

ANONYMOUS Anonymous, as ever, speaks for himself, this time from a source dating back to the 1840s, and there the trail peters out. This story, however, is a Yankee favorite that has appeared in a variety of forms over the years.

■ On the banks of the Hudson a bunch of village loafers were standing, seeing who could throw stones the farthest into the stream. A tall, raw-boned, slabsided Yankee, and no mistake, came up and looked on. For awhile he said nothing, till a Yorker in a tight jacket began to try his wit on Jonathan.

"You can't beat that," said the Yorker, as he hurled a stone away out into the river.

"Maybe not," said Jonathan, "but up in Vermont in the Green Mountains we have a pretty big river, considering, and t'other day I hove a man clear across it, and he came down fair and square on the other side."

His auditors yelled in derision.

"Well, now, you may laugh," said Jonathan, "but I can do it again."

"Do what?" demanded the tight-jacketed Yorker quickly.

"I can take and heave you across that river yonder, just open and shut."

"Bet you ten dollars on it!"

"Done!" said the Yankee. Drawing forth a ten-note, he covered the Yorker's shinplaster. "Can you swim, feller?" he asked.

"Like a duck," says tight-jacket.

Without further parley, the Vermonter seized the knowing Yorker stoutly by the nape of the neck and the basement of his pants, jerked him from his foothold, and dashed him heels over head into the Hudson. A shout ran through the crowd as he floundered in the cold water. He put back to the shore and scrambled up the bank.

"I'll take that ten-spot, if you please," said the shivering loafer, advancing to the stake-holder. "You took us for greenhorns, eh? We'll show you how to do things down here in York."

"Well," said Jonathan, "I reckon you won't take no ten-spot just yet, captain."

"Why? You lost the bet!"

"Not exactly. I didn't wager to do it the first time. Just said I could do it, and I tell you I can." And in spite of the loafer's utmost effort to escape him, he seized him by the scruff and seat and pitched him farther into the river than upon the first trial.

Again the Yorker floundered back through the icy water.

"Third time never fails," said the Yankee, stripping off his coat. "I can do it, I tell you!"

"Hold on!" said the victim.

"And I *will* do it, if I try till tomorrow morning," said Jonathan.

"I give it up!" shouted the sufferer between his teeth, which now chattered like a mad badger's. "T-take the m-m-money!"

"Oh well, if that's the way it's done in York State," said the Vermonter, pocketing the money and coolly turning away. ■■

Is This the Road to Freeport?

JUDSON HALE Judson Hale was born in Boston; raised in Vanceboro, Maine; and has spent most of his adult life in Dublin, New Hampshire, as editor of *Yankee* magazine. Hale inherited the job from his uncle, Robb Sagendorph, founder of *Yankee* and long-time editor of that quintessential New England publication, *The Old Farmer's Almanac*. Hale succeeded to that job as well. You can't get more New England than that.

In 1982 Hale put his impressions of the region into a book, *Inside New England*, in which he recalled, among other things, an invitation to address the Dublin Women's Club and the special introduction he received from the elderly lady who was program chairman: "It is indeed a pleasure to introduce and welcome Judson Hale, who will tell us about the *Yankee* magazine. After his talk, we will adjourn for refreshments and begin to enjoy ourselves."

That story alone qualifies Hale to discuss New England humor with authority.

MOTORIST: "Is this the road to Freeport?"
DOWN EASTER: "What part of Freeport do you want to go to?"
MOTORIST: "Well, I don't know—just Freeport."
DOWN EASTER: "Want to see someone?"
MOTORIST: (*annoyed but still patient*): "I was looking for a Mr. Anderson who runs a restaurant."
DOWN EASTER: "Mr. Anderson don't run the restaurant. He sold it to a man named Hawks."
MOTORIST: "Well, then, where is the garage?"
DOWN EASTER: "It ain't where the restaurant was. It's moved."
MOTORIST: (*purple in the wattles*): "And where has the garage moved to?"
DOWN EASTER: "I thought you wanted to see Mr. Anderson."

And so forth.

New England humor more or less starts, at least in the minds of most Americans, with the lost tourist or city person asking directions of some grizzled old Maine or Vermont country native and receiving in return a devastating one-liner.

Such as:

"I'd like to get to Orange."

"Don't know a thing to hinder."

Or:

"Does it matter which road I take to Portland?"

"Not to me it don't."

Or (and *everyone* in America knows this one):

"Can you tell me how to get to Wheelock?"

"Well, now, if I were going to Wheelock, I don't think I'd start from here."

Writer Bill Conklin tells a true "asking directions" story that occurred several years ago when he was moving from "away" to the town of Walpole, New Hampshire. He'd somehow wound up across the Connecticut River from Walpole, in the town of Westminster, Vermont, and although he could plainly see the church spires of Walpole, he couldn't find the road to the bridge that would get him there. Finally, he stopped to ask directions. The classic setup.

"Can you tell me how to get across to Walpole?" he asked an elderly gentleman walking along beside the road.

"Well, turn right a few hundred yards down this road, cross the bridge, and you'll be there," the man said in what appeared to be a very un-Vermontlike response to a tourist asking directions.

But then, after a short pause, he added, "I wouldn't go there, though."

"Why shouldn't I?" Bill asked, at once apprehensive.

"Didn't say *you* shouldn't," he replied. "Said I wouldn't."

Vermont and Maine are the only two New England states associated with New England humor, perhaps a bit unfairly. Cape Cod creeps in on occasion, but one seldom, if ever, hears a "New Hampshire story" or a "Connecticut joke." For that matter, no one has ever heard of South Dakota humor or Michigan humor. They are not *regions*. Vermont is a region. Maine is a region. Cape Cod is a region. Massachusetts is not a region, nor is Rhode Island or Connecticut. New Hampshire isn't, either. New England, as a whole, *is* a region. Texas is a region and so is the South. A "region," I submit, is an area with which its residents associate themselves with far more than ordinary pride. Thus I've found that at regional publishers' meetings I've attended around the United States, a New Hampshire person will say he or she is "from New England." A Vermont resident will say "from Vermont."

Incidentally, there is a New England Society in St. Louis (as well as other New England societies around the country), but I've never run across a St. Louis Society here in New England.

Keith Jennison of Castleton, Vermont, author of a few books on New England humor, says, "While my books on Maine and Vermont were selling well, I did one on New Hampshire. The book didn't sell copy one. I also did a book that had pure Massachusetts—Boston—humor in it. That didn't sell at all. I guess Maine and Vermont are magic words."

Well . . . Maine and Vermont are *regions*. Regional pride and regional humor go hand in hand. It may be, too, that the nonregional humor on television and radio has supplanted to some extent the country regional humor in the more urban areas of New England.

I'd make an exception with Boston, however. As Keith Jennison says, Boston humor may not sell—but I submit it is there. It's based on snobbism, certainly a common denominator to much humor all over the world.

For instance . . .

It seems a Boston man had lost his wife. As soon as telephone communication was established between the "Hub of the Universe," as Bostonians refer to it, and heaven, he put in a call to her.

"Hello!" he shouted. The connection wasn't all that good.

"Hello!" she shouted back from the other end.

"Is that you, Artemesia?"

"Yes, dear. It is."

"Well, my love, how do you like it up there?"

"Well, it's very nice," she replied, "but of course, it isn't Boston."

Boston's stories about Philadelphia have been for ages a part of the city's humor too. Today's sports rivalries between the two cities (the Boston Celtics versus the Philadelphia Seventy-sixers, for example) is in no way a recent phenomenon. The feud between Boston and Philadelphia goes back to the days of Benjamin Franklin, whom Philadelphia claims but who everyone knows was born in Boston.

Years ago I heard the story of the Bostonian proudly showing his native city to a friend from Philadelphia. Having taken his guest to all the historic points of interest, he asked him if he didn't think Boston a wonderful city.

"Yes, it's very nice," said the Philadelphian. "But I don't think it is so well laid out as Philadelphia."

"No," replied the Bostonian, "but it will be when it's as dead as Philadelphia."

Pretty harsh. But of course, true. In terms of balance, however, it could be mentioned here that Mark Twain, a Western writer often associated with the understated New England type of humor, once explained that Boston is known as the "Hub of the Universe" because the hub is the slowest part of the wheel.

• • •

E.B. White once wrote that "humor can be dissected as a frog can, but the thing dies in the process and the innards are discouraging to any but the pure scientific minds." The humor that occurs unconsciously may well be the very best indication of the nature of a region's humor. If a person isn't intending to be funny, then there are no preconceived notions influencing that person's ability to *be* funny. Like all spoken humor, unconscious humor requires the participation of at least two people—one to *be* funny, the other to *think* it's funny.

An undertaker friend of my sister's told her of the time he was summoned by a farmer living up in the hills of Albany, Vermont, a long way from town. He told the undertaker to please come and pick up the body of his wife. When the undertaker arrived at the farm after a rough drive up a winding dirt road, he was met by the farmer outside the front door of the house. "She ain't dead yet," he said, "but you can come in and wait."

The farmer was simply being practical, so practical as to be funny to at least the undertaker and my sister. And me.

As another example of raw, pure New England humor, consider this story that Bill Conklin swears occurred precisely as follows. And, surprise, it occurred in neither Vermont nor Maine!

"At an old barn on a back road in New Hampshire, my wife and I came upon an Antiques & Collectibles sign that led us into the barn and the presence of one of those Yankee proprietors right out of 'Bert and I.'

"I at once spotted a curious contraption, a rectangular pine platform mounted on four short legs. One end of it held a wooden upright with a hole cut out of the middle, exactly resembling a miniature stock for punishing, say, a midget of old New England days.

"On inquiring about its purpose, and waiting a long minute while the proprietor decided if he was going to tell me or not, there finally came a muttered, 'That's a goat-milking stand.'

"To me, newly transplanted from the flatlands, it seemed a marvelous piece of pure folk art.

" 'Look at that,' I exclaimed to my wife. 'You could use it for a planter, or a coffee table, or to display *objets.*'

"The silence was palpable. Then the flat, nasal, disgusted voice came from behind us, where the proprietor stood.

" 'You could *use* it,' he said, '*to milk a goat.*' "

Professor Edward Ives of the University of Maine, who has studied New England humor for many years, says it is very difficult to define New England humor as something that is found only in New England. "Nine times out of ten," he says, "you can find the same story somewhere else." Well, you might *find* the goat-milking-stand story somewhere else someday, but it couldn't have *happened* anywhere but here in New England.

Driving through Burlington, Vermont, one night, I spotted a twenty-four-hour diner, went in, and allowed a grizzly old counterman to wipe my elbow with a damp cloth while I studied the menu.

"I'll have apple pie à la mode."

"Want ice cream on it?"

"I *said* à la mode."

"Well, *that's* with ice cream."

I wonder who was laughing at whom?

One attribute of the bona fide New England punch line is that there isn't a single word that can be appropriately said afterward. When you've been Down Easted or Vermonted, that's that. The next spoken words must begin conversation on an entirely new subject. I recall the time an unconscious blast of New England humor rendered me speechless for the remainder of the time I was with the person I had dropped in on—and to this day I cannot conjure up a suitable retort.

It was during the years I was editing *Yankee's* monthly column "Small Business and Crafts," and a woman in Stoddard, New Hampshire, wrote me about her button collection, which I decided to go over to see and photograph. She took me into her living room and invited me to examine the contents of a very large button basket. Seated in the room was an elderly gentleman who uttered not a word. When the woman briefly introduced us (it was her father), he simply nodded. While the button collector and I discussed various unusual button specimens in the basket, the silent spectator slowly rocked and unashamedly stared at the sight of a grown man who would waste his time talking to a woman about buttons. After a rather long period of time, his curiosity finally overcame his Yankee reticence. He looked me straight in the eye, and completely without facial expression, said:

"Ain't you got no folks?"

Then there is the *conscious* type of New England humor, which most often involves a gentle or devastating put-down. Done deliberately. Maybe even with malice! Those people we New Englanders enjoy putting down with humor are: (1) tourists; (2) wealthy people (even wealthy New England natives—there are plenty of them, you know, even though they are never, *ever* labeled as such); (3) outsiders or "outlanders" and city people; (4) the federal government; (5) Democrats; and (6) ourselves.

I've already discussed tourist put-down humor. It's mainly the "asking directions" line of stories. Others involve old chestnuts, such as the tourist asking the local storekeeper if she has lived in the area all her life and the storekeeper replying, "Not yet."

Wealthy people are the butt of put-down humor all over the world. That's simply one of the prices a wealthy person must pay for being wealthy. New England humor is no exception. Perhaps that's *one* of the reasons many old-time New England natives of wealth wear clothes until they become threadbare, drive ordinary (but quality) cars, and have an ingrained tendency toward stinginess in everyday matters. There is a horror at being "fancy." But of course, all that accomplishes very little. As far as New England humor is concerned, the rich *are* fancy. Period.

Here's a typical example, extracted from the detached pages of an old nineteenth-century book I've had in my files for years. You'll note that not only is the punch line a put-down of rich, fancy people, but the entire tone of the telling is pretty darn belligerent as well. It's a little dated, but the sentiments are still around. . . .

> Men may be important on Wall Street and their very presence may cause city men to tremble. But those big fellows are just human beings to the average New England countryman. A pompous, chesty, egotistical city man only makes a fool of himself when he tries to show off. One such man, who thought of himself as a big shot, had to leave his summer home in the mountains in a hurry and telegraphed to the president of the railroad asking to have the 10:24 southbound stop at a certain nearby rural station. Upon reaching the station that night, he asked the station agent if he had received orders to flag down the 10:24. "No, I hain't." "Well, aren't you going to flag that train?" "No, I hain't." The big shot was all of a dither, for he heard the train approaching in the distance. As the train hove into sight far down the track, he grabbed a lantern the agent had left sitting on the platform and swung it violently up and down in his best imitation of a railroader. The 10:24 came to a stop. "You'll hear about this," said the big shot to the agent.
>
> "Teehee," snickered the agent. "If you hadn't been so high and mighty, I might have told you the 10:24 always stops here."

Outsiders overlap the wealthy to a certain extent—probably because if someone can either move to the country or travel, he must have money. So an outsider is most often a summer person.

"Nice little town, so old and quaint. But I suppose you have a lot of oddballs too."

"Oh yes, quite a few. You see 'em around. But they're mostly gone after Labor Day."

The federal government is the butt of New England put-down stories because the federal government often offends the old-time New Englander's attitude of frugality. In fact, of the thousands of Calvin Coolidge jokes, 90 percent involves his legendary frugal attitude toward money or the simple frugality of his words. And the juxtaposition of this supposedly stingy, dry Vermonter heading up the big-spending federal government, so often snarled in the wordiness of red tape, easily created a humor situation over and above the good sense of humor manifested by Cal himself.

"Let's walk and save a nickel," said a friend to then ex-President Coolidge, as they were leaving their New York hotel for Grand Central Station.

Replied Cal, in reference to the higher cost of a Fifth Avenue bus ride back then, "Let's walk down Fifth Avenue and save a dime."

But the typical federal-government put-down could be exemplified by the story of the man whom a policeman in a New England town observed throwing ten-dollar bills out the window of his car. Stopping the driver, the policeman said he intended to arrest him.

"On what grounds?" the man asked.

"Insanity is the charge, mister."

"Insanity, nothing," came the angry retort. "I'm just as sane as you are. I guess I have the right to throw my money from my car if I please."

"Well, then you must be drunk. Nobody sober goes down my street throwing money away like that."

"I beg your pardon," the man replied, "but it so happens I haven't had a drink in five years. Any of my friends will tell you that."

The exasperated policeman paused, but suddenly came up with the solution to his problem.

"OK, no more of your back talk now. You're under arrest for impersonating a federal officer."

Since the days of Roosevelt and even beyond, the Democratic party has been associated with the antithesis of New England thrift, and so, like the federal government, which the Democrats have been in charge of off and on, the Democrats are a favorite subject of New England humor. I should quickly add that Democratic jokes cannot be turned around to become Republican jokes. Democratic jokes are not like worldwide ethnic jokes, in which, often, most any ethnic minority can be substituted for another ethnic minority.

For instance, if "Republican" were substituted for "Democratic" in the following story told by former New Hampshire governor Sherman Adams, it would not be funny.

The governor's story concerns a boy in a Vermont village near his hometown (Adams was raised in Vermont) who decided to go to college. His parents were willing to help him but were unsure about some of the ideas he might pick up.

"Sure enough," said Governor Adams, as recorded on tape for a *Yankee* article by writer Richard Meryman, "the boy came back from college a Democrat. The family was very upset about that and considered he had been under the auspices of evil. To make matters worse, the boy founded the local Democratic movement and on the Fourth of July organized a parade. His father pulled down all the shades in the house and wouldn't let anybody look out to see what was going on. But then he got curious and picked up just the corner of the shade and took a peek. In horror, he turned to his wife and said, 'My God, Samantha, they've stolen our flag!' "

Here's one more, as told by the late Professor Allen Foley of Dartmouth College and involving a Texas Democrat and a Vermont Republican. It takes place in Texas and has a double whammy because New Englanders enjoy putting down Texans (and I'm sure the reverse is true—Texas is a bona fide *region* after all) just about as much as they enjoy putting down Democrats.

"How come you are a Republican?" the Texas Democrat asks the visiting Vermont native (there's no such thing as a native Vermont tourist).

"I come from Vermont and my father was a Republican," replies the Vermonter.

"Oh, I see," says the Texas Democrat. "So I suppose if your father had been a horse thief, you would have been a horse thief too."

"No," says the Vermonter. "In that case I would have been a Democrat."

There are, of course, thousands of Democrats in New England. In fact, at this writing, every governor in New England, save one, is a Democrat. So how do New England Democrats counter all these old-time New England "Democrat stories"? Well, one of their most effective means is to utilize the "wealthy, fancy people stories" and substitute "Republican." Maybe that's not always fair, but fairness and accuracy have nothing whatsoever to do with New England or any other kind of humor.

It might well be that all these put-down stories would constitute a sort of mean streak in New England humor if it were not for the fact that the group of people we enjoy putting down most of all is ourselves. Every so-called New England trait—such as frugality, independence, laconism, shrewdness, elderliness, reluctance to be beholden to anybody—is turned around and used in the punch lines of New England jokes.

"Good morning, Mr. Spence, and how are you this lovely morning?"

" 'Tain't none of your business and I wouldn't tell you that much if you wasn't my neighbor."

Movie producer Frank Pierson, in another Dick Meryman interview for *Yankee*, said that New England jokes are told with little morals "masquerading behind the laughter." He tells about two Maine fishermen who lose contact with their mother-ship and drift for days and weeks in their dory. For food, they grab sea birds that land on their heads, and drink the blood. Finally, far off on the horizon, they see the smoke from a passing steamship. One of the fishermen tears off his shirt and is waving it in the air and screaming and crying. The other one says:

"Jed, don't do nothing to make you beholden to them."

And writer Edwin Valentine Mitchell, in his book *It's an Old State of Maine Custom*, recalls the story of the stranger being shown around town who remarked to his guide how extraordinarily old the townspeople seemed to be.

"Seems as if everybody we meet is old," says the stranger.
"Yes," the guide admits, "the town does have a lot of old folks."
"I see you have a beautiful cemetery over there," remarks the stranger.
"Yup," is the laconic answer. "We had to kill a man to start it."

Like sex, use of a dialect is also not an essential ingredient of New England humor. It's used a lot, but misused far more often. After all, the word "ayuh" isn't particularly funny to someone who often says "ayuh." And unless you *do* say "ayuh" as part of your natural way of speaking, there is no possible way you can say "ayuh" and have it sound authentic. No possible way in the world. The sound of the word is far too subtle to be picked up.

However, dialect can be *written*. Many of the nineteenth-century New England humorists—such as Seba Smith, creator of "Major Jack Downing of Downingville, Way Down East," or Josh Billings, born and buried in Lanesborough, Massachusetts ("About the hardest thing a phellow kan do, iz tew spark two girls at onst, and preserve a good average"), or Charles Farrar Browne, otherwise known as Artemus Ward—many of these pioneer humorists wrote in heavy dialect. And while I believe the dialect used in even the written New England stories of today more often than not seriously obstructs the humor, the likes of Smith, Billings, and Artemus Ward made dialect work for them.

For example, in 1860 Artemus Ward, who once referred to Ralph Waldo Emerson as "a perpendicular coffin," described his experience as a census taker in characteristic fashion, even to his jumbled orthography:

> The Senses taker in our town being taken sick he deppertised me to go out for him one day, and as he was too ill to giv me informashun how to perceed, I was consekently compelled to go it blind. I drawd up the follerin list of questions which I proposed to ax the people I visited:
> "Wat's your age? Whar was you born? Air you marrid, and if so, how do you like it? How many children have you . . . ? Did you ever have the measels, and if so how many? Wat's your fitin wate? Air you trubeld with biles? Do you use boughten tobacker? Is Beans a regler article of diet in your family? Was you ever at Niagry Falls? How many chickens hav you, on foot and in the shell? Was you ever in the Penitentiary?"
> But it didn't work. I got into a row at the fust house I stopt to, with some old maids. Disbelieven the ansers they giv in regard to their ages I endevered to look at their teeth, same as they do with hosses, but they floo into a violent rage and tackled me with brooms and sich. Takin the senses requires experiunse, like any other bizniss.

The line between successful and unsuccessful regional humor is, of course, infinitesimally narrow, depending on timing, voice inflection (if spoken), surprise, and the precise choice of words utilized. The latter is probably the most important. I remember a party my wife and I recently attended in which an elderly New Hampshire friend of mine had perhaps one more drink than he should have had. As we were leaving, he and his wife were just ahead of us, and I could hear her gently admonishing him for "being drunk," although he seemed to be walking along all right. I really didn't mean to be eavesdropping, but on the other hand, I'm glad I caught his answer, because I consider it a classic.

"Betsy, a man ain't drunk," he said, "so long as he can lay down, hang on to the grass, and keep himself from rolling over."

Strangely enough, the humor here is enhanced by my *overhearing* it rather than having had it spoken to me directly. Successful humor is often puzzlingly subtle, be it the New England variety or that found anywhere in the world.

But as to actually demonstrating New England's own identifiable brand of humor, you're on the safest ground using those brief, understated, droll, devastatingly blunt one-liners typical of the "lost-tourist-asking-directions" and the "put-down" stories. Regional tall tales notwithstanding. The circulation manager of *Down East* magazine sent a letter to Abner Mason of Damariscotta, Maine, notifying him that his subscription had expired. The notice came back a few days later with a scrawled message: "So's Abner." Nothing complicated there. Its simplicity and frugal choice of words is its key to modest success.

That and many other favorite Maine stories are recorded by Jim Brunelle in *Over to Home and From Away*. However, Jim starts out with a puzzling story about a lost tourist asking a Maine farmer if he knows the way to the town hall.

" 'Ayuh,' the farmer replies, setting up his victim for some crushing Down Eastism. But the tourist sees it coming and neatly dodges.

" 'Just checking!' he cries and drives off."

What's so funny about that? ■

You Take the Highway: I'll Take the Back Way

MARGUERITE HURREY WOLF Writer and lecturer Marguerite Wolf lived nearly ten years in Vermont, where her husband was dean of the medical college at the state university. Even after they moved out of the state, residing at various times in Boston, New York, and Kansas City, the Wolfs continued to summer in Jericho, Vermont.

Out of this experience came two popular books, *Vermont is Always With You* and *I'll Take the Back Road*, from which the following selection is taken.

■ If you prefer a smooth wide road where you can cruise steadily at the legal limit in all seasons, stay on the interstate highway. In fact, I wish all the tourists would so that we rural types could enjoy our golden tree tunnels and silent arches of snow-laden pines in quiet. But from the advent of the first Model T, the questing tourist has managed to get himself lost on Vermont back roads and has unwittingly provided Vermonters with anecdotes to evoke chuckles from their neighbors at the general store or post office.

Walter Hard captured one of these moments in his poem when octogenarian Steve Henderson, ruminating quietly on the post office steps, was accosted by a baffled traveler.

"Can you tell me how to get to Stockbridge Corners?"
"Nope."
"You mean you can't tell me how to get to Stockbridge Corners?"
"Nope."
"Would you mind telling me why you can't give me this information?"

Steve humped his shoulders and twisted his face
Into his nearest approach to a smile
Firing (tobacco juice) again and then chewing rapidly he said,
"You're there."

It might have been the same store where a touring car full of summer folk stopped to inquire the way to the Blodgett farm. The storekeeper of course knew where the Blodgetts lived and exactly how to get there.

"Go ten miles until you come to a covered bridge. Take the turn three miles before you reach the bridge. When you go up their road if you come to a white church, you've gone too far."

In the early days when the little Morgan mares could maneuver through mud that mired the carriages and wagons, the census around the cracker barrel was usually reduced to those within walking distance of the store. News traveled slowly, and the farther the raconteur had to walk, the more time he had to embellish his story.

Eben Fuller clumped up the steps of the store, and all heads around the stove turned towards the door, hoping for a bit of verbal refreshment.

"Morning, Eben, what's new up your way?"

"Not too much. I just passed Foster Davis's hat down in the mud waller."

"Where was Foster?"

"Well, his head and shoulders were right there, under the hat, but he was up to his waist in mud."

"Reckon we should get a team and haul him out?"

"No, by Judast, I don't. I ast him did he want a hist and he said, 'What fer? I still got my horse under me.'"

The expression "You can't get there from here" is funny only to those "from away." The back roads usually followed the path of least resistance. Inasmuch as the resistance is the state-long Green Mountain range, there are a good many locations where you can't get from a town on the western side of Vermont to the parallel one in the Connecticut Valley without detouring a hundred miles to the nearest gap. Most of the roads run north and south, avoiding the mountains or following a stream. But occasionally a road will make a loop that lengthens its route for no apparent reason. One example was right in front of our house in South Burlington. It would have been more direct for Hinesburg Road to slant northwest from the Wright farm past our house toward Burlington. Instead, it went close to Rollin Tilley's house and then turned sharply west. The explanation turned up in an old record. Rollin's house had been a tavern shortly after the Revolution, when the road was being hacked out by every able-bodied man along its route. The tavern keeper saw that the proposed (more direct) route would divert travelers from his hostelry, so he offered the work crew a keg of rum and a keg of Holland gin to dogleg the new road right through his dooryard.

Ralph Hill tells my favorite back-road story with suitable straight-faced understatement.

A tourist stopped at a fork in the road where both signs read "To Londonderry." Mystified by this ambivalence, he noticed a farmer plowing in the adjoining field, and waiting until he was within earshot, he shouted, "Does it matter which road I take to Londonderry?"

The farmer finished his row, studied the tourist at length, turned the plow and starting back down the next furrow, called out over his shoulder, "Not to me, it doesn't!" ■

Cape Cod Humor

WALTER S. HINCHMAN Author, essayist, poet, and educator, Walter Swain Hinchman was a prominent prep-school professor of English in New England during the early part of this century.
In the 1920s, while teaching at Milton Academy, he served as a
contributing editor of *The Forum* magazine. Writing under the
pseudonym of "The Pedestrian," Hinchman delivered rambling,
informed commentaries on a variety of subjects including, at one
point, the local humor of the Massachusetts region where he
maintained a summer retreat.

■ Once, when I had so far abandoned my pedestrian convictions as to
accept a lift in a flivver (compassionate reader, it was a hot, sandy road in
New Jersey), I noticed that the driver leaned overboard and looked past the
windshield. In fact, he couldn't see *through* it, it was so dirty.

"The sun on that glass," I remarked sympathetically, "makes it difficult
to see, doesn't it?"

"Well," replied the driver, with no suggestion of mirth in his tone, "you
kin almost see through it. I'll have to give it a coat o' paint pretty soon."

The pronunciation betrayed him, to be sure, as did his lean, weather-
beaten face, but I think it was the type of his jest that chiefly prompted my
next question. "You come from Cape Cod?" I queried.

"Not far from there," he answered matter-of-factly. "Born and brought
up in Falmouth."

Every serious reading circle comes, sooner or later, to a debate in
regard to wit and humor. It never seems to occur to the debaters that you
might as well try to define poetry or generosity as to attempt to label humor
in general. Only in its specific manifestations can it be ticketed. You may
describe dramatic poetry or Robinson's generosity with some accuracy; and
just so you may approximate a label for Scotch humor, or Cockney humor,
or Cape Cod humor. But though the sum of different kinds of poetry or of
different degrees of generosity may give you a rough idea of poetry or of

generosity, you have to recognize, with the sad example of the debating club before you, that the sum of all the particular kinds of humor will not add up to a definition of the abstract quality, Humor. That is perhaps the most humorous thing about humor; its expressions are so concrete; it, itself, is so uncapturably abstract. We offer, therefore, no encouragement whatever to the debating societies; we are concerned with specific manifestations.

Now the most obvious thing about Cape Cod humor (*pace* Chesterton) is that it is humorous because it isn't humorous. It may have much in common with other New England varieties, but it has two particular differences. Most New England humor of the "dry" variety emerges in an incongruous seriousness; in fact, it takes its life from that seriousness. But generally it betrays, by a twinkle of the eye or a peculiar emphasis, that it is not meant to be taken in absolute earnest. You, the listener, are given a chance to share in the suppressed merriment. But your Cape Cod humorist never vouchsafes a sign. To do so would be to deny his nature and to spoil the jest. The merriment is so wholly suppressed that it is not only inaudible but absolutely invisible.

The other particular difference is that, whereas most humor is made partly for someone else's benefit, Cape Cod humor is made solely for the maker's delight. In fact, much of it depends on its not being recognized. You are never asked to share; you are not even given a chance. You must *take* a share. If you do so in the right way, you may almost please the originator (vanity reaches even to Chatham Bars); but you mustn't laugh, you must answer in kind—a trifle drier if possible. The true Cape native will then show his delight by making no sign whatever. If he should laugh, it would be out of politeness; he would recognize for your sake that you thought you were making a joke. Only uproarious silence signifies perfect rapport.

The prime quality, then, is seriousness exaggerated to an absolute point, complete suppression of any sign of intended mirth. If my friend of the flivver had changed his tone in the slightest, if he had stressed the word "almost" or "see" never so little, the joke might have been a good one from Hartford east to Maine, but not from New Bedford to Harwichport.

I remember, for example, a story of a Vermonter's humor.

"What," he cried, "you never saw Mrs. Smith? Well, she was Hen Smith's wife, and of all the ugly, ornery-lookin' wimmin, she took the cake. Why, whenever the conductor wanted to lead a train by their house, he had to ask Hen to call her in off the veranda." Then after a pause: "Well, I s'pose, ef you went fer enough back in hist'ry, you might find she was descended from the human race, but there warn't no indications of it in her countenance."

Clearly, this raconteur was a conscious humorist, with an audience. Dry, but not so dry that almost any listener might not get a bit of refreshment from it. There must have been a twinkle or a twitch that betrayed him.

The same may generally be said, I think, of other typically American humor of the dry variety. One may be sure Lincoln indulged in an inward chuckle that showed in tone or eye if not in actual laughter. When Mark Twain said, on receiving an honorary degree, that he never doctored any literature, he may have enjoyed his little joke, but he certainly counted on his audience's enjoying it too. And when Whistler retorted in print to one of his critics, "Who ever supposed you were a real person?"—he must have hoped that the critic would wince *just because* others would see the joke. Of your dyed-in-the-wool Cape humorist, on the contrary, it can be said that he gets rather more pleasure if you don't see the joke. He is not quite at home with a responsive audience.

Now I don't mean to be doctrinaire. There are no exact boundaries to humor, and the genuine Cape Cod variety appears in somewhat diluted form in other parts of New England. But it rarely goes west of the Berkshires. Once in the Hudson Valley, during an exceptionally dry, hot spell in June, I passed some workmen toiling near a dazzling concrete walk. "Guess we'll be cutting ice on that sidewalk today," one of them said to me with a serious drawl. From long acquaintance with more eastern folk, I responded, quite as seriously as he, "Ought to get quite a crop." Perhaps they do not speak of an ice *crop* along the Hudson, but from the contemptuous glance the man gave me, I feel sure he was disappointed with my sense of humor. He had made a joke, and instead of laughing I had taken him seriously!

One of the best examples of what I have designated as Cape Cod humor, but in this case made outside the sacred precincts, is the reply ascribed to Mr. Coolidge when, as vice-president, he was rallied at a dinner party by a lady who assured him that she had a bet she could make him converse.

"Well, ma'am," he is reported to have said, "you've lost your bet."*

But, though Cape Cod humor takes its merit from its complete lack of what is humorous elsewhere, a visitor to southeastern Massachusetts makes a great mistake if he supposes that these Cape folk don't mean to be funny. Sometimes he laughs at them, if the thrust is not too personal, as he laughs at unintentional Scotch humor. But he is grossly in error. When your genuine clam-digger on the Cape delivers himself of preposterous incongruities with a straight face, you may not see the joke, but it is there, even if you don't see it—*especially* if you don't see it. From other New England humor it may differ in degree rather than in kind, but it alone is the simon-pure, sand-dry, salt-cured article.

The most perfect instance I know is the reply of a Buzzards Bay native

*Editor's note: This shows how an academic can mangle a perfectly good story. Most versions have the woman saying, "Mr. President, when my husband found out I would be sitting next to you tonight, he bet that I couldn't get you to say three words. What do you think of that?" Replied Coolidge: "You lose."—J.B.

to President Cleveland. Cleveland had missed his way after a long day's fishing. It was pouring rain; he was afoot. When he knocked at the door of a lonely farmhouse, a voice from a second-floor window asked him what he wanted.

"I want to stay here tonight," called the President.

"Well," replied the voice, "stay there." ■■

Cape Cod Yesterdays

JOSEPH C. LINCOLN Novelist, story teller, and self-described "Cape Cod author," Joseph Crosby Lincoln (1870–1944) liked to recall an old saying about the people of the New England coastal area where he grew up. The Cape Codder born and bred, he said, "was perfectly certain of three things. First, that Cape Cod was the finest place in the world. Second, that Cape Codders were the finest people in the world. Third, that he himself was finer than any other Cape Codder."

In *Cape Cod Yesterdays*, one of dozens of books he turned out during a long and productive writing career, Lincoln provided some choice, first-hand examples of Cape Cod humor.

■ This captain, so our friend said, had the reputation, spread by the unlucky foremast hands who had sailed with him, of being a "poor provider." He was a first-rate skipper and fisherman, but he fed his crews in meager fashion. A cook who shipped with him one trip—I never heard of any cook shipping with Captain Ote for more than one trip—swore that, the second day out, he asked the skipper what he should prepare for the crew's supper.

"Well," drawled Ote, "if you go below, you'll find a ham hangin' up. Cut off a couple of slices and fry 'em."

The cook obeyed orders and, so he said, found a ham *bone* hanging from a nail, but with absolutely not a shred of meat left on it. He came on deck again and reported the results of his finding. Captain Ote pulled his beard.

"Ain't nothin' on it, eh?" he queried.

"A little gristle, that's all."

Captain Ote reflected. "Humph!" he grunted. "Then maybe you better bile it."

• • •

He is a queer bird, Cyrenus [Small]. Lives all alone in a little house away up on the Punkhorn Road, and there are all sorts of stories told about him.

Grandmother remembered that, when he was a lad in the "down-stairs" school, the teacher asked the children if they knew what was meant by the summit of a mountain. Cyrenus held up his hand; *he* knew. "Where is the summit?" asked Teacher. "Halfway up," declared Cyrenus, with the pride of certainty.

The boys in his neighborhood tormented him a good deal. He was accustomed to carry in his truck-wagon a long rope for use in lashing heavy loads. The boys, led by one older individual who "went mackereling" in the summer months, borrowed this rope one night and spliced the ends together, the older boy doing the splicing so neatly that the joining was scarcely discernible. About nine the next morning, so the story goes, a neighbor found Cyrenus seated in the truck-wagon, pulling the loop of rope around and around through his hands and talking to himself.

"What's the matter, Cy?" asked the neighbor.

Cyrenus looked up. "Some of them everlastin' young ones," he sputtered, "have gone to work and cut the end clean off my cart rope."

Oh, yes, we were talking of the peddler who sold fish from a carryall; that was it. He did so sell them. He had removed the rear seat and rigged an icebox in its place.

He was a peculiar specimen. All Codders of the vintage of the 1880s and 1890s will remember him. A garrulous talker and deaf as a haddock. That comparison is used because it fits the subject we are supposed to be—or should be—discussing, and because "deaf as a haddock" is a common expression alongshore. How deaf a haddock may be, or how anyone knows he is deaf at all, are questions I will not presume to answer.

But this fish peddler was deaf; there was no doubt of that. And his imperfect hearing was not altogether a curse—in business. One summer he made weekly calls at our back door and sold fish each time. At the end of the season, when he presented his bill, there was a decided difference between his footings and ours, a difference much in his favor. After protesting for twenty minutes or so that there could be no mistake, he was prevailed upon to go over the figures with us. When, at last, forced to acknowledge that we were right and he was wrong, he shook his head.

"Well, now, ain't that a shame," he observed sadly. "That's what comes of bein' hard of hearin'. I'm gettin' so plaguey deef nowadays I can't add."

Once, toward the latter part of his life, our motorcar caught up with his fish carryall in a narrow, across-the-Cape road. Until he moved to the side, there was no room to pass and for almost a mile we crept along behind him, blowing our horn persistently. At last a bewhiskered face protruded beyond the edge of the carryall curtain and turned in our direction, and a melancholy voice came from the mouth behind the whiskers.

"I'm deef," it explained sadly. "I don't hear ye."

The face disappeared and we crept on for another half-mile until the road widened and we could squeeze by.

Last summer a friend told us of a recent happening in the community where he lives. During the winter it is a small community indeed, but from June to September it swarms with summer cottagers and vacationists. Among the town's residents, winter as well as summer, are two men named—well, named anything you like—"Williams" will do well enough. One Williams is a prosperous, well-to-do cranberry grower and banker, member of the Board of Selectmen, and prominent in town affairs. The other is a veteran clam-digger, weir-tender, and longshoreman. The first Williams is a fine-looking gentleman; the other is, as our friend described it, "homelier than a sculpin with the mumps."

Among the town's summer cottagers was a lady with a strong aesthetic sense. This was her first summer in that neighborhood; she knew few of the year-round residents; but she had already fallen in love with the place, planned to spend many, if not all, of her remaining summers there, and she wished to show her appreciation in some tangible way. She conceived an idea and she spoke to some of her friends about it.

They told her that she should see Mr. Williams. He had lived there all his life and his opinion was greatly respected by the permanent population. She had never met Mr. Williams, but she set about meeting him immediately. At the bank, where she inquired, they told her he had gone down to the wharf and she would probably find him there.

So to the wharf she went and asked the first lounger she met there if Mr. Williams was in the vicinity.

"Why, yes, ma'am," was the reply. "There he is, right over yonder."

The man he pointed out to her was not the banker Williams, but the other, the sunburned, leather-necked old longshoreman. The lounger of whom she inquired had taken it for granted that she wished to buy clams or lobsters, as did so many summer housekeepers. She crossed the wharf and approached the veteran, who was winding a length of cod line about the cracked handle of a clam hoe.

"Excuse me," she asked, "but are you Mr. Williams?"

He raised his wrinkled, unshaven, ugly old face and regarded her from under bushy, bleached eyebrows.

"Yes, ma'am," he replied.

"Oh, I'm *so* glad to meet you. They told me you might be at the wharf."

"Yes, ma'am, here's where I most ginerally be—when I ain't somewheres else."

"Now, Mr. Williams, I won't take but a little of your time, I promise you. You've lived in Wellmouth all your life, haven't you?"

"Yes, ma'am."

"Oh, I'm so glad! You are *just* the man I want to talk with. I want to ask your advice. You see, this is my first summer here, but I am in love with the place and I want to help it in some way, to *do* something for it, if you know what I mean."

Williams had not the least idea what she meant, but he said "Yes, ma'am."

"My idea is very vague, but it is something like this: It occurred to me that some of us summer people—myself among the number—might sub-scribe a sum of money to be used in beautifying Wellmouth. We can't be too extravagant, of course, but we would like to do something, some little thing which would make this charming town more lovely, if that is possible, than it is now. They told me to come to you, because your suggestions would be valuable. Now can you suggest anything—anything not too expensive? If you can, I shall be so much obliged."

Williams took off his shabby, fish-scale-spotted old cap, and ran his fingers through what was left of his grizzled old hair. Of course, he realized the mistake she had made, that it was the other Williams to whom she had been sent for counsel; but he, characteristically, did not tell her that. He chewed methodically.

"Well, now, ma'am," he drawled. "Let's see if I've got this straight. You want to make this town prettier than 'tis now, but you don't want to spend much money. Is that right?"

"Yes, yes, that is exactly right. Have you an idea? Oh, I hope so!"

"Well, ma'am, I don't know's I ain't got one. It would make Wellmouth consider'ble more pretty and 'twould be cheap, too."

"Splendid! What is it?"

"Why, ma'am, you give me fifty cents and I'd move to Ostable." ■

GROWING UP

The Elder Shute Rescues a Chicken and Rebuilds a Barn

HENRY A. SHUTE The stories of Plupy, the Real Boy were tremendously popular among young readers at the turn of the century. They were, in fact, semifictional accounts of the boyhood life of Judge Henry A. Shute, based upon a schoolboy journal he kept while growing up in Exeter, New Hampshire.

Shute was graduated from Harvard in 1879 and admitted to the New Hampshire bar three years later. While waiting for his law practice to develop, he killed time by writing editorials and obituaries for the local newspaper. This eventually led to a series of reminiscences from which the Plupy books emerged.

Although Shute was encouraged to quit the law for a literary career after the success of his first books, he could not bring himself to give up what he called "the intense interest and almost infinite variety of the general practice of law." He became a municipal judge in Exeter and spent forty-three years on the bench.

■ From the preceding sidelights on the character of our friend, Plupy, one may have gained the impression that he was not only a mischievous boy but far worse, a cruel lad. Any such impression was an injustice to him. Far from being cruel, he was extremely kind-hearted and affectionate, as were most of his companions and acquaintances.

When Plupy landed a hard green apple under the ear of an innocent and inoffensive old gentleman and transformed that dove of peace into a ravening wolf thirsting for the blood of any small boy on the street, he had no thought of the pain he inflicted, of the mortification of the old gentleman when he dispassionately reviewed his bursts of language, of the danger of apoplexy caused by the rush of blood to his head due to his rapid passage over fences and down alleys in futile pursuit of his prey.

No, he only felt a justifiable pride in his marksmanship and a keen and unalloyed delight in the sinful profanity and wondrous agility of the mark.

Again, when a smooth pebble or a couple of buckshot impelled with terrific force from his slingshot impinged upon a dog or cat peaceably taking the air, the shrill yelp of the canine and the loud yawl of the feline and their frantic leaps for safety gave him such delight that he rolled on the ground with laughter. And yet, the idea of pain never entered his head, and if the same dog or cat were drowning or caught in a trap, he would go to any length to save or relieve them.

The highly colored spatter that a rich, ripe, and juicy tomato would make when propelled with judgment between the shoulders of a friend dressed in his Sunday suit on a weekday was to him not only interesting from an artistic view and delightful from a humorous standpoint, but thoroughly justifiable, for, as he expressed it, "No feller hadn't got no business to wear his best clothes on a weekday, and any feller which done it had ought to be plugged."

No, Plupy was not cruel, only a bit, perhaps, thoughtless, with a very keen sense of the ridiculous and possessing an active imagination. On one occasion, being the fortunate possessor of a wing-tipped partridge, he spent all his half-holidays for a month in excursions to the woods in football season, where he painfully gathered partridge berries and other woodland plunder, scratched himself with briars, mired himself to the eyebrows in bottomless bogs, smeared his clothes and hands with pitch, and impaled himself on hidden stubs in order to nurse and care for his pet.

He would toss his rooster over the fence into a neighboring hen yard and watch the contest which immediately ensued, with soul-absorbing interest, and the fight once decided, whether for or against his bird, he would bathe, salve, and care for the bruised and bloody gladiators with the greatest care and patience.

He was always bringing home diseased dogs which invariably developed fits and had to be killed, or cats that had fleas and drove the entire family to scratching and complaining.

He was fond of frogs, toads, mice, squirrels, birds, worms, beetles, slugs, snakes, and all sorts of crawling, creeping, biting, stinging, and otherwise unpleasant vermin, to which he was invariably kind and attentive, although his ministrations to their needs usually resulted in their untimely deaths.

He was particularly fond of chickens and always had several broods every spring and summer, which he watched over like a guardian angel.

Plupy inherited this fondness for animals from his father, who had a mania for purchasing spring-halted and spavined old plugs and treating them with a variety of decoctions of his own inventing, which, when applied, although warranted to remove the cause of lameness or disease, removed nothing but the hair and ofttimes the hide of the afflicted but patient animals.

He would buy cows that promptly developed garget, horn-ail, or sevenfold indigestion in every one of their stomachs at once, and in time he would succeed in removing them from a sinful world by judicious and kindly intentioned treatment.

And so one night when Plupy brought him the appalling intelligence that one of his newly hatched chickens had been buried in a corner of the barn beneath the superincumbent weight of about a ton and a half of hay, the old gentleman was all sympathy, and with him sympathy meant action.

Armed with a couple of forks, Plupy and his father mounted to the barn loft. "Listen, father," said Plupy, breathing heavily through the nose from his haste in mounting the stairs.

"Howjer spose I can listen, when you are breathing like a planing mill?" retorted the old gentleman. "Shut up, and praps I can hear something."

Thus adjured, Plupy held his breath. Sure enough, they heard a distant, muffled peep from one corner where the hay was piled the highest.

"There he is," said Plupy's father, and with great vigor began to pitch huge forkfuls of fragrant hay on poor Plupy, with stern parental command to stow it away and be lively. Indeed, had not Plupy been in the highest degree lively and energetic, he would soon have shared the fate of the imprisoned chicken. Indeed, it was only by taking advantage of the frequent intervals when the old gentleman's wind gave out, that Plupy by hard work managed to keep his head above the surface. As it was, he was hard put to keep up, and his tongue hung out like a panting dog while he inhaled hayseed, dust, and a variety of foreign substances that made him sneeze thunderously and wheeze like a grampus.

For an hour they worked with short intervals of rest and refreshment, without incident. The feeble peeping became nearer and stronger; the mound of hay decreased steadily while that behind Plupy became mountainous. Finally they removed the last forkful. "There he is, father," shrieked Plupy, "grab him, quick!"

Both Plupy and his father dashed forward and grabbed frantically at the small mite. Their heads came together with a thud. "Ow! ow! ow!" howled Plupy as he went over backwards, striking his head resoundingly on the bare boards.

"What in thunder you trying to do, you numbhead?" roared Plupy's father, holding his nose with both hands and blinking through a flash of fireworks.

Plupy arose warily and ready to dodge the expected cuff, but it came not, for his father stood staring at a small hole in the side wall of the barn and with his eyes bulging out like walnuts.

"Well, I swear," he growled, "that infernal little cuss fell down that hole."

Instantly hostilities were suspended and they listened intently. Sure enough, from the depths of the hole came the feeble, frightened peeping of the little prisoner.

"Whacher goin' t' do now, father?" queried Plupy.

"Let the little idiot rip," snarled Plupy's father. "Whaddier think, I'm goin' to crawl down that hole like a thunderin' garter snake?" he replied with fine sarcasm.

"I guess not," he continued, without waiting for a reply. "I've broke my back and strained both arms pitchin' over more'n fifteen tons of damp hay that weighed three thousand pounds to the ton, and I've breathed in a half-bushel of hayseed and cobwebs, and I'm not going to lift a finger if that cussed chicken peeps until doomsday," and Plupy's father, snorting with disgust, tramped heavily down the creaking stairs, followed by the reluctant Plupy, almost in tears.

"Aw, come on now, Father," he pleaded. "What's the good of leaving the poor little thing in that hole?"

"I tell you I've done al! I'm goin' to," said Plupy's father.

"Howdjer like to be in a hole like him?" queried Plupy.

" 'F I didn't know any better than to fall down a hole when somebody was tryin' to save my life, I ought to stay there," retorted Plupy's father grumpily.

"But I think it's mean to leave a poor little chicken to die down in a black hole like that. Jest like's not a big rat will get him," said Plupy mournfully, "it's mean as dirt, so now!"

"Not another word, sir," said Plupy's father warningly, "unless you want to get your ears boxed."

Plupy discreetly said no more but went down by the side of the barn and listened. Pretty soon he shouted, "Say, Father, he's right inside here, and if we can pull this board out about an inch or two we can get him."

"Git a crowbar over to Sam Dyers and we will try it. Hurry up now," said Plupy's father, again laying off his coat.

Plupy ran for the crowbar and returned in half a minute. Then Plupy's father inserted the point of the bar in the crack and sprung it back an inch or so, whereupon Plupy, to assist, promptly put his fingers in the crevice thus made. Just at this point Plupy's father, seeing a better place, removed the crowbar, and the board sprang back and cruelly pinched poor Plupy's hands.

"Ow! Ow!! Ow!!! I'm caught, Father, you're pinchin' my fingers off! Ow! Ow!!" he roared.

"You thunderin' fool! Whatcher put them in there for?" stormed Plupy's father, rushing back with the bar and prying the boards apart, while Plupy, wailing loudly, pressed his injured fingers between his knees and alternately bent double and straightened out in dire anguish of spirit.

"Come! come!" said Plupy's father impatiently, "you are not killed quite yet, so stop howling."

"Guess you'd howl if you had all your fingers jammed into puddin'," groaned Plupy.

Finally, however, he calmed his troubled spirit and with his father turned again to rescue the imprisoned.

The next move was to put the point of the bar under a board, and Plupy's father straightened up. The board did not give or spring. Again he heaved like a Titan. No result. Then giving utterance to a gruntingly expressed determination to "start the cu-cu-ssed thing if he bub-bub-broke the bar," he strained and tugged until the cords in his neck stood out and his eyes became bloodshot.

Still no result. Plupy's father was puzzled, until he found that he had placed the bar beneath the stone foundation and was trying desperately to lift the entire building single-handed and alone, whereupon he cursed heartily.

Next he carefully placed the bar in the right place and threw his weight on it. Crack! the board came off so quickly that he fell on his hands and knees with his hands under the bar.

Plupy did not laugh. He knew better than that. Plupy's father should not have said such things as he did in Plupy's hearing.

Now, Plupy's father was a man of determination, and right there he registered a solemn vow to get that chicken if he tore that barn down, and he went about his task promptly and vigorously but with a singular absence of skill and neatness.

Plupy watched his father with bated breath as clapboards, sheathing, and studding fell in showers and the crack and shiver of rending wood filled the air. Finally Plupy's father got the chicken. It ran out into the grass and boards under Plupy's father's feet. They hunted some time for it and finally found it. Plupy's father had accidentally stepped on it. Plupy's father weighed two hundred and fifteen pounds. The chicken was very small, but after it was stepped on it spread out over a considerable space.

The carpenters came next day and the day after and the day after that.

Plupy's father was a kind-hearted man, but nobody in the family said anything to him about it. It would not have been well to do so. ■

When Nudism Came to New Hampshire

NEWTON F. TOLMAN "It is well known that to get anywhere, you have to have a profession," wrote Newton F. Tolman. "Mine is that of an unsuccessful writer, and my wife is an unsuccessful painter."

Still, along the way Tolman managed to eke out a comfortable living through various enterprises in the rural New Hampshire town where he spent his life, including writing humorous pieces for *The Atlantic Monthly, Boston Globe*, and other publications.

He also turned out at least a couple of popular books on country life in New England, although he insisted that all the most successful "country" writers were urban exiles. "I could never qualify as a country writer," he said, "because I was *born* in our old farmhouse—we didn't have to buy one."

■ Somebody asked me the other day, "Is it true you once had a nudist colony up here?"—about the way you would ask whether we'd ever had a colony of cannibals or maybe some cult that practiced human sacrifice.

The question had been sparked by an item in the daily newspaper, and I was happy to be reminded of this chapter from our local history.

According to the news item, a man was arrested recently while driving in his car stark naked. It seems he had taken a swim on a deserted stretch of beach and was about to get dressed. But, on seeing a prowl car approaching, he panicked and drove off at high speed. Such was his funk in this dilemma, the police had to fire bullets through the back of his car to stop him.

If this unfortunate "Nude Male Driver Caught in Car Chase" had ever read a certain book I once owned, he wouldn't have been so nervous about being surprised in the buff. The book was our inspiration and operating manual in the heyday of our nudist group some thirty-five years ago—a scholarly work entitled (as I recall it) something like *Adventures in Nakedness*, by a man whose name escapes me now.

My copy has long since disappeared, stolen no doubt by some good friend, but a fairly vivid impression of it remains. The author, with the air of one bringing a Great Message to his fellow Americans, describes a tour of European nudist centers. He sets out just to observe but soon becomes an ardent convert. In sober, scientific detail, he records the moral and physical benefits of nudism in a mixed society. The lonely and impoverished stenographer, for example, at a nudist camp finds herself on an equal footing with the rich daughter of a prominent family.

Many photographs bore out his theme, showing nude crowds of both sexes, old and young, dancing, swimming, playing volleyball, turning cartwheels, and standing on their heads (the last seemed to be a favorite pose). There were also scenes with elderly, stout burghers and their wives dining or playing bridge. Much of this action took place in Germany, where Hitler had not yet put everybody in uniform and where, incidentally, clothing was then very expensive. (Wonder what would have happened had Hitler become a nudist, instead of a Nazi . . . ?)

The author also found flourishing nudist establishments in Scandinavia and elsewhere. France didn't seem to go for the idea much; maybe there was too much competition from the Folies Bergère. And in the British Isles the cultist missionaries got nowhere at all, the English stuffily clinging to their traditional love of raiment for all occasions.

In one memorable passage the author arrives at a nudist camp somewhere in Germany. After checking in at the gate and leaving his clothes, he sets out for a stroll on the crowded beach. He is hailed by a middle-aged lady with a nicely tanned figure (the various components of which are described objectively in some detail) who is sunbathing on the sand. They converse for a time, but he is quite embarrassed because, while she calls him by name, he cannot place her at all.

Then, laughingly, the lady reminds him that they became acquainted only a few days before while traveling to Hamburg on the same ship together—fully clothed. And he realizes that her ordinarily drab and unimpressive personality has suddenly become so enlivened, so vivacious—by the simple act of removing her glasses and all her clothing—that he didn't recognize her. (What a difference one or two little things can make!)

It was not this book, however, that gave us the idea for starting our own version of a nudist club. We had already drifted into it by ourselves. It evolved out of an earlier summertime fraternity, all male, known for some years as the Woodpeckers. Most of us were still of school or college age when we formed this rather informal group.

Physical culture in all forms was flowering in those days. Bernarr Macfadden was making millions promoting the body beautiful. Men had begun to go swimming in trunks without uppers, and girls—who but recently had adopted "knickers"—in one-piece bathing suits without stockings. Getting well tanned was the first preoccupation of every arrival at the summer colonies.

On another lake a couple of miles from the one where our farm was located, a boys' camp had been started. It was soon followed by many others. The camp boys lived in tents and played Indian, naked, all summer. Actually they wore breechclouts or shorts, but no woman was allowed within miles, except for Sunday visiting hours.

Our old farmhouse had been enlarged into a sort of inn, and we built a dozen cottages for rent. "The Pond" became a full-fledged summer colony, with the usual mixture of artists, business or professional people, millionaires, and other oddballs. But the whole community was dominated socially, at least as far as possible, by the Proper Bostonians who had got there first.

So when it began to be known that the Woodpeckers were working in the fields, hiking, swimming, and holding picnics in the woods with no clothes, we were considered to be definitely subversive, at best. Naturally, this added a certain zest to our meetings.

Much of the credit for founding the Woodpeckers must go to Sandy Lewis, a part-Hawaiian art student who worked at the farm a few summers. The farm work gang consisted of six or eight school or college boys and was often joined, for the fun of it, by several other boys from vacationing families around the area. In those days we hayed largely by hand, and while shaking-out, raking, cocking, and loading, we used to take off all our clothes, to keep them free of hayseed and sweat. Then we would swim in the nearest pond or stream.

Sandy was a remarkable athlete: a great swimmer and diver, of course, also a gymnast, a boxer, a weight-lifter, an expert at all games, and a natural leader with lively imagination and wit. One day when two new arrivals from the city, with their white skins, joined our sun-blackened gang, Sandy decided we should "initiate" them. Since we had to have something to initiate them into, we invented the club. Nobody remembers who thought up the name Woodpeckers, or why.

We decided to meet in the woods behind the farm at noon on Sunday. The new recruits would be required to hike the two miles to the village, circle completely around it, and return, wearing only tennis shoes and carrying one sock. (The latter was for cigarettes, etc.) All the rest of us would go along, too—similarly clad, of course—just to see that they didn't welsh on us.

The initiation proved such a success that it became a regular custom every summer thereafter. Whenever a prospective member arrived at the farm, the next Sunday all hands would take the village initiation hike.

There were usually adventures of one sort or another. A dozen or fifteen strong, we would march along the main highway until we heard someone approaching, then scatter into the foliage until the danger had passed. Once we all walked for half a mile in stealthy silence behind a buggy in which an old couple was driving to the village, some of us actually holding on to the back of the buggy. The old man and his wife never looked around, and I always wondered what their reaction would have been if they had.

Another time we trotted around the corner of a house we knew was unoccupied, only to step into the midst of two families picnicking on the lawn. Some of our members ran all the way home cross-country, never daring to stop for breath.

Then there was the day when, at a crossroads, Sandy bet Charley Nason ten dollars Charley wouldn't dare stand on top of the signpost until the first car went past. Charley, who was broke at the time, accepted readily. But he made the condition that he could hold his hands over his face.

When we boosted him up on the post, he looked like a Greek statue. He'd just arrived from Philadelphia, and his skin was lily-white in the bright sun. The rest of us crouched behind the stone wall and waited.

Presently we heard a car approaching. Charley didn't so much as twitch a muscle. But as it drew close, he saw through his fingers that it was an open car containing the three Emerson girls, their mother, and a couple of other women. This was too much for Charley, who fancied himself as a social lion with the mothers and daughters of the summer colony. He spun around and took a wild leap, racing off through the pines like a startled faun.

When the Woodpeckers were a little older and two or three had married, we decided to become coeducational. Somebody had got hold of *Adventures in Nakedness* at about this time. So we launched New Hampshire's first real nudist club, and for all I know it may have been the last.

It flourished for only three or four happily exciting summers. Our innocent outings split the whole summer community violently down the middle: pronudist and antinudist. Nothing ever provoked so many fights in the whole long period between Woodrow Wilson and the Spanish Civil War.

At one front-porch session, a young matron from Xenia, Ohio, announced that she just could not believe such horrible things could really happen. She and her husband, she asserted, always undressed in complete darkness or in separate rooms. And she went on to tell about the time, when she was seventeen, that her sister had surprised her in the bathtub after she'd forgotten to lock the door, and she'd fainted dead away.

At times we heard rumors somebody was going to prosecute us, but we always met in remote fields and pastures where ambush would be difficult. And, guerrilla-fashion, we kept changing our meeting places.

Sometimes approval came from unexpected sources. One day Sandy Lewis and I were delivering ice to the cottage of Miss Bellew, an elderly spinster. She was a retired history teacher. Miss Bellew told us she had heard we held outings in the woods, where we picked berries and sun-bathed in the nude.

Bracing ourselves, Sandy and I didn't deny the charge. She then said, "I've always thought it would be a splendid idea—so natural and healthful! If you wouldn't mind, I would love to join your group. . . . " And, When did we plan our next meeting? and, Where should she meet us? and so on.

We were not equal to the compliment. Miss Bellew was very formidably stout of build and more ancient than any of the matrons pictured in *Adventures in Nakedness*. We just couldn't face up to the thought of her in the nude, trying to frolic around with our members in some mountain pasture. Mumbling that we would "let her know some time," we hurried away. I still feel guilty about it. She was a better sport than we were.

Usually we didn't allow clothed persons at our rendezvous, but we made an exception of Edgar Frude, a young prep-school teacher who fancied himself as a great intellectual. We all liked to kid him. While we would all be lying out in some field taking a sunbath, Edgar would show up in sharply creased flannels and, without even removing his bow tie and straw hat, sit stiffly on a rock and lecture to anybody who would listen. The game was to taunt him about his prudishness, bookishness, and general lack of manly qualities.

He would retaliate with prosy and clinical speeches. We were, he said, typical American nonintellectual types, mere exhibitionists, extroverts of the most obvious sort. His favorite phrase was "prurient youth."

Edgar had always been a loudly self-proclaimed misogynist. But some of us were sure he came to our conclaves for one reason only: to get a look at the anatomy of the more shapely girls. He must have liked what he saw, because a little later he married a female psychologist.

There were, of course, many rumors about our immorality. Nothing could have been further from the truth. Most of the girls didn't even smoke. Anything but the most coldly impersonal relations between the sexes would have been completely out of line at any meeting of the Woodpeckers. Our whole creed would have been undermined.

In any case, we were too busy eluding the local constabulary, the deacons of the village church, and the irate mothers of the summer colony.

Our most reluctant recruit was a prim, rather snobbish girl named Agatha Britonhouse. She was about nineteen when she first landed at the farm to spend the summer. She quickly let it be known that she was one of the *Virginia* Britonhouses—apparently a rare and superior subspecies of Britonhouse.

Aggie's small figure was perfection in all respects, and she could not walk without switching her hips, looking from the rear like Ann Corio going onstage to do a strip. But her face, while not unpretty, had in repose a sort of pouting look and seemed to promise that she would snarl or even snap at anybody who came too close. It was more than a promise, as the boys soon found out. And we came to the conclusion, sad as it was, that Aggie was a born old maid—one of nature's more ironical pranks, it seemed, when you saw her in a swim suit.

We all used to work on Aggie, that summer and the next, trying to persuade her to join up. Nobody had the slightest idea she ever would, but it was a sort of game. She loved the attention but remained elaborately scornful of us.

Toward the end of the third summer everybody had long since tired of arguing with Aggie, and nobody had been taking much notice of her. Then one afternoon as we were assembling, she abruptly announced she was coming along. But only to watch, she added in her precise, prim little voice.

Our plan that day was to play volleyball in a clearing back in the woods. There was a big sawdust heap left by a portable sawmill, ideal for lying around and sunbathing. We had found that the clean, slightly fermenting stuff, if you dug into it, produced a combined steam bath and alcohol rub.

After everybody else had disrobed, Aggie, no doubt feeling a little out of place, took off her dress and lay down in the sawdust wearing only pink panties and bra. This gave her a decidedly sexy look compared to the three or four other girls, wholesome and natural in their altogether. But Aggie would make no further concessions.

After a time, when we were all replete with exercise and lying half asleep on the warm and fragrant pile, Ken Williams crept up behind Aggie. Ken was a big, good-natured kid from someplace in New Jersey, and he was always kidding Aggie.

Now he suddenly grabbed her feet and dragged her along for several yards through the sawdust. It had the desired effect. Coarse sawdust is pleasant against the skin only when not confined, and after Aggie had done some squirming and dancing around, her two garments still clung like the poisoned robe of Hercules. Finally she ripped them off entirely.

Nobody paid any attention to all this. But taking the final step evidently went to Aggie's head. She climbed up to the top of the pile and waved her arms, shouting, "I'm free, I'm free! Look, everybody, I'm free!"

Ken had gone back to his couch in the sawdust, and the only comment came from Sandy Lewis, who said without opening his eyes, "She may be free, but she's nuts. Tell her to shut up, so I can go back to sleep."

That was the last outing of the summer and, as it turned out, one of the last formal gatherings of the Woodpeckers. I never saw Aggie again, so I never learned what effect, if any, her new-found freedom may have had on her. ■

Coming of Age
in Decency

PETER DeVRIES A British critic has called Peter DeVries "the authentic, troubled voice of educated East-coast America, with all its appalling confusions and unspeakable hang-ups." He also happens to be one of America's funniest contemporary writers.

DeVries, a long-time member of the editorial staff of *The New Yorker*, has turned out at least two dozen comic novels, primarily dealing with life in the suburban Connecticut region where he resides.

His stories, characterized by a stylish word play, usually involve comic collisions between the sophisticated sensibilities of his characters and the cultural realities of their surroundings. An early example comes from the opening chapter of his 1956 novel, *Comfort Me With Apples.*

■ I think I can say my childhood was as unhappy as the next braggart's. I was read to sleep with the classics and spanked with obscure quarterlies. My father was anxious to have me follow in his footsteps—if that is a good metaphor for a man whose own imprints were largely sedentary—and he watched me closely for echoes of himself that were more felicitous than most. He advised people to have intellect and to look beneath what he called "the epithelium of things," though he did discourage scrutiny of his own motives.

Living on a little money my grandmother had left him, he spent his time exercising a talent which was more or less in his own mind. He wrote essays of a philosophical nature which he sent to those periodicals off which he tried to rub some of the bloom on me. They were all returned. This gave him a feeling of rejection (rather than one of submission) and he developed internal troubles. He went to a hospital for observation, but they found nothing worse than what they called a sensitive colon, which is I suppose an apt enough ailment for a man as meticulous about punctuation as he was.

The hospital library was nothing to brighten his stay, and he rather truculently offered to "send over something decent" as soon as he could, a promise he set about fulfilling the minute he got home.

He drove back to the hospital two days after he was discharged, with a few cartons of selections from his own shelves. I rode along and helped carry them in through the emergency ward, from which the basement room where the ladies' auxiliary handled books was most conveniently accessible. It was an icy day in late winter, and I picked my way carefully behind my father with a small boxful—he toting a rather large packet on his shoulder, like a grocery boy with an order. The walk we traversed sloped upward across a short courtyard, and at a turn in it my father's foot shot out from under him and, loudly exclaiming "Damnation!" he went down, spilling culture in every direction and breaking a leg.

The bone was set free by the hospital, which also gave him a room without cost ("No it is not handsome of them to do this—it would be outrageous if they did not!"), and soon he was propped up in the same bed again dipping into his old copy of Plutarch, available to him from a trundled cart of books now noticeably enriched as to contents.

What displeased him constitutes a history of our time. He could not abide typewritten correspondence or most people's handwriting. He hated radio and couldn't wait for television to be perfected so he could hate that too. The very word "psychosomatic" was enough to send him into symptoms for which no organic cause could be found; the decline of human teeth he laid to the door of toothpaste, "surely chief among the sweets properly arraigned as villains," as he asserted through dentures which clacked corroboratively. He hated everything brewed in the vats of modernity. He hated music without melody, paintings without pictures, and novels without plots. In other words, a rich, well-rounded life.

The house on the outskirts of Decency we lived in was built around a silo, which became my father's library. Swiss cheese, except for the silo, comprised the principal masonry, as the dank airs which continually stirred the draperies attested; the wiring was, to put it no lower, shocking; the fireplace drew briskly but in the wrong direction, sending out ashes which settled like a light snow on our family and on the strangers within our gates, for in those years my parents loved to entertain. They had lived originally in a dinette apartment in town but had begun to drift apart and needed more room. The capacious new house did in fact ease their relations, getting them out of one another's pockets I suppose, and I can still hear my mother wailing over some new kitchen crisis, "Oh, God," and my father answering cozily from the silo, "Were you calling me, dear?"

He believed that the art of conversation was dead. His own small talk, at any rate, was bigger than most people's large. "I believe it was Hegel who defined love as the ideality of the relativity of the reality of an infinitesimal portion of the absolute totality of the Infinite Being," he would chat at dinner.

It was my father's example which, more than any other single factor in my life, inspired in me my own conversational preference: the light aphorism.

I belonged in adolescence to a clique of pimpled *boulevardiers* who met at a place called the Samothrace, a restaurant and ice-cream parlor run by a Greek who let us pull tables out on the sidewalk and talk funny. The Greek's name was Andropoulos, but he had Americanized it to Nachtgeborn, which blended in better with the heavy German population that dominated that end of town and which he therefore thought better for business reasons. He was a prickly sort who was always complaining that this country was commercial, especially when trade was slack and he was more irritable than usual. We expatriates, be that as it may, could be seen there every evening loitering over coffee and pastry, or maybe toying with a little of what the Greek called fruit compost. I often wore my topcoat with the sleeves hanging loose, so that the effect was like an Inverness cape, when it was not like that of two broken arms. An earnest youth on the high-school debating squad, who got in with our set by mistake one *soir*, tried to interest me in politics by speaking of the alarming layoffs then occurring in the Department of Agriculture.

"I had thought," I said, smiling round at my disciples as I tapped a Melachrino on the lid of its box, "that the Department of Agriculture slaughtered its surplus employees."

This attitude grew into a *fin-de-siècle* one of cultivated fatigue and bored estheticism, marked by amusement with the colloquial mainstream. I would lie full-length around the house and with a limp hand wave life away. My mother took this as an indication that I had "no pep" and urged a good tonic to fix me up.

"No, no, no!" my father said. "This is what they call Decadence. It's an attitude toward life." He turned and looked down at the horizontal product of their union, disposed on the sofa with a cigarette. "He'll come to his senses."

"Instead of coming to one's senses," I airily returned, "how much more delightful to let one's senses come to one."

My mother, a thin, sentimental woman who often broke up funerals with her weeping, tried to get me interested in "healthy" books like the jumbo three-generation novels she herself couldn't put down.

"The books Mother cannot put down," I said, "are the ones I cannot pick up."

"He *is* run-down. Now I don't care."

Seventeen. Slightly above medium height, slender, with clothes either too casual or too studied—it makes no difference now. I had a pinched-in, pendulous underlip, like the pouring lip on a pitcher, which must have conferred an air of jocularity somewhat at odds with my intention to be "dry." Anyhow, to sit and say "Thomas Wolfe is a genius without talent" was a lot less trouble than was gone to by my contemporaries, who got their effects by riding around in old Fords on the sides of which were painted SEVEN DAYS IN THIS MAKE ONE WEAK.

My best friend was a schoolmate named Nickie Sherman, and he needed a good tonic too. Between the two of us we wrote a junior-college class play that realized far more fully than anything Oscar Wilde ever did the Wilde ideal for a perfect act as one in which there was no action whatever. Ours was laid in the drawing room of an English country house known as Wise Acres, where fabulous wits foregathered and paradox was so far the order of the day that the cook complained the upside-down cakes came out right-side-up. Often seen at Wise Acres, which gave the play its name, was a celebrated detective named Inspector Vermouth. Our one concession to occurrence was in the form of a murder which, however, Vermouth forewent solving because he admired the malefaction so.

A man at the piano entertaining the weekend guests was shot by a pistol secreted within the instrument and wired to go off when a certain chord was struck, a combination of notes so avant-garde as to be likely to appear only in the music of Villa-Lobos, which the murderer knew only that guest was likely to perform. Inspector Vermouth declined to seek out the perpetrator on the ground that he might find him. "And it would be a shame to send him to the gallows," he said. "It was a capital crime."

That our pursuit of nuance was causing even greater strain under Nickie's roof than under my own was brought home to me when his father phoned me, one morning when Nickie was in New York, and asked me to come over—he wanted to talk to me. Mr. Sherman owned a tailor shop a mile from our place where he pressed people's pants while they waited. It being a slow morning with no customers, he was pressing his own pants, while he waited. He stood at the steam iron in his shirttails and shook his head as he told me how Nickie had been worrying him lately.

"Ecks all the time tired and listless—*and* talks odd," he added through a cloud of steam as he bore down on the press. With his foot on the pedal he regarded me over a pair of half-specs, like those worn by the man on the Old Grand Dad whisky label.

"How, odd?" I asked, drawing up a chair. "Can you give me some examples?"

Mr. Sherman turned a pants-leg over and ruminated. "Oh, he's loving life far too much to take part in it, there's too much nature obscurink the billboards . . . I don't know. He's always been a bright boy, but now that he's educated, half of what he says sounds fibble-minded."

I explained perversity and paradox to him—without recourse to *Wise Acres*, which Mr. Sherman hadn't seen. Fortunately the illness of his wife, a woman of Spanish–Irish extraction, had kept them both home the night of the production.

"Paradoxes are where everything sounds the opposite of what it should," I discoursed. "You're not supposed to take them too seriously. That business about loving life far too well to participate in it—Nickie means that he wants to be an observer of the passing scene so he can enjoy it more. They call that esthetic. Nickie's precious."

"He's dollink. Always was dollink boy. But what's going to hepp'm should he stay in the anesthetic? I want he should snap out of it."

"He will, Mr. Sherman."

"I hope so." Drawing on his now crisp trousers, Mr. Sherman ran a critical eye over mine. "Take off your pants and I'll press them so it shouldn't be a total loss you came down here."

I demurred but he insisted. And while he gave my trousers the hot sandwich, I strolled about in shirttails elucidating further what I could of the attitude he had encountered in his son. "It's what they call *fin-de-siècle*. That means the end of the century," I said.

"Dot's how menkind will talk in de future?" he asked, peering at me over the half-glasses.

"No, no, the end of the *last* century, not this one. But it *is* modern in the sense of the *way* he says things. That's known as 'understatement.' "

"He shouldn't lay it on so thick."

As Mr. Sherman overturned my trousers on the iron he seemed also, in his mind, to be revolving the phenomenon just touched on, as the symptom of a larger and more far-reaching decay in human sensibility.

"Poems got no rhyme, books got no stories," he mused in a sudden uncanny echo of my own father's pet peeves, "and now jokes got no point. I was riddink in a magazine about the latest, those hairy-dog stories. Dot's high-class? *Phooey!*" He gestured at my trousers on the iron. " 'When they saw how tight his pants were they thought they'd split.' That's by me humor. I think jokes and stories used to be funnier in my time," he finished with a considered terseness.

"Can you remember some others?" I asked, sitting down again.

Mr. Sherman accepted the challenge. He lit himself a cigar and then immediately set it down in an ashtray nearby.

"There was this fellow from the old country. Immigrant," he began. "He did his best to learn the customs here. But he says to his friend one day, says, 'I don't know. One minute they tell you do one thing and the next something else.' Friend says, 'How do you mean?' Fellow says, 'Well, the other day I'm sitting in church and they all sing, 'Stand up, stand up for Jesus.' The next day I go to the ball park and behind me everybody is yellink as loud as they can, 'For Christ's sake, sit down!' "

I ran all the way home as from a revelation still bursting volcanically behind me, and for days was shaken by the glimpse of a humor more visceral than any I had dreamed had existed since the cave-man days. At the same time, my father cracked down on the offbeat as represented in my nuances, on the ground that they were disrespectful to my mother, who could never possibly hope to understand them. I was finally punished for epigrams and paradoxes by being sent to my room. Here is the way that worked.

One evening at dinner my younger sister Lila and my mother were teasing me about a girl named Crystal Chickering whom I had been dating. My mother remarked she'd have guessed I'd have preferred Jessie Smithers because "Jessie laughs at absolutely everything a person says."

"That is because she has no sense of humor," I said, buttering a roll.

My father stiffened in his chair. "I'll ask you to apologize to your mother for that."

I think that behind this, more than a chivalrous regard for her capacities, was a sense of compunction he himself felt over having neglected her all these years, leaving her to what he eruditely called her "needlepwah" while he sat with his nose in Goethe or went off on vacations by himself.

"If I'd made a fool of the mother who bore me, my father would have given me short shrift. Explain to your mother what that last so-called paradox means. I think I'll insist on that."

The fact was that he didn't understand it himself, and so, while pretending to be indifferently worrying a fishbone out of his mouth, he listened alertly to the exegesis I was glad to give.

"I simply meant that a sense of humor implies discrimination, selection," I said. "So laughing at everything, as Jessie Smithers does, isn't the same as having a sense of humor."

"That clear it up for you, dear?" On receiving an affirmative nod, my father returned to his food.

But my mother went on:

"You mustn't think I *mind* not understanding what the boy says, Roebuck. Goodness gracious, let him talk over my head the same as I talked over my mother's. That's progress."

Feeling perfidy in the form of aphorisms to be uncoiling everywhere about him, my father came to dinner in a Norfolk jacket. We had a dog, Pavlov, who lived for our table scraps: I mean those mealtime squabbles to which he listened with soft thuds of his tail and a look of seeming comprehension. One evening as we sipped our coffee in the living room, I crossed my legs and remarked in regard to poise: "There are only three women in Decency who know how to enter a restaurant."

My father made a truncheon of his *Yale Review*. "Is your mother one?"

"I don't know, Popper, I've never seen her enter a restaurant. I'm always the one who's with her when she does."

"That does it—upstairs. For myself I don't care—paradox away. But I will not have you insulting your mother with language fit for nothing but a Mayfair drawing room. Upstairs!" he repeated with a flourish of his billy.

That allusion to his neglect of my mother had gone home! I rose and, kissing her good night, went up to my room, glad to get away from the hurly-burly.

That Sunday evening at supper my mother remarked on the very trait in me that was unstringing my father, though touching on it obliquely in a reference to Nickie Sherman, whom we'd had to dinner the day before.

"He should learn that when you get *too* smart and clever, it isn't much better than being what you boys call corny," she said.

I nodded. "Excessive subtlety does negate itself. It is like being winked at with both eyes."

"You'll apologize to your mother for that last remark," my father said, his face red from bad claret and a lifetime of plain damn exasperation.

"But I'm agreeing with her!" I protested.

"Yes, but she doesn't know that. That poor woman doesn't understand a word you're saying. Agreeing with her is no excuse for talking over her head, sending her own words back over her head. I've warned you about this matter for the last time. Grieving her mother heart with words so elliptical—"

"What does elliptical mean?" my mother asked him.

"—so in excess of what she can comprehend—"

"Now who's running her down?"

"Upstairs!"

"But I've got a date," I objected.

"You should have thought of that sooner."

Rather than waste precious time arguing, I went up and started serving my "sentence" without delay. It was usually about an hour for epigrams, somewhat longer for a paradox. It wasn't till nine o'clock that I was let out tonight, after apologizing for the obscurity of my rejoinder and promising never to do it again. By that time, of course, I was dressed. I was now half an hour late for my date with Crystal Chickering, toward whose house I legged it, as a consequence, with commendable pep. ■

CHARACTERS

Anger and Enumeration

JAMES M. BAILEY James Montgomery Bailey, "The Danbury News Man," was a native of Albany, New York. After serving in the Union Army during the Civil War, he settled in Danbury, Connecticut, where he became a newspaper editor. Like many editors of the time, he wrote a humorous column about the political and social life of his community and periodically collected these into anthologies. Unlike many editors of his time, Bailey was able to give a universal quality to his parochial observations, and his books proved popular with the American public.

Bailey cheerfully acknowledged a lack of originality in producing the books. *Life in Danbury*, an 1873 collection from which the following piece is taken, carried this disclaimer: "Carefully compiled with a pair of eight-dollar shears, by the compiler."

■ A Danbury man named Reubens recently saw a statement that counting one hundred when tempted to speak an angry word would save a man a great deal of trouble. This statement sounded a little singular at first, but the more he read it over the more favorably he became impressed with it, and finally concluded to adopt it.

Next door to Reubens lives a man who has made five distinct attempts in the past fortnight to secure a dinner of green peas by the first of July, and every time has been retarded by Reubens's hens. The next morning after Reubens made his resolution, this man found his fifth attempt to have miscarried. Then he called on Reubens.

He said, "What in thunder do you mean by letting your hens tear up my garden?"

Reubens was tempted to call him a mud-snoot, a new name just coming into general use, but he remembered his resolution, put down his rage, and meekly observed:

"One, two, three, four, five, six, seven, eight . . . "

Then the mad neighbor, who had been eyeing this answer with a great deal of suspicion, broke in again:

"Why don't you answer my question, you rascal?"

But still Reubens maintained his equanimity and went on with the test.

"Nine, ten, eleven, twelve, thirteen, fourteen, fifteen, sixteen . . . "

The mad neighbor stared harder than ever.

"Seventeen, eighteen, nineteen, twenty, twenty-one . . . "

"You're a mean skunk," said the mad neighbor, backing toward the fence.

Reubens's face flushed at this charge, but he only said:

"Twenty-two, twenty-three, twenty-four, twenty-five, twenty-six . . . "

At this figure the neighbor got up on the fence in some haste, but suddenly thinking of his peas, he opened his mouth.

"You mean, low-lived rascal; for two cents I could knock your cracked head over a barn, and I would . . . "

"Twenty-seven, twenty-eight, twenty-nine, thirty, thirty-one, thirty-two, thirty-three . . . "

Here the neighbor broke for the house and, entering it, violently slammed the door behind him; but Reubens did not dare let up on the enumeration, and so he stood out there alone in his own yard and kept on counting while his burning cheeks and flashing eyes eloquently affirmed his judgment. When he got into the eighties, his wife came to the door in some alarm.

"Why Reubens, man, what is the matter with you?" she said. "Do come into the house."

But he didn't let up. She came out to him and clung tremblingly to him, but he only looked into her eyes and said:

"Ninety-three, ninety-four, ninety-five, ninety-six, ninety-seven, ninety-eight, ninety-nine, one hundred—go into the house, old woman, or I'll bust ye!"

And she went. ■

Never Bet the Devil Your Head

EDGAR ALLAN POE It is hard to think of the Boston-born Poe—poet, critic, and innovator in the short-story form—as a humorous writer. He is best known for his tales of horror and his dark poetry. Still, from time to time Poe turned out funny pieces for the periodicals of his day, even though the humor more often than not reflected his peculiar fancy for the macabre.

■ It is not my design to vituperate my friend, Toby Dammit. He was a sad dog, it is true, but he himself was not to blame for his vices. They grew out of a personal defect in his mother. She did her best in the way of flogging him while an infant—for duties, to her well-regulated mind, were always pleasures, and babies, like tough steaks, are invariably the better for beating.

But—poor woman! She had the misfortune to be left-handed, and a child flogged left-handedly had better be left unflogged. The world revolves from right to left. It will not do to whip a baby from left to right. If each blow in the proper direction drives an evil propensity out, it follows that every thump in an opposite direction knocks its quota of wickedness in.

Thus it was that no matter how often and severely he was cuffed, Toby Dammit grew worse and worse. At six months of age I caught him gnawing a pack of cards. At seven months he was in the consistent habit of catching and kissing the female babies. So he went on, increasing in iniquity, until I went down on my knees and, uplifting my voice, made prophecy of his ruin.

Perhaps the worst of all his vices was a propensity for cursing and swearing and for backing his profane assertions with bets. He could scarcely utter a sentence without interlarding it with propositions to gamble. However, I will do my friend the justice to say that with him the thing was a mere formula—nothing more—imaginative phrases wherewith to round off a sentence. No one ever thought of taking him up.

For poverty was another vice which the peculiar deficiency of Dammit's mother had entailed upon her son. He was detestably poor. This was the reason, no doubt, that his expressions about *betting* seldom took a pecuniary turn. I will not be bound to say that I ever heard him make use of such a figure of speech as "I'll bet you a dollar." It was usually "I'll bet you what you please," or "I'll bet you a trifle," or else, more significantly still, "I'll bet the Devil my head."

This latter form seemed to please him best—perhaps because it involved the least risk. His head was small, and thus his loss would have been small, too. In the end he abandoned all other forms of wager and gave himself up to "I'll bet the Devil my head," with a pertinacity and exclusiveness of devotion that displeased not less than it surprised me. I am always displeased by circumstances for which I cannot account. Mysteries force a man to think, and so injure his health.

One fine day, having strolled out together arm in arm, our route led us in the direction of a river. There was a bridge, and we resolved to cross it. It was roofed over by way of protection from the weather; and the archway, having but few windows, was uncomfortably dark. At length, having passed nearly across the bridge, we approached the end of the footway, when our progress was impeded by a turnstile of some height. Through this I made my way quietly, pushing it around as usual.

But this would not serve the turn of Toby Dammit. He insisted upon leaping the stile and said he would cut a pigeon-wing over it in the air. Now this, conscientiously speaking, I did not think he could do. I therefore told him in so many words that he was a braggadocio and could not do what he said.

He straightway offered to bet the Devil his head that he could.

I was about to reply, when I heard close at my elbow an ejaculation, "*Ahem!*" I started and looked about me in surprise. My glance fell into a nook of the framework of the bridge and upon the figure of a little lame old gentleman of venerable aspect. Nothing could be more reverend than his whole appearance, for he not only had on a full suit of black, but his shirt was perfectly clean and the collar turned very-neatly down over a white cravat, while his hair was parted in front like a girl's. His hands were clasped pensively together over his stomach, and his two eyes were carefully and piously rolled up into the top of his head.

I perceived that he wore a black silk apron over his small clothes. This was a thing I thought very odd. Before I had time to make any remark, however, he interrupted me with a second "Ahem!"

To this observation I was not immediately prepared to reply. The fact is, remarks of this laconic nature are nearly unanswerable. I am not ashamed to say, therefore, that I turned to Mr. Dammit for assistance.

"Dammit," I said, "what are you about? Don't you hear? The gentleman says 'Ahem!' "

If I had shot Mr. D. through and through with a bomb or knocked him in the head with a copy of the *Poets and Poetry of America*, he could scarcely have been more discomfited than by those simple words. "You don't say so?" he gasped at length. "Are you quite sure he said *that*? Well, at all events, I am in for it now, and may as well put a bold face on the matter. Here goes then—*ahem!*"

At this the little old gentleman seemed pleased, God only knows why. He left his station at the nook of the bridge, limped forward with a gracious air, took Dammit by the hand and shook it cordially, looking all the while straight up in his face with an air of the most unadulterated benignity.

"I am quite sure you will win, Dammit," said he, "but we are obliged to have a trial, you know, for the sake of mere form."

With a deep sigh, my friend took off his coat. The old gentleman now took him by the arm and led him more into the shade of the covered bridge—a few paces back from the turnstile.

"My good fellow," said the little old gentleman in black, "I make it a point of conscience to allow you this much run. Wait here till I take my place by the stile, so that I may see whether you go over it handsomely and don't omit any flourishes of the pigeon wing."

Here he took his position by the stile, looked up—and, I thought—smiled very slightly, then tightened the strings of his apron, saying: "One—two—three—and away!"

Punctually at the word "away" my friend set off in a strong gallop. I saw him run nimbly and spring grandly from the floor of the bridge, cutting the most awful flourishes with his legs as he went up. I saw him high in the air, pigeon-winging it to admiration just over the top of the stile; and, of course, I thought it an unusually singular thing that he did not *continue* to go over.

But the whole leap was the affair of a moment, and before I had a chance to make any profound reflections, down came Mr. Dammit on the flat of his back, *on the same side of the stile from which he had started*. At the same instant I saw the old gentleman limping off at top speed, having caught and wrapped up in his apron something that fell heavily into it from the darkness of the arch just over the turnstile.

At all this I was much astonished, but I had no leisure to think, for Mr. Dammit lay particularly still, and I concluded that his feelings had been hurt and that he stood in need of my assistance. I hurried up to him and found that he had received what might be termed a serious injury. The truth is, he had been deprived of his head, which, after a close search, I could not find anywhere. A thought struck me, and I threw open an adjacent window of the covered bridge, when the sad truth flashed upon me at once. About five feet just above the top of the turnstile and crossing the arch of the footpath so as to constitute a brace, there extended a great iron bar. With the edge of this brace it appeared evident that the neck of my unfortunate friend had come precisely in contact.

He did not long survive his terrible loss. I bedewed his grave with my tears, worked a bar sinister on his family escutcheon, and for the general expenses of his funeral sent in my very moderate bill. When payment was refused it, I had Mr. Dammit dug up at once and sold him for dog's meat. ■

Soft Sawder

THOMAS C. HALIBURTON Thomas Chandler Haliburton was a prominent judge and politician in the Canadian province of Nova Scotia during the early nineteenth century. He is best known, however, for his comic stories about Sam Slick, a traveling clock salesman from New England.

Haliburton had a specific political and social purpose in mind when he created the Sam Slick character; he hoped to awaken Nova Scotians to what he regarded as their backwardness and lack of enterprise by satirically contrasting them with the quick-witted, energetic Yankee peddler from the United States. The stories eventually took on an international popularity, being translated into several languages, and Haliburton's reformist intentions were—thankfully—lost in the process.

■ "How is it," said I to Sam Slick, "that you manage to sell such an immense number of clocks, which certainly can't be called necessary articles, among people with whom there seems to be so great a scarcity of money?"

Sam looked me in the face and said in a confidential tone, "Why, I don't care if I do tell you, for the market is glutted and I shall quit this circuit. It's done by a knowledge of soft sawder and human nature.

"Here is Deacon Flint's. I've got but one clock left and I guess I'll sell it to him."

At the gate of a most comfortable-looking farmhouse stood Deacon Flint, a respectable old man who had understood the value of time better than most of his neighbors, to judge by the appearance of his place.

After the usual salutation, an invitation to alight was accepted by Sam. He said that he wished to take leave of Mrs. Flint before he left Colchester, Nova Scotia.

We had hardly entered the house before Sam, pointing to the view from the window, said, "If I was to tell them down in Connecticut that there was such a farm as this away Down East here in Nova Scotia, they wouldn't believe me. Why, there ain't such a location in all New England!" Sam praised the fine bottom land and admiringly said that the "water privilege" alone must be worth three or four thousand dollars—"twice as good as that Governor Case paid fifteen thousand dollars for. I wonder, Deacon, you don't put up a carding mill on it. The same works would carry a turning lathe, a shingle machine, a circular saw. . . . "

"Too old," said the Deacon. "Too old for all these speculations."

"Old!" repeated Sam. "Not you! Why, you're worth half a dozen of the young men we see nowadays. You're young enough to . . . " Here he said something in a lower tone of voice, which I did not distinctly hear, but whatever it was, the Deacon was pleased. He smiled and said he did not think of such things now.

"But your beasts," the Deacon said. "Your beasts must be put in and have a feed."

As the old gentleman closed the door after him, Sam drew near to me and said in an undertone, "That's what I call soft sawder."

He was cut short by the entrance of Mrs. Flint.

"Just come to say goodbye, Mrs. Flint," he told her.

"What!" said she. "Have you sold all your clocks?"

"Yes, and very low, too. Money is scarce and I wished to close the concern. I'm wrong in saying *all*, for I have just one left. Neighbor Steel's wife asked to have the refusal of it, but I guess I won't sell it. I had but two of them, this one and the feller of it that I sold to Governor Lincoln. General Green, the Secretary of State for Maine, said he'd give me fifty dollars for this here one. It has composition wheels and patent axles. It's a beautiful article, a real first chop and no mistake, genuine superfine. But I guess I'll take it back. And, besides, Squire Hawk might think kind of hard that I didn't give him the offer."

"Dear me," said Mrs. Flint. "I should like to see it. Where is it?"

"Oh, it's in a chest of mine over the way at Tom Tape's store. I guess he can ship it on to Eastport."

"Just let's look at it," said Mrs. Flint. "That's a good man."

Sam Slick, willing to oblige, soon produced the clock, a gaudy, highly varnished trumpery affair. He placed it on the chimney piece, where its beauties were pointed out and duly appreciated by Mrs. Flint, whose admiration was about ending in a proposal to buy when Deacon Flint returned from giving his directions about the care of the horses.

The Deacon praised the clock. He too thought it a handsome one. But the Deacon was a prudent man. He had a watch, he was sorry, but he had no occasion for a clock.

Sam said, "I guess you're in the wrong furrow this time, Deacon. It ain't for sale. And if it was, I reckon Neighbor Steel's wife would have it, for she gives me no peace about it."

Mrs. Flint said Mr. Steel had enough to do, poor man, to pay his interest without buying clocks for his wife.

"It's no concern of mine," said Sam, "what he has to do, as long as he pays me. But I guess I don't want to sell it. And, besides, it comes too high. That clock couldn't be made at Rhode Island under forty dollars."

Suddenly Sam started and said, "Why, it ain't possible!" He looked at his watch. "Why, as I'm alive, it's four o'clock, and if I ain't been two hours here! How on earth shall I reach River Phillip tonight? I tell you what, Mrs. Flint. I'll leave the clock in your care until I return on my way to the States. I'll set it a-going and put it to the right time."

As soon as this operation was performed, he delivered the key to the Deacon, telling him to wind it up every Saturday night.

When we were mounted and on our way, Sam said, "That I call human nature. Now, that clock is sold for forty dollars. It cost me just six dollars and fifty cents. Mrs. Flint will never let Mrs. Steel have the refusal, nor will the Deacon learn until I call for the clock how hard it is to give up.

"We can do without any article of luxury we never had, but once we've had it, it's not in human nature to surrender it voluntarily. Of fifteen thousand sold by myself and my partners in this province, twelve thousand were left in this manner. And only ten clocks were ever returned when we came back around."

Said Sam Slick, "You see, we trust to soft sawder to get the clocks *in* the house and to human nature that they never come *out* of it." ■

The Chip on Grandma's Shoulder

ROBERT K. LEAVITT When Robert Keith Leavitt, a writer and historical researcher, set down his reminiscences of growing up in a small Massachusetts community, he admitted frankly that his informal recollections were "utterly untrustworthy."

After comparing his most vivid memories with those of his boyhood friends, he found that they differed considerably. Furthermore, old photographs, news clippings, and other records showed them all to be wrong. "So I gave over trying to verify details," he wrote. "To hell with documentation. If I remembered a thing such-and-such a way, that was the way it was going to be."

The result was a warm, funny, and reasonably credible memoir of small-town New England in the early 1900s.

■ My grandmother, a frail and silver-seeming little old lady, carried an invisible chip on her shoulder.

This was easier to get away with in the opening years of the present century, and in the town of Bradford in the Old Colony of Massachusetts. For those were the last, sunlit hours of an unsuspecting era, and that was a green-and-golden backwater of intelligent, unhurried life. Time and place combined to make gentlemen gentle. They rarely yielded to the natural impulse to clip a combative old lady on the point of her outthrust jaw.

On the other hand, my grandmother was considerably limited in the indulgence of a natural taste for pugnacity during the half-dozen years she lived with us. She was the acting mother in our home.

My own mother had died early in 1902, leaving my father with two small boys of five and six. Until then my grandmother, as the widow of a clergyman, had been living comfortably in the back farming districts of York County, Maine. In this section, though it is thinly populated, she had an ample supply of fond adversaries by kinship, propinquity, or business.

Moreover, she had leisure to feud happily with them, for she had inherited a modest income from her father, once a redoubtable country lawyer of those parts. However, on being called to preside over her son's bereft family, she resolutely put aside the pleasures of retirement and lit out for Bradford with a trunk solid-packed with her choicest possessions. Figuratively, too, she stowed away and clamped down in this trunk—which she never entirely unpacked during her time with us—all her purely sporting targets of attack, bringing forth for use only those she considered practical and workaday.

These, to be sure, were numerous. They included conspicuously: the Demon Rum and his procurer, Tobacco; cruelty to animals; misbehavior in church; suspected skulduggery on the part of grocers, butchers, and others; inhumanity of man to man; and imposition upon the family under her charge by anyone soever. She also dealt vigorously with inanimate objects that presumed to defy her—such as a stove that smoked or a pipe that froze—and if her battles with these often resulted in a double knockout, at least she always floored them, sometimes for keeps.

On advancing to any attack, she looked much like George Washington in the famous Gilbert Stuart "Athenaeum" portrait. Put a lilac-flowered bonnet on Stuart's Washington, draw his fluffed-out hair silkily close to the head, and you would have my grandmother in the instant before battle: the same icy-blue eyes under thin, half-lowered, hemispheric lids; the same high, determined beak; the same ruddy, country-bred complexion; the same grim mouth all set to let off a low-voiced blast fit to lift you right out of your seat, curl your hair, and make a Christian out of you—sincerely rueful, if temporary.

To see my grandmother's George Washington gaze come to rest on any miscreant was like the present-day experience at sports newsreels of watching a fast middleweight measure some blissfully inept opponent for the knockout punch. You know what the cavorting victim-to-be doesn't: that in a matter of seconds he will be flat on the canvas, toes up, and dreaming of Jerusalem the Golden.

Just so, Dicky Hathaway and I once watched my grandmother walk up to an itinerant peddler who was beating a horse stuck on a steep grade. "Gorry!" said Dicky, whom my grandmother had once socked on the nose for misbehavior in her Sunday-school class, "that man better watch out." Instead, the fool dismounted and faced my grandmother with his hands— one holding the whip—on his hips and a silly grin on his face. There was a flicker of black bombazine, too rapid for the eye to follow. In the next instant the whip was in my grandmother's fist and working so fast the fellow collected a dozen welts before he could get out of range, which he did at high speed on an uphill course. My grandmother then led the horse right-about, mounted the wagon, and drove the equipage down to the

Square, where she interned it with Nick Banton, who was Chief (and half) of Bradford's police force.

Her usual or nonembattled expression was also Washingtonian, but with a subtle difference: she looked as Washington might if he had suddenly remembered an irresistibly funny experience while sitting to Stuart and was trying to keep a straight face over it. To her the world was full of quiet amusement. She was forever abrim with secret laughter.

This was the face which she turned almost invariably upon my brother and myself, though people who knew us all too well were at a loss to understand how she could maintain it. Other relatives on whom we were parked for even brief periods were accustomed to employ the hairbrush from the second day on, and my father, though naturally a mild, affectionate man, found himself obliged to develop the technique of barehand spanking to an extraordinarily fine point in order to exist under the same roof with us without taking total leave of his wits. Yet my grandmother, who never laid a hand in wrath on either of us for six mortal years, not only kept us out of reform school but even extracted from us prodigies of useful labor around the house.

Partly this was because she loved us very greatly and, being greatly loved in return, found it easy to overlook our merely venial sins. Most of the others she sidetracked by ingenuity instead of by trying to suppress them.

She knew how to keep two active larvae on the move and out of mischief. In this she was aided by four very special characteristics: a surprising reserve of physical strength; a habit of pooh-poohing difficulties; a weird, piebald knowledge of primitive mechanics; and the gift of being both interested and interesting. She was also sustained in moments of trial by the consolations of culture as manifest in the fine and applied arts.

Her vigor and stamina were amazing in so slight a person. She could saunter up to a heavy-laden trunk; ease one thin, wrinkled hand beneath its strap handle; and in a flash have it up-ended, ready to roll, baggage-man fashion, across the attic floor. She could walk the legs not only off a pair of small boys but off many grown men as well.

In her late sixties she traipsed over Europe with a crony of equal years, and there the two of them had guides begging for mercy in five languages and a dozen dialects. Going out for a stroll from Lucerne one day, they dragged a Swiss who had misunderstood their intentions or underestimated their capabilities clear to the top of Pilatus—a bush-league Alp, to be sure, but higher than anything in the east of this country. They descended in a snowstorm, ambling along in high-buttoned shoes, with their reticules flopping, and assuring the poor anxious guide that this was nothing to the snows on Mt. Washington.

This pooh-poohing technique made life strenuous for my brother and me. There was no such thing as being too tuckered to finish a job if she was bossing it—no such thing, even, as sitting down for a rest. She went at housecleaning—with us for skirmishers, infighters, and moppers-up—in the manner of Grant flushing the Confederates out of the wilderness. And though we and the house took as thorough a beating in the process as the Army of the Potomac and the forest lands of Virginia did, she always beat the eventual tar out of Disgraceful Circumstances.

Often, in the course of these operations, she had to move—or thought she did—some prodigious weight, such as a granite-slab doorstep or a cast-iron stove. Whenever one of these trifles was too massive to be snatched around with a Yo Heave Ho, my grandmother took swift thought of the basic principles of primitive mechanics, beginning with the lever and fulcrum, the roller, the inclined plane, and so on, if necessary, to very involved contraptions of block and tackle, with a jack thrown in for good measure.

She had first become a fan for these mysteries upon learning in young womanhood how the Egyptians had wrassled together the enormous stones of the Pyramids without other power than that of Israelite slaves. While still deeply impressed by these triumphs of mind over matter, she had picked up a copy of Luce's *Seamanship* at Edgartown, on the island of Martha's Vineyard, where my grandfather had filled a youthful pastorate. This fat volume was intended to give shipmasters in the days of sail exact instructions for rigging tackle by which a handful of sailors at the capstan could jackass around incredible weights of masts, anchors, guns, and chain cable. From Luce my grandmother, though salty in no other respect, had picked up a considerable lore of slings, blocks, braces, purchases, whips, guys, parbuckles, and preventers; and she could rig a double Spanish burton with the best of them.

In this art and science she reached her high point during the transfer of a great, round, cast-iron parlor stove from retirement in the woodshed, up the steep, narrow, angled back stairs to the hired girl's room—with only boy-power to move it.

Even so she would have failed, and the stove would be there yet, if she had not added resourcefulness in morale to ingenuity in mechanics. For my brother and I quickly grew exhausted at playing Children of Israel, and a change of role to that of Athenians building the Acropolis only served to wedge the whole contraption at the sharp bend near the stair top. Rigging a preventer at this point, my grandmother adjourned for brief study of a section of Luce she had hitherto neglected—one on the art of giving commands.

When she reappeared we found ourselves sailors before the mast and under her shrill whoops of "haul aft!" and "sway away!" laid on at the end of a complex arrangement of block and tackle to such effect that presently, with a sound of crackling wood and falling debris, the angle of the wall gave way and the stove bounded aloft in a cloud of dust, bringing with it shreds of wallpaper, slabs of plaster, pieces of lath, and a yard-long section of two-by-four framing wrenched from the very vitals of the house.

My grandmother dearly loved such proofs of the validity of culture. She had been born and brought up in a great, flat-roofed Palladian house with fanlight windows over the doors and yard-wide pumpkin-pine paneling, in the southwest corner of Maine. There she had absorbed simultaneously the frugality and the classicism of Down East New England. She could make soap and translate Horace with equal facility and mordant effect. She learned at one and the same time the art of drawing clear water from a well-sweep well in summer when water is very low and the genteel female accomplishment of drawing pictures by copying fashionable chromos.

At this she was only passably fair, for she had no artistic talent whatever. But she had an eerie, unconscious gift for exaggerating some minor feature of each work of art she was put to copying, with astounding results. Given as model the picture of a lovely, innocent child holding a cat, she unintentionally bestowed on that cat such an expression of agonized ferocity as you would find only on a trapped panther. She once copied a landscape with weeping willows over a tomb by which two lovers lingered, and unwittingly gave the lovers every apparent posture and expression of Messalina and Don Juan about to leap into the nearby thicket of laurels for purposes which I am sure neither the original artist nor my grandmother intended.

Marrying out of this backwoods cultural milieu into the churchly towns of Massachusetts, she had lit neatly on her feet in Tuesday Afternoon Culture Club circles. There she had listened to innumerable papers (and written her share) on Ruskin, Millais, and Turner; Tennyson, Browning, and Emerson. She had gazed upon God knows what phantasmagoria of lantern slides showing the art and architecture of the Old World, and had acquired a considerable collection of books on cathedrals, sculpture, and painting, together with a number of ghastly plaster-cast reproductions of Greek medallions.

At the period of which I write she had long been released by widow-hood from compulsory attendance at deliriums of culture. But, unable to shake off the habit altogether, she still took an occasional swig out of Ruskin or Philip Gilbert Hamerton and went on benders in the Boston Museum of Fine Arts, then located on Copley Square where the Sheraton Plaza is now.

It must have been on one of those occasions that she struck up an acquaintance with the lady representative of a firm which rented out fine-arts exhibitions to schools. These were not, you understand, original hand-painted pictures; they were cardboard-mounted lithographic reproductions of Great Masters, arranged in linked chains so they could be draped over the walls of schoolrooms or hung from steel-pipe frames between the aisles.

The lady, catching my grandmother in a debauched mood, persuaded her to sell the idea of an exhibit in the Pratt School to Bella Barrie, its principal; and Bella, who had a weakness for such heady stuff, fell in with the plan.

This was all very well for my grandmother and Bella; for Wesley Mather, highflown and civic-minded editor of the Bradford *Monitor*; and for the several hundred females of the town who flocked in at ten cents a head to "Oh" and "Ah" before the Masters all day one Saturday. Bradford had never had such an orgy of art. But the proceedings made no hit with the boys of the fifth, sixth, and seventh grades, who had to put up the pictures under Bella's eye on Friday afternoon and take them down again early Monday morning, and less than no hit with me, for all my friends, suspecting my grandmother's hand in the business, took surreptitious pokes at me as we hung up endless strings of Raphael Madonnas, Corot landscapes, Landseer animals, and the like. To this day I cannot see a reproduction of Rosa Bonheur's "Horse Fair" without the horrid fear that some justly outraged contemporary is about to pinch me in the fundament.

She was not above skulduggery to achieve an end she considered worthy. Once, in the interest of art, she took a slingshot to editor Mather's buggy horse.

The occasion was a Sunday afternoon committee meeting at our house. My father had been appointed to a group charged with advising the selectmen on a proposal that the town buy one of those standardized stone statues of a Civil War infantryman, as put out many years before by enterprising firms in the mortuary monument business. Bradford had never bought one of these. Hundreds of other towns had bought them and put them up, but ours had always declined on the grounds of individuality, strongly supported by frugality. Also there were many citizens who believed that the stock statues, considered purely as art, were pretty awful. Now, however, the remainder of an old lot of such figures was being offered at close-out prices so seductive that frugality caught fire, individuality was strongly tempted, and Art found itself in a tight corner.

What my father was doing on this committee I can't say. He knew little about art. But then, most of the other members knew even less. To a man, however, they held strong opinions. And those opinions were evenly divided. Some, like Judge Dearden, scoffed at the stony figure, though acknowledging, as Union veterans themselves, that it was correct in every detail of uniform, arms, and accoutrements. Others, led by Wesley Mather, were all for anything civic. Mather was no veteran, but he was a powerful pleader, and as soon as he discovered that no one present was able to gainsay him, he assumed the position of the committee's art expert.

My grandmother had, of course, been excluded from the meeting. But she listened to its proceedings from the adjoining sitting room. And as Mather unloaded one preposterous pontification after another, she began to sizzle at the seams and hiss at every pore. At anybody else's house she might have barged into the meeting to set matters straight. But here hospitality restrained her.

She seethed in her rocking chair until she could stand it no longer. Then she got up and went outside for air. Coming to the front of the house, she saw editor Mather's horse and buggy standing across the street, facing downhill. Mather was one of the few people in town who, for business reasons, drove his own rig. His horse was a burly beast named Caesar. Caesar, for all his might, was unenterprising, so Mather was accustomed to let him stand untethered while he was newsgathering.

My grandmother, strolling and contemplating Caesar with distaste, stepped on a something in the lawn. It turned out to be my brother's slingshot. She eyed it for a moment speculatively and then considered Caesar with particular respect to range and exposure. Then she picked up the slingshot, selected a sharp-cornered stone from the driveway, and retired to a discreet emplacement among the hydrangeas. From there, with a nice eye for trajectory and a little allowance for windage, she let Caesar have it.

The stone, traveling fast, took him just where she had aimed—in a tender spot in his southwest area. And Caesar took off like a jackrabbit. Of course he made more noise, for his hoofs were enormous, and there was the clatter of the iron-tired buggy to help him. He raised more dust, too, and may have traveled faster. At any rate he was only a cloud in the distance by the time the alarmed committee poured out the front door.

Mather set out in pursuit, accompanied by my father as the spriest of the conferees. The rest sat down on the front piazza to wait. Here they were presently joined by my grandmother, inquiring what was the fuss. One explanation led to another, and soon the talk worked back to the subject of the committee's deliberations. So my grandmother sat down, too.

Half an hour later, when Mather and my father drove up in the rig—retrieved intact from the sanctuary of Mather's own barn—the matter of the statue was settled right where the committee sat, by a vote of seven to one against the editor.

And that is why the town of Bradford, almost alone among Old Colony towns, has not, to this day, a monument to its Civil War soldiery. ■

Black Walnut and Red Plush

GEORGE WOODBURY A one-time archeologist in Harvard's Peabody Museum, George Woodbury abruptly changed careers in the late 1930s. He returned to the land in New Hampshire that had been held by his family for nearly two centuries and restored an ancient water-powered saw and gristmill originally built by his great-great-great-great-grandfather. In "John Goffe's Mill," Woodbury told the story of that restoration and how it led to his conversion from archeologist to sawmill operator and furniture maker.

In "John Goffe's Legacy," he went into greater detail about the history of the region of his forebears and the characters it harbored—such as Civil War veteran Saxy Pike.

■ And there was Saxy Pike, the blacking peddler, who was a regular at the door each year. He was different from the others. Old soldiers from the war were plentiful and a common sight. Many carried with them stirring tales of reckless bravery and courage which got better as the years rolled by. But none had so unique or so bizarre a record as the blacking peddler, ex-Drum Major Saxon Pike, once of the Sixth Massachusetts Volunteers. And unlike most veterans, he did not talk about the war.

He neither looked nor acted the way other peddlers did. The tall erect figure with iron-gray beard that reached his waist strode into the yard under the arching elms, his boots crunching on the gravel with a self-confidence none ever gainsaid. The leather straps that held his pack box were curved and shiny-black with wear. When he swung the box to the ground before him and opened the lid, producing a squat blacking bottle, it was always with the statement, "Your blacking, Ma'am." It was not a request, not a demand, but a simple assertion that here was something you were waiting for. He accepted his money with the same detached air, fumbling through his pockets before announcing he did not have the change "just now." Then he produced a worn black notebook and the stub of a pencil, wet it on his tongue, and carefully made the entry. "Next time" he would have the change. But of course next time he never did. The sober pantomime was repeated every year, as it had been for years past and probably would be for years to come. He accepted a glass of milk and a doughnut, discussed the weather, and resumed his journey. No other peddler was ever treated like him; there was no other like Saxon Pike.

The elders knew Saxon Pike years ago, and he was no blacking peddler then. He was a dashing, daring, and frequently inebriated volunteer fireman in the years before the war. Also he was the drum major of the firemen's band and no ordinary drum major either. Drum majors had been for years content with their impressive aspect and their strut, but Saxy Pike had higher aspirations. In this part of the world at least, he was the first to introduce baton twirling as an adjunct to his art. Practice and application made him a master of the craft. At Fourth of July and Firemen's Musters, his skill and dexterity were the marvel of all beholders. The unbelievable quantities of hard cider, applejack, and tanglefoot whiskey he consumed seemed to increase rather than impair his talents. His stunts with the spinning baton were infinite in variety and daring in conception, and he never fumbled or missed a beat no matter how much or what mixture of assorted alcohols rippled within his ample frame.

Though born and bred a small-town sport and local hero, Saxy was destined to a larger stage and more vital role. The echos of Fort Sumter's guns had hardly rolled away before the Sixth Massachusetts Volunteers were called to arms and then into immediate service. With them as drum major of the regimental band went Saxon Pike, baton twirler par excellence, black bearded then and in his prime, a tall majestic figure with a profound thirst for showmanship and liquor.

At this first beginning of the War Between the States, the city of Washington, capital of the Union, lay in a singular situation. Virginia, just across the Potomac, had seceded into full-scale rebellion. Maryland, which lay between Washington and the northern states, wavered in a delicate balance of loyalty. Baltimore, the sole railroad connection with the North, was strongly sympathetic to the secession cause. Mobs of Rebel sympathizers had succeeded in cutting off Washington from the North, which amounted almost to severing the head from the body of the Union. A contingent of Pennsylvania troops hurrying to the relief of the capital had been met and turned back by the Baltimore mob. Troops—loyal troops in force—were urgently needed in Washington. It was not going to be easy to get them there. The railroad did not run through Baltimore at that time. Passengers had to change trains and cross the city to the Camden station to entrain for Washington. The Sixth Massachusetts Volunteers were already on the way to Baltimore when the news reached them of the repulse of the Pennsylvania troops.

As the crowded troop train rattled on through the rich farmland, dark with the first warmth of spring, the orders were read out:

> The regiment will march through Baltimore in column of sections, arms at will. You will undoubtedly be insulted, abused, and perhaps assaulted, to which you must pay no attention whatever, but march your faces square to the front and pay no attention to the mob, even if they throw stones, bricks, or other missiles; but if you are fired upon and any of you is hit, your officers will order you to fire. Do not fire into any promiscuous crowd, but select any man whom you may see aiming at you and be sure to drop him.— (signed) Edward F. Jones, Col. 6th Mass. Vols., April 19, 1861.

The band would go first, of course, and as Saxy Pike led the band, a lot would depend on him. Saxy had withdrawn from the group and was busy applying himself to the battered case bottle he carried in his coattail pocket. He remained aloof as the train puffed through the dark stone tunnel and into the Baltimore station, and it was not even certain that Saxy realized the nature of the reception waiting for them.

The broad street leading from the depot's main entrance was choked with people, men and boys, mostly ragged and ill fed, but with a smattering of more prosperous citizens. This sea of humanity that had somehow lost its humanity moved with a slow viscous motion in aimless currents to and fro. Its voice was the voice of many, the undulating rumble of many dissonances, senseless, inhuman, and charged with evil. The cobbled street had provided most of the weapons, but here and there clubs and pistols waved high above shouting faces. Right up to the entrance gate the surging mob ebbed and flowed. There a cordon of police, pistols in hand, held them back, but only by the tradition of their authority. There was no real authority but that of violence. The mob was master and knew it.

In the enclosure behind the cordon the regimental band formed in the accustomed ranks. Twenty-five terrified young men fingered their futile instruments and faced the human surf breaking beyond the barrier.

Suddenly a towering resplendent figure strode forward through the open files. He was head and shoulders above them all, and his bearskin shako made him appear even taller than his six foot six. The crimson jacket laced with gold, the white crossbelts and pipeclayed pants stood in sharp contrast to the grimy background of the station walls. A heavy baton, like a weaver's beam but glittering with silver and gold, lay balanced in one ham-like hand.

"Number five!" roared Saxy in a voice of thunder.

"Not that, Saxy, for God's sake!" wailed the second trombone in an agony of terror.

"Git into that goddam sliphorn—and toot!"

At the pulsing double roll of the snare drums, Saxy faced the band, his baton rising and falling to the beat. The baton, spinning like a propeller now, shot heavenward to an astonishing height. (A double squeal of the fifes and a clash of cymbals.) Empty handed, Saxon Pike spun on his heel facing the angry mob and caught the baton behind his back as it fell, true to the beat. His head and shoulders seemed surrounded by a blur of ebony, silver, and gold as he stepped forward, whirling the whistling baton. The surging roll of drums and blare of horns rose with the bellow of the mob.

The baton spun, rising and falling, first in front of, then behind the majestic marching figure—now high over the heads of all, now caught and shot upward once more like a whirling bubble. Baltimore had never seen anything like this before; neither had his regimental band. Saxy was doing the impossible, and that easily it seemed, with either hand. Instinctively the massed mob gave ground before the magnificent apparition that marched so confidently toward them. They would have known what to do against lowered arms or bayonets. The whizzing baton produced total surprise combined with profound astonishment and admiration. They parted, not knowing just what to do. A dead cat rose in a parabola from the thick of the mob and fell at Saxy's marching feet. His expressionless eyes were focused far away and paid no more attention to it than to the baton, which spun and leaped around him like a St. Elmo's fire. A furrow opened before him in the dense-packed, astonished mob.

Was it "Hang Jeff Davis," or "John Brown's Body," or "Glory, Glory, Hallelujah"? No one cared or even listened as the band trailed on behind. Saxy had caught his public and caught it by surprise. He was too good a showman not to know it.

The band had passed one block, dividing the motionless mob in two. Its hostile roar had softened and was lost in the throb and blare of the band. The activity of hate was submerged in the immobility of total astonishment. All eyes and all attention were riveted on the transfigured form of Saxon Pike, whose baton went from one miracle into another faster than anyone could count. He, himself, seemed to grow in stature, becoming taller and more imposing under the rapt stare of so many once hostile eyes. If he was monumental before, he was something of Homeric proportions now. As if hypnotized, the mob now slowly turned and followed him. A telegraph wire hung high above the strange procession at the corner of Light and Charles streets. When the baton spun from behind his back, rocketed up and over and was caught on the other side, there arose a murmur that was almost a cheer. Saxy's eyes looked straight ahead. He never wavered, hesitated in his majestic stride, or missed the fraction of a beat.

Two more blocks, then a third, tramped the long column's marching feet. They were through the thickest of the mob now. A scamper of small boys, their brickbats forgotten in their hands, tried to keep step with Saxy's stride in whole-souled admiration. Then four blocks, and at the fifth, Saxy with a gorgeous gesture swung his band around the corner. Ahead of them gaped the protecting gates of the Camden depot—and safety. They would make it now. Straight on they went without the slightest change in pace. The band, deployed to one side of the station yard, played on, and Saxy, stationary now, still spun his baton as though he had forgotten how to stop. Company after company of blue-clothed infantry, bearded men and fresh-faced country boys, tramped by and glanced toward Saxon Pike as they vanished into the dark safety of the station walls. It was as if he were some visiting potentate and these were troops being passed for his review. It was that and much more. There was gratitude mixed with whole-hearted admiration for the one man who, of all of them, was the foremost, the most defenseless, and the most alone. Only the last of the column had been handled at all hard. The charm had worn thin by then. Six were dead and over thirty injured.

Saxon Pike alone brought the Union troops through Baltimore and relieved beleaguered Washington. There were many sung and unsung heroes in the long years of war that followed, but there never was another like the drum major of the Sixth Massachusetts Volunteers. Some said that Saxon Pike was so drunk he really thought the Baltimore mob had turned out just to see him, and was as surprised as anyone when he found out afterwards what their real intentions were. Others said he knew perfectly well the gravity of the situation and acted out of courage of the highest order.

But Saxy Pike was a showman, and showmen never tip their hands. He himself never referred to the incident. Drunk or sober, Saxon Pike had led the troops to the relief of Washington, perhaps had saved the nation's capital and altered the whole course of the war. He was forever after respected for what he had done, however he had managed to do it.

Aesthetically deplorable perhaps, the black walnut and red plush period was nevertheless sensitive to human values. ■

Spoiled Picnic

WILLIAM M. CLARK William M. Clark's column, "Some Logrolling," appeared on the editorial pages of the Guy Gannett Publishing Company newspapers of Maine for more than three decades, until his death in 1988.

Clark's witty and perceptive commentaries on the political and cultural life of Maine were often cast in the form of stories about Cedar River, a fictional upriver community whose colorful residents added a country wisdom to his observations. In addition, Clark produced four volumes of Cedar River tales in which the adventures and misadventures of the townspeople were chronicled in highly entertaining—not to say hilarious—style.

Clark described himself as "a country boy with country leanings." He was also one of New England's most skillful writers of rural humor.

■ A town that is not positive or even concerned with the duration and the necessity and the reality of its own existence will have one automatic asset. It will have no false ideas of its importance to the world. The world may be with it, late and soon, but it will rarely be with the world.

So Cedar River has its own ideas about status and sanity, but it is not particularly perturbed when it finds that there are other ideas in other places. The only thing it questions is the necessity for crusades.

Down the river, near or far according to the mood of Cedar River, lies Cranston, more populated and more eager. The *Cranston Gazette* crusades constantly for better schools, more business, cleaner sidewalks, and more adequate concealment of immorality. Cedar River scoffs, because the crusades are usually short and ineffective. Only two had notable success. The *Gazette* editor felt that a liquor store would bring trade to Cranston Avenue. He worked for one and he got it. When it was opened, the Salvation Army Lassies, who try to repair some of the damage that liquor causes in the intemperate, started standing in the entry with their collection boxes. When cold weather came, they moved inside. The *Gazette* campaigned against this practice.

So in Cedar River the crusading editor is known as the man who got the liquor store into Cranston and the Salvation Army out of the liquor store. Cedar River isn't really positive that these things benefited mankind.

Anyway, Cedar River doesn't wish to be saved by outsiders with ideas. If it can find salvation by clinging to its own concepts, it would prefer salvation to the other fate. But if too great a change is indicated, and if there is too much challenge to the old institutions, Cedar River would prefer to be left alone and condemned.

Only Jonas P. Hall constantly mourned the loss of the Cedar River message to the barbarians in other towns. Jonas was a Cedar River booster. Could he have found such a thing, he would have worn a bigger button than Babbitt.

Jonas was a poet and an inventor. His inventions had the timelessness of his town, and they were usually outdated before he made the models. He constantly invented things that had been replaced by new designs fifty years before. Part of this was because Jonas was crazy, but part of it was because he conceived of progress as a great big circle, where going forward was also going back. If he had been designing women's dresses, he could easily have been an innovator by being a twenty-year reverter. But he couldn't do this in such things as sawmills and vehicles.

As an inventor, Jonas was fairly futile. As a poet, he brought glory in unorthodoxy. Most of his poems extolled Cedar River. He had a home-town image that he had conjured up by blacking out all the vices and exaggerating the virtues.

The townspeople thought Jonas was wonderfully loyal, but they knew that America wasn't ready for him. They hated to see him work so hard with such futility.

But still Jonas worked. He once wrote a letter to six candidates for state offices, suggesting that they adopt the campaign pledge, "Every Town Another Cedar River." The candidates thanked him, but they wanted to get elected, so they used his slogan in a kind of reverse manner. They accused their opponents of wanting to make every town another Cedar River.

My uncle Jake and Jonas P. Hall had a running feud for ten years over the fact that Jonas had written a long poem for the Labor Day picnic. When Jonas pre-read his masterpiece, Uncle Jake noticed that he wasn't even listed in the also-rans.

"You ain't done nothing for posterity," said Jonas.

"What's Deak Trembley done for posterity?" asked Uncle Jake. "He ain't done no more than I have, but you used his name."

"He had children."

"Holy smoke, that's a blow, that ain't a benefaction. A man in this town that don't have children is probably doing the world a favor. Put me down as a man who loved the world more than he loved Cedar River."

But Jonas had refused. Uncle Jake smarted. He never forgot the slight. He maintained that he could have been squeezed into the last few lines. He had a point. The last lines were a rush of miscellaneous inclusions, thusly:

> And others in this fine assembly,
> Ernest Thompson, old Deak Trembley.
> Reggie Gage and Joe Caruthers,
> Andy, too, for they are brothers. . . .

I don't remember the whole thing. Actually all anybody ever got was the pre-reading. The poem was supposed to be recited after the eating was all over, just before the singing of "God be with you 'til we meet again." But there wasn't any singing. The eating was never finished. The picnic ended too soon.

Deak Trembley's mother, Minnie, ended the picnic. She wasn't in the poem, either, but she didn't know it yet, so nobody thought she was demonstrating her protest by her dramatic demise.

It was a beautiful day that Minnie Trembley spoiled. Of course, it never would have been a guidepost in the chronology of future reminiscences if she hadn't spoiled it, and some guideposts are needed to determine the dates of other guideposts.

Anyway, Minnie couldn't help it.

The sun lit up the shale banks of the running brook. Paper plates and corn cobs steamed and smouldered in the untended ashes. Deak Trembley pushed home the last mouthful of blueberry pie and scratched his back against a rock. He yanked at his sweat-stained cap and he winked at Andy Caruthers.

"I done it, by jumpers," said Deak. "Even the women is happy."

Andy Caruthers looked around. Andy was tall while Deak was short, but both were raw-faced and bony-handed. Both were knobby-muscled like a boulder-spotted brook. Both were lean and tough like a rangy white ash. Both were full of picnic food and waiting their turn to slip into the ledge crevice where Uncle Oscar and Francis Gage were supervising each other in the custody of a keg of whiskey.

"Beats the hell out of last year," agreed Andy. "Last year was a doozie."

Deak nodded. "Town's getting smaller. River grove was getting too big."

There was a sadness in the admission. Surface was surface and truth was truth. Time meant nothing, but it went by. It took people with it when it went, and the new time that came didn't seem to be as full of people as of memories. The fields were getting old and the days of the clearings were done. No Cedar River man would admit that he cared.

"Fewer people? What the hell? Make more room."

But there had been too much room at the river grove the year before. There'd been so much room that it seemed as though the Labor Day picnics were dead.

The river grove had been a perfect picnic site for as long as any man could remember. But that was when there had been kids and ball games and a need for fringe brush for courting purposes. Some towns could have picnicked in the river grove anyway, just by using a smaller part of it. But when Cedar River had room, it used room. It was too close in time to the raucousness of the river drivers. It was a town of joviality which lacked restraint. It couldn't remember that age should develop dignity.

So the year before, the picnic had been, as Andy Caruthers said, "a doozie."

There had been a mass fight because everybody wanted to be partners with the widow Anstruthers in the three-legged race.

Reggie Gage had wrestled my uncle Waldron right into a whipped cream cake. Aunt Margie had clipped Reggie with a pickle bottle, and when Joe Hanrahan had tried to move the chicken salad so the blood wouldn't soak past the top layer, Margie had thought he was stealing it and had banged him with the bean pot. When he fell, he put a fork through his ear.

That was why Doc Yates had been too busy with his bandages and his needles to protest the risks in a lottery that was based on the length of time that Francis Gage could stay under water.

It was all right for Francis to go under water. Any Gage could stand a bath. But Francis had started to break surface after two minutes, and Jubal Dean had needed another three seconds to win the two dollars and thirty cents. Naturally Jubal had jumped in and tried to hold Francis down. Eight men had ended up in the river, each making an effort to enforce his own concept of fairness.

After Francis had been dragged out and given artificial respiration, the lottery prize was gone anyway. Andy Caruthers had been holding the change in his fist, and he had dropped it when he finally grabbed Francis by the collar and pulled him from beneath four strugglers.

But during the disruption Uncle Oscar had poured a pitcher of whiskey into the ladies' punch. The ladies loosened up and told each other things that they thought they should know for their own good, things they ordinarily would have told to someone else. It took a month for the ladies to get adjusted to new battle alliances, and in a sudden freshet of information, they confided in denied friends all winter.

The ladies had agreed on only one thing, "No more picnics."

Some had added private picturesque definiteness.

But Deak Trembley had hated to see the picnics go. He hung to tradition because he had an unexplainable feeling that with each function Cedar River lost, Cedar River moved one degree toward being lost itself. He had suggested Big Brook Gorge, where the confinement would inhibit activity, where everyone could be peaceful as cows in a pasture.

There had been reluctant agreement. There had been doubts, but there had been a series of slow surrenders. And the change of location had seemed to solve the problem. All through lunch murmurs had been at a minimum.

Deak scratched again and chuckled. He raised his voice to let everyone know who deserved the plaudits for the peace.

"Just took thinking, folks," he said. "Today we ain't going to have no trouble at all."

Joe Caruthers shouted him down. "Jesus H. Christ, shut up." But the mountain gods had heard. They laughed and stirred and smote.

Minnie Trembley rose to her feet, reached for a watermelon, swayed off plumb, and sprawled conclusively onto the rocks.

She went down like an undercut boulder in a gravel bank, not fast, but not stoppable either. Of course nobody tried to stop her. Movement was away, not toward. Minnie was a big woman.

At the end of her fall there was this thud, and Minnie rolled half over on her back and lay still.

Doc Yates was beside her right off. He did what he could. It wasn't a long fall, and Minnie was padded, but she had a bad heart, and she'd had palpitations, and she'd had blood pressure trouble and hot flashes and dizzy spells. She'd evidently got a fright, too, when she felt herself falling. The fright may have done the trick.

She's always been afraid of falling, or perhaps not so much afraid as prophetic. She had narrated the probable details on many occasions, relishing the descriptions.

"Some day I'm going to fall down," she'd said, "and something's going to smash, because, you know, there's a lot of me to fall. I'm going to fall and smash my gizzard, probably. That's what happened to Deak's father. His gizzard failed up on him. He turned purple and red right before my eyes. That's what I'll probably smash . . . my gizzard."

She had never seemed to disapprove particularly of this method of dying, but Doc Yates had discounted it.

"People don't even have gizzards," Doc had said. "Fred Trembley died from drinking green home-brew until he burned out his stomach. Minnie can't smash something she don't have. She'll likely die in bed, anyhow. Most people do."

Doc may have been right about the gizzard, but he was wrong about the bed. Minnie had fallen and she'd smashed something. She lay right there on the shale, not moving at all.

Doc straightened up and shook his head. Laughing stopped. Deak Trembley's wife had the first word.

"There," she said to Deak, "now you've done it. You had to come to this treacherous territory. Now you've killed your poor old mother."

Deak didn't answer. He stood looking down at the result of his efforts to preserve the old traditions for the town and the town for time. His mother had paid for his picnic insistence.

"She really dead, Doc?" he asked.

"Yes, she's dead."

"You sure?"

"Of course I'm sure. Would I tell . . . never mind, Deak, never mind. Yes, she's dead. But it wasn't your fault. Annie, it wasn't Deak's fault at all. If Deak did anything, he made her last minutes happier. I don't like to say this, but Minnie's been swallowing the steps to heaven for thirty years. I warned her about eating so much, but she wouldn't stop."

"Ma always was hearty," said Deak.

"Hearty? My soul, Deak, she must weigh better'n two fifty."

"Three hundred and seven on Turner's scales, carrying five pounds of sugar. Got to figure it from there, because that's what she was doing, testing the sugar weight. She weighed herself and the sugar and then she handed the sugar to Jonas Hall, and he pressed down with his foot because he was feeling frolicky, and Ma weighed three-eighteen without the sugar, so she didn't know what the hell to figure Turner was putting in his sugar bags and . . . "

"Deak," said Annie, "stop it. Stop it right this minute. Your poor mother's not even cold and you start telling stories."

Deak patted her hand. "I'm sorry," he said. He shook his head. "Well, I guess this picnic's over. If you women will pack up, we'll . . . we'll . . . "

He stopped talking. So did everybody else. Nobody said anything at all. Everybody knew what everybody else was thinking. There wasn't any need to talk.

Big Brook Gorge was a half-mile from the road. It was bounded on two sides by waterfalls, one up, one down, both about twelve feet high. The other two sides were shale banks, not cliffs, but not gradual slopes either. There just wasn't room for enough men to get the handholds on Minnie Trembley that were needed to carry her up the trail. That trail was as twisted as a bureaucrat's logic.

Minnie had really fixed her friends. She'd been afraid of falling for ten years, and then, when she fell, she fell right where she could give the most possible trouble to her survivors.

Deak finally phrased the question.

"How are we going to get her out of here?" he asked.

Three men cleared their throats. A few more looked questioningly around, but Big Brook Gorge wasn't built for unnoticed escape.

It was Uncle Oscar who made the first move, and that startled a lot of people because Uncle Oscar had been in the crevice with the whiskey and he might have been expected to stay there. Uncle Oscar simply wasn't a natural volunteer for work. Cedar River folks said that the only way to get any work out of Uncle Oscar was to cremate him and put his ashes in an hourglass.

But he came out of that rock crevice carrying a tarpaulin. The men recognized the tarpaulin. They'd had it wrapped around the whiskey keg as a kind of cushioning sling when they'd lowered the keg down into the gorge the night before.

Uncle Oscar walked over to Minnie and made his suggestion.

"Least we can do is to cover her up," he said. "Lay this down and roll her over and bind her in."

"Seems kinda informal," said Deak.

Andy Caruthers took the tarpaulin and started the covering rites. "It's got to be informal," he said. "She didn't die in no parlor. She died in a damn canyon, and it's going to kill two or three other people, probably, getting her up the bank. We got to do the best we can, formal, informal, or barefoot."

Francis Gage eyed the canvas bundle, lashed at both ends.

"I bet that'd float," he said. "If it was spring, we could pop her right in the brook and bring her to the bridge on the freshet."

"It ain't spring," said Jeb Seekings. He hefted Minnie's feet. "Hell, she'd draw better'n sixteen inches of water, and six-inch pulpwood would ground in this brook right now. . . . "

"Judas jumpers," said Deak. "It don't matter how much water there is in the brook. Nobody ain't making a log drive outa my mother."

"I got an idea," said Francis Gage.

"Oh, nuts," said Andy. "Any idea you got is probably so poopbrained . . . "

"Now, wait a minute," said Doc Yates. "We need ideas. I want you men to stop arguing and do some thinking. If Francis has a suggestion, let him tell it."

"It ain't an idea on how to move her, Doc," said Francis. "It's a theory . . . well . . . I was just going to say . . . well . . . she was lying down while she was eating, see? And she ate pretty good. She ate six chicken sandwiches and five hard boiled eggs and three helpings of ham and potato salad. She ate about a quart of baked beans and I don't know how much cornbread. She had a half a cake and a couple of pieces of pie and a quart of coffee. . . . "

"Christ," said Andy Caruthers. "How come you lost track on the cornbread? Did you lose your goddam notebook?"

"I ain't interested in no narration of what Ma ate," said Deak. "I ain't interested at all. . . . "

"But that's why she fell," said Francis. "She was lying down and that stuff didn't have no chance to get to the right place to ballast her. So when she got up to get that melon, she was topheavy and . . . "

"Francis," said Doc Yates, "why don't you go home?"

"No, Doc," said Andy Caruthers, "nobody is going home. I mean, you can be the boss, but nobody is going home, especially Francis. I think that's what the son-of-a-bitch is working for. He ain't going to get away with it. We need everybody. Now, Doc, if you got some method in mind . . . "

"I haven't. You know more about this than I do."

"All right. Then I'll handle it. Deak, first I want you to know that I respect the dead just as much as anybody else. I got a deep reverence for the dead, a real deep reverence. But there ain't no carrying your mother up that trail. If she was solid, me and Joe might have a go at it. But she's all limp and floppy and she'd slop all over the place. You know how it is trying to carry something without no shape to it. It'd be like bringing a dead cow up the attic stairs. . . . "

"This is respecting the dead?" said Deak. "This is deep reverence? You ain't talking about no cow. You're talking about my mother, my mother who raised me and took care of me. . . . "

" . . . and then packed on the pounds so they'll have to put four extra handles on the coffin," said Francis Gage.

"Shut up," said Andy. "Shut up, or I'll flatten you right alongside of her, and then we can have a regular damn parade of corpses up that cliff."

"I ain't sure you're man enough. . . . "

"I'm going home," said Doc Yates, "and make my report to the county coroner. The report is going to include the fact that ten or twelve grown men are standing over the body of a poor dead woman, fighting about her disposal, and that my sincere prayer is that the cliffs close in and bury the dead and the living both, or that a flash flood is sent by some horrified power to carry all parties concerned downstream to the River Styx."

"There ain't no sticks in the river, Doc," said Andy. "The drive's over. But you're right. There's no need of fighting. I already sent Joe for his horse."

"What for?" asked Deak.

"Because he's closest. Deak, we got to skid her out. There ain't no other way. With a long line and a plank, we can snatch her right outa here like a stump from a cornfield. I mean . . . we can snatch her . . . I mean, nice and easy, Deak . . . just gentle, like a . . . like a . . . "

"Yeah, like a log from a ledge. I been with you when you snatched things out nice and easy. My soul, what would Pa think if he knew that all his good neighbors were going to yank my mother out of a brook bed with a skidding horse?"

"He'd think it was damned practical," said Uncle Oscar. "Andy, that's a good idea. I'll tell you what. There's a two-inch plank upstream, washed ashore. If the rest of you want to get up top and cut the brush back and find a place to pull from, I'll get the plank and tie it under Minnie, and you can just throw the line down when you're ready and I'll guide her up."

"I better stay with you," said Francis. "I mean, she might snag up somewhere and have to be twitched around. I hope Joe'll remember to bring a peavey."

"You ain't using no peavey," said Oscar.

"You're pretty damn bossy, Oscar. You telling me what to do?"

"Yes, I am. It's my tarpaulin. I don't want it full of holes."

"Your tarpaulin?" said Deak. "My God, Oscar, it's my mother."

"Ain't no use to use profanity. Your mother would be pretty upset by that."

"My mother would be upset by getting skidded on a plank, too."

"We can't help that. But he's right, Francis. You wouldn't want nobody sinking peaveys into your mother, if that was your mother laying there in that nice, almost new tarpaulin, waiting to get a first-class funeral just as soon as she was skidded out of the woods."

"If that was my mother, she wouldn't have to be skidded. My mother only weighs ninety-eight pounds. If that was my mother, I could carry her right outa here over my shoulder. Here, Deak, you weigh more'n my mother. Just let me get you in a fireman's carry, and I'll show old Oscar what I could do if that was my mother."

"Holy heaven," said Andy Caruthers, "how does everything in this damned town always get so twisted up? Deak, Francis and you come along with us. Let Oscar get his rigging ready. When we get all set, you can come back down and help Oscar steer the . . . you can help guide."

It was twenty minutes before a half-inch line was tossed over the edge and came snaking down to Uncle Oscar. He had the line secured before Deak came scrambling to help. Francis slid down, too.

"Take her away," shouted Oscar.

"Easy now," pleaded Deak, "just easy."

The tarpaulin-wrapped bundle started up the slope, tipped over the first ledge, and snubbed on an outcropping. Uncle Oscar gave a heave on the trailing end. He was sweating and he was panting. Francis Gage was puzzled. Uncle Oscar should have been up top, switching the horse or something. All Uncle Oscar's history negated the possibility of his being trapped into the hardest job of all. Francis looked at the pudgy figure and felt the Gage version of pity.

"Oscar," he said, "don't you want to come and ease this line and let me do that heaving and tugging?"

Uncle Oscar heaved again as the plank approached a boulder outcrop. "No," he said. "You stay up there . . . stay in front. I'm Deak's friend. I'm willing to do this much for good old Deak."

Deak Trembley said nothing. Deak was familiar with Uncle Oscar's history, too. He wondered what the price of this new friendship would be.

Bit by bit, Minnie was worked up the slope. She hung and she slid and she was maneuvered around the rocks and the roots. She was near the top of the bank when she snubbed one more time and the plank dug into a crevice in the ledge.

Uncle Oscar threw his weight against the back of the bundle. It didn't move. The rope stretched.

"Whoa," shouted Francis.

"Whoa," shouted Deak. The line tension eased.

Francis left Deak and grabbed with Oscar. The end started to swing.

"What are you doing? You taking her up feet first?" asked Francis.

"Shut up," said Uncle Oscar.

"What do you mean, feet first?" said Deak. "This here's her head. I can feel it through the tarp."

"She's got two heads, then," said Francis.

"Goddammit," shouted Deak, "all you've done is to make nasty remarks about my mother ever since she fell. I ain't going to . . . whoa . . . whoa . . . oh, Jesus, there she goes. . . . "

The horse had made a lurch forward and the line had snapped. Minnie started back down the slope. Deak braced his feet and hung to the broken rope. Minnie picked up speed. Francis Gage and Uncle Oscar were knocked to one side. Deak was dragged on his face for a few feet and then he let go. Minnie hit the last ledge hard, with a solid smack, hung for a few seconds, swung full around, and slid the rest of the way head first.

The three men got to her and rolled her around again as the faces peered over the edge of the bank.

"Can't you hold that horse?" shouted Uncle Oscar. "That line won't pull no solid ledge. We was getting her clear."

"He jumped," said Andy. "We'll knot the line and give it another try."

"My golly jumpers," said Deak, "we've smashed her all up. She's bleeding like a fountain. Wait a minute . . . that ain't blood."

"Don't be morbid," said Uncle Oscar. "Don't go analyzing her. You ain't no chemist."

"I don't need to be a chemist to know what's leaking out of that tarp," said Francis Gage. "It's whiskey."

"There you go again, you damned ghoul," said Deak. "Ma never took a drink in her life."

"I never said she did. I ain't saying it now. I just said . . . hey . . . that's why I thought I had hold of the side of her head. It wasn't her head at all. It was . . . "

"Stop jawing and let's get this line on again," said Uncle Oscar.

"Open up that tarp," said Deak.

"What for? Those men are waiting."

"So am I. Open that tarp."

"Oh, all right," said Oscar. "So what good would it have done to have left a half a keg of whiskey down there for some sneak to snaffle? A few pounds don't make no difference to that horse. He don't mind skidding my whiskey."

"It wasn't your whiskey," said Francis. "We all kicked in for it. Holy smoke, I wish I lived where somebody had some kind of decency. Now you've stove up our whiskey just by trying to steal it. What kind of morals is them?"

"I don't give a hoot about the whiskey," said Deak, "but you didn't need to make it a part of my mother's funeral procession. Andy would have taken another hitch and pulled it up, and we could have had it for the burying. Now it's all over Ma. The W.C.T.U. will read her right off their lists. What the hell are you doing now?"

"I thought maybe if it had gathered in the end of the tarp, I could find a bucket or something and ... "

"What's holding you up down there?" called Andy. "We got to get her to the road before dark. Hurry up."

"There's a pail down there where the fire was," said Francis. "But you don't want to open the whole end. The way to do it is to make a little hole in the tarp, so if there's too much for the pail I can hold my finger over the hole until you can get another one. That way ... "

"If you men don't get that keg out of there right now," said Deak, "so help me, I'll put a slip noose around both of your necks and have them drag you up first."

"Oh, my soul," said Oscar.

He untied the lashings on the end of the tarp. A flood of whiskey poured over the shale. Deak scooped out the broken staves. He scooped out the hoops. He hooked on the line.

They made better time on the second hoist. Minnie was more manageable. With one final surge she went over the edge and lay at last on level ground.

""Bring back the horse and we'll take a shorter hitch," said Jeb Seekings. "We ought to hook real short so the end don't dig."

"Ain't you going to get a wagon in here now?" asked Deak.

"Hell, there ain't been a wagon road through these woods for forty years," said Joe Caruthers. "It would take us a full day to cut a road. This here is Denniston Company land. If they gave us permission to clear the trees, they'd expect us to peel the pulp and pile it. I don't figure it's part of a man's funeral obligation to peel eight or ten cords of pulp."

"In this weather, she wouldn't last that long anyway," said Andy. "We got to be practical, Deak. Doc Yates has gone to town to send back the hearse. All we got to do is to skid her just a half-mile, and then we can load her and bring her home a-rooping. Holy Jesus, what's that smell?"

"Mind your manners," said Uncle Oscar.

"Can't we even get a stoneboat?" asked Deak. "Damn it, it just don't seem decent to skid my mother out of the woods like a pine log."

"That plank's just as decent as a stoneboat," said Andy. "Come on. Let's go."

The plank slid easily over the matted pine needles. The sun started to go down behind old Deer Mountain. Deak Trembley, his head respectfully bowed, plodded along behind the body of his mother. Uncle Oscar and Francis Gage followed Deak.

"Poor old Ma," said Deak. "Well, one thing, anyway. She went to the last Labor Day picnic Cedar River'll probably ever have."

Francis Gage shoved his elbow into Uncle Oscar's ribs.

"Thanks to you," said Francis, "she probably had the last drink of the day, too."

"Oh, shut up," said Oscar.

They rounded the last bend in the trail. The hearse was waiting. They untarped Minnie and lifted her reverently into place.

Uncle Oscar and Francis Gage stood at a careful imitation of attention as the procession headed for town.

"Well," said Uncle Oscar, "I guess Deak's pretty mad. But he'll get over it. And there's one thing about his being mad right now. It's the best time there is. He ain't going to ask me to be a pallbearer."

"I don't expect he'll ask me, neither," said Francis. "He seemed upset at me all afternoon. So I guess we're both all right. Lord, the Trembley lot is clear over by the cemetery fence. It's a good two hundred yards from where they'll have to stop the hearse. Somebody's arms is going to ache for three days."

"Where you going?" asked Uncle Oscar.

"Back to town, I suppose."

"Nuts. We're going to Big Brook Gorge. I poured out a jugful of that whiskey before I wrapped up the keg in the tarp. I ain't damn fool enough to put all my eggs in one basket and not make no provision for the unforeseen. Come on and we'll have a drink to Minnie Trembley."

"Might just as well," said Francis. "Minnie had one on us." ■

EVERYBODY TALKS ABOUT IT

Speech on the Weather

MARK TWAIN Mark Twain did *not* say, "Everybody talks about the weather, but nobody does anything about it." (His friend, Charles Dudley Warner, did.) But Twain, an adopted New Englander who did much of his best writing as a resident of Hartford, Connecticut, said just about everything else about the weather—and hundreds of other topics—which appear in all the standard books of quotations.

This discourse on weather was given before the New England Society's seventy-first annual dinner in New York City on December 22, 1876.

I reverently believe that the Maker who made us all makes everything in New England but the weather. I don't know who makes that, but I think it must be raw apprentices in the weather-clerk's factory who experiment and learn how, in New England, for board and clothes, and then are promoted to make weather for countries that require a good article, and will take their custom elsewhere if they don't get it.

There is a sumptuous variety about the New England weather that compels the stranger's admiration—and regret. The weather is always doing something there, always attending strictly to business, always getting up new designs and trying them on the people to see how they will go. But it gets through more business in spring than in any other season. In the spring I have counted 136 different kinds of weather inside of four-and-twenty hours.

It was I that made the fame and fortune of that man that had that marvelous collection of weather on exhibition at the Centennial, that so astounded the foreigners. He was going to travel all over the world and get specimens from all the climes. I said, "Don't you do it; you come to New England on a favorable spring day." I told him what we could do in the way

═ **143** ═

of style, variety, and quantity. Well, he came, and he made his collection in four days. As to variety, why, he confessed that he got hundreds of kinds of weather that he had never heard of before. And as to quantity—well, after he had picked out and discarded all that was blemished in any way, he not only had weather enough but weather to spare, weather to hire out, weather to sell, to deposit, weather to invest, weather to give to the poor.

The people of New England are by nature patient and forbearing, but there are some things which they will not stand. Every year they kill a lot of poets for writing about "Beautiful Spring." These are generally casual visitors, who bring their notions of spring from somewhere else, and cannot, of course, know how the natives feel about spring. And so the first thing they know, the opportunity to inquire how they feel has permanently gone by. Old Probabilities has a mighty reputation for accurate prophecy and thoroughly well deserves it. You take up the paper and observe how crisply and confidently he checks off what today's weather is going to be on the Pacific, down South, in the middle states, in the Wisconsin region. See him sail along in the joy and pride of his power till he gets to New England, and then see his tail drop. He doesn't know what the weather is going to be in New England. Well, he mulls over it, and by and by he gets out something about like this: Probable northeast to southwest winds, varying to the southward and westward and eastward, and points between, high and low barometer swapping around from place to place; probable areas of rain, snow, hail, and drought, succeeded or preceded by earthquakes, with thunder and lightning. Then he jots down this postscript from his wandering mind, to cover accidents: "But it is possible that the program may be wholly changed in the meantime."

Yes, one of the brightest gems in the New England weather is the dazzling uncertainty of it. There is only one thing certain about it: you are certain there is going to be plenty of it—a perfect grand review, but you never can tell which end of the procession is going to move first. You fix up for the drought, you leave your umbrella in the house and sally out, and two to one you get drowned. You make up your mind that the earthquake is due, you stand from under and take hold of something to steady yourself, and the first thing you know you get struck by lightning. These are great disappointments, but they can't be helped. The lightning there is peculiar; it is so convincing that when it strikes a thing it doesn't leave enough of that thing behind for you to tell whether—well, you'd think it was something valuable and a Congressman had been there. And the thunder. When the thunder begins to merely tune up and scrape and saw and key up the instruments for the performance, strangers say, "Why, what awful thunder you have here!" But when the baton is raised and the real concert begins, you'll find that stranger down in the cellar with his head in the ash-barrel.

Now as to the *size* of the weather in New England—lengthways, I mean. It is utterly disproportioned to the size of that little country. Half the time, when it is packed as full as it can stick, you will see that New England weather sticking out beyond the edges and projecting around hundreds and hundreds of miles over the neighboring states. She can't hold a tenth part of her weather. You can see cracks all about where she has strained herself trying to do it. I could speak volumes about the inhuman perversity of the New England weather, but I will give but a single specimen. I like to hear rain on a tin roof. So I covered part of my roof with tin, with an eye to that luxury. Well, sir, do you think it ever rains on that tin? No, sir, skips it every time. Mind, in this speech I have been trying merely to do honor to the New England weather—no language could do it justice.

But, after all, there is at least one or two things about that weather (or, if you please, effects produced by it) which we residents would not like to part with. If we hadn't our bewitching autumn foliage, we should still have to credit the weather with one feature which compensates for all its bullying vagaries—the ice-storm: when a leafless tree is clothed with ice from the bottom to the top—ice that is as bright and clear as crystal—when every bough and twig is strung with ice-beads, frozen dewdrops, and the whole tree sparkles cold and white, like the Shah of Persia's diamond plume. Then the wind waves the branches and the sun comes out and turns all those myriads of beads and drops to prisms that glow and burn and flash with all manner of colored fires, which change and change again with inconceivable rapidity from blue to red, from red to green, and green to gold—the tree becomes a spraying fountain, a very explosion of dazzling jewels; and it stands there the acme, the climax, the supremest possibility in art or nature, of bewildering, intoxicating, intolerable magnificence. One cannot make the words too strong. ■

The Eye of Edna

E.B. WHITE The spare, elegant writing style of E.B. White graced the pages of *The New Yorker* from the time of the magazine's founding. He helped start the witty "Talk of the Town" column and contributed hundreds of essays, poems, squibs, and fillers to the magazine over a period of decades.

"He is a hard man to classify," commented author Edward Streeter. "Every time I get him pinned as a humorist he wriggles out from under and turns up as a philosopher. Perhaps the best way out is to classify him as an artist."

Eventually White moved out of New York City and took up permanent residence on a coastal farm in Maine. For several years he wrote the "One Man's Meat" column on country topics for *Harper's*. White published more than twenty books, including the best-selling children's stories, *Stuart Little* and *Charlotte's Web*, and edited a widely circulated revision of William Strunk, Jr.'s *The Elements of Style*.

Allen Cove, September 15, 1954

Two hurricanes have visited me recently, and except for a few rather hasty observations of my own (which somehow seem presumptuous), all I know about these storms is what I've heard on the radio. I live on the Maine coast, to the east of Penobscot Bay. Formerly this coast was not in the path of hurricanes, or if it was we didn't seem to know it, but times change and we must change with them. My house is equipped with three small, old-fashioned radios, two of them battery sets, one a tiny plug-in bedside model on which my wife sometimes manages to get the Giants after I have turned in. We do not have TV, and because of this curious omission we are looked upon as eccentrics, possibly radicals.

Hurricanes, as all of us know to our sorrow, are given names nowadays—girls' names. And, as though to bring things full circle, newborn girl babies are being named for hurricanes. At the height of the last storm, one of the most dispiriting crumbs of news that came to me as the trees thrashed about and the house trembled with the force of the wind was that a baby girl had been born somewhere in the vicinity of Boston and had been named Edna. She is probably a nice little thing, but I took an instant dislike to her, and I would assume that thousands of other radio listeners did, too. Hurricanes are the latest discovery of radio stations, and they are being taken up in a big way. To me, Nature is continuously absorbing—that is, she is a twenty-four-hour proposition, fifty-two weeks of the year—but to radio people, Nature is an oddity tinged with malevolence and worthy of note only in her more violent moments. The radio either lets Nature alone or gives her the full treatment, as it did at the approach of the hurricane called Edna. The idea, of course, is that the radio shall perform a public service by warning people of a storm that might prove fatal; and this the radio certainly does. But another effect of the radio is to work people up to an incredible state of alarm many hours in advance of the blow, while they are still fanned by the mildest zephyrs. One of the victims of Hurricane Edna was a civil-defense worker whose heart failed him long before the wind threatened him in the least.

I heard about Edna during the morning of Friday, September 10, some thirty-six hours before Edna arrived, and my reaction was normal. I simply buttoned up the joint and sat down to wait. The wait proved interminable. The buttoning-up was not difficult—merely a couple of hours of amusing work, none of it heavy. I first went to the shore, hauled my twelve-foot boat up above high-water mark, and tied it to a stump. I closed and barricaded the boathouse doors. Then I came back up through the meadow, tolled the sheep into the barn, hooked the big doors on the north side, and drove nails in next to the hooks, so they couldn't pull out when the doors got slatting around. I let the geese in and fed them some apples—windfalls left over from Hurricane Carol. There was no good reason to shut the geese in, as they had roamed all over the place during Carol, enjoying the rough weather to the hilt and paying frequent visits to the pond at the height of the storm, but I shut them in from tidiness, and because the radio was insisting that everyone stay indoors. I got a couple of two-by-fours and some pegs and braced the cedar fence on the west side of the terrace. Anticipating power failure, I drew extra water for drinking and cooking, and also set a pail of water next to each toilet, for a spare flush. My wife, who enters quickly into the spirit of disaster, dug up a kerosene lamp, and there was a lot of commotion about cleaning the globe and the chimney—until it was discovered that there was no wick. The potted fuchsia was moved indoors, and also the porch rocker, lest these objects be carried aloft by the wind and dashed against windows. The croquet set was brought in. (I was extremely skeptical about the chance of croquet balls coming in through the window, but it presented a vivid picture to the imagination and was worth thinking about.) The roof of the pullet house had blown off during Carol, and the pullets had developed a prejudice against hurricanes, so I shut them up early. I went to bed that night confident that all was in readiness.

Next morning everything was in place, including the barometric pressure. The power was on, the telephone was working, the wind was moderate. Skies were gray and there was a slight rain. I found my wife curled up in bed at ten of seven with her plug-in going, tuned to disaster. In the barn I received an ovation from the geese, and my failure to release them caused an immense amount of gossip. After breakfast the whole household, with the exception of our dachshund, settled down to the radio, not in a solid family group but each to his own set and his own system of tuning. No matter where one wandered, upstairs or down, back or front, a radio voice was to be heard, bringing ominous news. As near as I could make out, the storm was still about a thousand miles away and moving north-northeast at about the speed of a medium-priced automobile. Deaths had been reported in New Jersey. A state of emergency had been declared in New London, Connecticut, and in Portland, Maine. Something had happened to the second shift at the Commercial Filters Corporation plant in Melrose, Massachusetts, but I never learned what. A man named Irving R. Levine wished me "good news." The temperature in Providence, Rhode Island, was sixty-eight degrees.

It became evident to me after a few fast rounds with the radio that the broadcasters had opened up on Edna awfully far in advance, before she had come out of her corner, and were spending themselves at a reckless rate. During the morning hours they were having a tough time keeping Edna going at the velocity demanded of emergency broadcasting. I heard one fellow from, I think, Riverhead, Long Island, interviewing his out-of-doors man, who had been sent abroad in a car to look over conditions on the eastern end of the island.

"How would you say the roads were?" asked the tense voice.

"They were wet," replied the reporter, who seemed to be in a sulk.

"Would you say the spray from the puddles was dashing up around the mudguards?" inquired the desperate radioman.

"Yeah," replied the reporter.

It was one of those confused moments, emotionally, when the listener could not be quite sure what position radio was taking—*for* hurricanes or *against* them.

A few minutes later I heard another baffling snatch of dialogue on the air, from another sector—I think it was Martha's Vineyard.

"Is it raining hard there?" asked an eager voice.

"Yes, it is."

"Fine!" exclaimed the first voice, well pleased at having got a correct response.

At twenty-one and a half seconds past eleven o'clock, a New England prophet named Weatherbee, the WBZ weatherman, reported that the storm was moving north-northeast at fifty miles an hour and said that New England as a whole would not get the sustained force of the wind. This prediction was followed by a burst of inspirational music, and I wandered away and into the kitchen, where I found Mrs. Freethy mixing up a sponge-cake. "Heard from Edna?" she asked with wry amusement as she guided the electric mixer on its powerful way through the batter. Mrs. Freethy takes her hurricanes where she finds them.

When I returned to the radio, a man was repeating the advice I had heard many times. Fill the car with gas before the pumps lose their power. Get an old-fashioned clock that is independent of electricity. Set the refrigerator adjustment to a lower temperature. I weighed all these bits of advice carefully. The car had already been fueled. The clocks in my house have never been contaminated by so much as a single jolt of electric current. And I decided against monkeying with the refrigerator, on the ground that the control knob was probably buried behind about eighteen small, hard-to-handle items of food left over from previous meals and saved against a rainy day like this one.

I switched to Rockland, 1450 on my dial. The town manager of Camden was speaking. He said preparations had been made for mass feeding and that you could get fed at either the Grange Hall or the Congregational Parish House, and you were invited to bring your own food. A bulletin said the core of the storm would pass to the east of Rhode Island. From Bangor the news was that the Gene Autry show would continue as planned. The Boston Fire Commissioner advised me to keep calm and follow instructions, and I thought again about my obstinacy in the matter of the refrigerator. In Nantucket, winds were seventy-seven miles per hour.

At noon I took a short vacation from the radio and looked out at the familiar scene, which, because it bore so little relation to the radio scene, assumed a sort of unreality. It was thirty hours or more since I'd slipped into a hurricane mood, and I could feel the telling effects of such sustained emotional living. I went outdoors. A light breeze was blowing from the southeast. Rain fell in a drizzle. The pasture pond was unruffled but had the prickly surface caused by raindrops, and it seemed bereft without geese. The sky was a gloomy gray. Two rosebushes bowed courteously to each other on the terrace. I got a berry basket and walked out to the pullet yard, where I collected a few damp eggs. The pullets stood about in beachcombing attitudes, their feathers in disorder. As I walked back to the house, I measured with my eye the point on the roof where the biggest balm-of-Gilead tree would strike when it toppled over. I made a mental note to evacuate my people from front rooms if the wind should shift into the west, but was doubtful as to my chances of evacuating my wife from any room whatsoever, as she doesn't readily abandon well-loved posts, especially if they are furnished with traditional objects that she admires and approves of; and she is inclined to adopt a stiff-backed attitude about any change of location based on my calculations. Furthermore, she can present an overwhelming array of evidence in support of her position.

Back indoors, the storm, from which I had enjoyed momentary relief by taking a stroll in it, was on me again in full force—wild murmurings of advance information, almost impossible to make head or tail of. Edna's eye was at sea, and so was I. The eye was in New Jersey. No, it was in Long Island. No, it was not going to hit western Long Island or central Massachusetts. It was going to follow a path between Buzzards Bay and Nantucket. (This called for an atlas, which I produced.) All of New England will get the weaker part of the storm, but the Maine coast, "down Bar Harbor way," can be hit hard by Edna late this afternoon. I bridled at being described as "down Bar Harbor way."

Not only were the movements of the storm hard to follow but the voices were beginning to show the punchy condition of the poor, overworked fellows who had been blowing into their microphones at seventy miles per hour for so many hours. "Everything," cried one fellow, "is pretty well battered down in Westerly." I presumed he meant "battened down," but there was no real way of knowing. Another man, in an exhausted state, told how, in the previous hurricane, the streets of Providence had been "unindated." I started thinking in terms of unindated streets, of cities pretty well battered down. The wind now began to strengthen. The barometer on my dining-room wall was falling. From Rockland I got the "Top of the Farm News": 850,000 bales of cotton for August, a new variety of alfalfa that will stand up to stem nematode and bacterial wilt, a new tomato powder—mix it with water and you get tomato juice, only it's not on the market yet. Low tide will be at 4:23 this afternoon. The barometer now reads 29.88 and falling. A chicken shoot is canceled for tomorrow—the first chicken shoot I had ever heard of. All Rockland stores will close at three o'clock, one of them a store carrying suits with the new novelty weave and novel button and pocket trim. If this thing gets worse, I thought, I'll have to go outdoors again, even though they tell you not to. I can't take it in here. At 1:55 P.M. I learned that visiting hours at the Portsmouth Hospital, two hundred miles to the southwest of me, had been canceled, and, having no friend there, I did not know whether to be glad about this or sorry.

The time is now two o'clock. Barometer 29.50, falling. Wind ESE, rising. It seems like a sensible moment to do the afternoon chores—get them over with while the going is good. So I leave the radio for a spell and visit the barn, my peaceable kingdom, where not a nematode stirs.

When I resumed my vigil, I discovered to my great surprise that Rockland, which is quite nearby, had dropped Edna for the time being and taken up American League baseball. A Red Sox–Indians game was on, with the outfield (I never learned which outfield) playing it straightaway. My wife, who despises the American League, was listening on her set and dialing erratically. I heard a myna bird being introduced, but the bird failed to respond to the introduction. Then someone gave the rules of a limerick contest. I was to supply the missing line for the following limerick:

> I knew a young lady named Joan
> Who wanted a car of her own.
>   She was a sharp kid
>   So here's what she did
>
>   . . . .

The line came to me quickly enough: She ordered a Chevy by phone. I was to send this to Box 401 on a postcard, but I didn't know what city and I wasn't at all sure that it was a General Motors program—could have been a competitor. The whole thing made no sense anyway, as cars were at that moment being ordered off the roads—even Joan's car.

At 2:30 it was announced that school buildings in the town of Newton were open for people who wanted to go to them "for greater personal security or comfort." Ted Williams, who had been in a slump, singled. WBZ said the Boston police had lost touch with Nantucket, electric power had failed in South Natick, Portland was going to be hit at five o'clock, Wells Beach had been evacuated, a Republican rally for tonight in Augusta had been canceled, the eye of Edna was five miles north of Nantucket, a girl baby had been born, Katharine Cornell had been evacuated by police from her home on Martha's Vineyard, and all letter carriers had been called back to their stations in Boston on the old sleet-snow-wind theory of mail delivery. I made a trip to the barometer for a routine reading: 29.41, falling.

"The rain," said the mayor of Boston in a hearty voice, "is coming down in sheets."

"That gigantic whirlpool of air known as Hurricane Edna," said Weatherbee, from his South Shore observation point, "is over the town hall of Chatham." Weatherbee also dropped the news that the eastern end of the Maine coast would probably get winds of hurricane velocity about six hours from now.

"Weatherbee," said a proud voice from the WBZ Communications Center, "is still batting a thousand." (At this juncture I would have settled for Ted Williams, who wasn't doing nearly so well.)

The rest of the afternoon, and the evening, was a strange nightmare of rising tempest and diminishing returns. The storm grew steadily in force, but in our neck of the woods a characteristic of hurricanes is that they arrive from the southwest, which is where most radio lives, and radio loses interest in Nature just as soon as Nature passes in front of the window and goes off toward the northeast. Weatherbee was right. The storm did strike here about six hours later, with winds up to ninety miles an hour, but when the barometer reached its lowest point and the wind shifted into the NW and began to tear everything to pieces, what we got on the radio was a man doing a whistling act and somebody playing the glockenspiel. All the livelong day we had had our mild weather to the sound of doom, and then at evening, when the power failed and the telephone failed and the tide flooded and the gale exploded, we heard the glockenspiel. Governor Cross, a Republican, who also lives to the westward, had already announced that the worst of the storm was over and that, except for a few benighted areas along the coast, everything was hunky-dory. I notice he got voted out of office a couple of days later, probably by an enormous outpouring of Republican turncoats from the coastal towns to the east of him, whose trees were being uprooted at the time he was speaking.

My own evening was an odd one. As Edna moved toward me across the Gulf of Maine, I watched the trees and the rain with increasing interest, albeit with no radio support except from the glockenspiel. At half-past six I evacuated my wife from the front room, without police action, and mixed us both a drink in a back room. At 6:55 she leaned forward in her chair and began neatening the books in a low bookshelf, pulling the volumes forward one by one and lining them up with the leading edge of the shelf, soldiers being dressed by their sergeant. By half-past seven the wind had slacked off to give Edna's eye a good peep at us, the glass was steadying, and ten minutes later, watching the vane on the barn, I saw the wind starting to back into the north, fitfully. The rain eased up and we let the dachshund out, taking advantage of the lull. (Unlike the geese, she had no use for rough weather, and she had obeyed the radio faithfully all day—stayed put under the stove.)

At 7:45 the governor of New Hampshire thanked everyone for his cooperation, and Logan International Airport announced the resumption of flights. At eight o'clock my barometer reached bottom—28.65. The governor of Massachusetts came on to thank *his* people, and somebody announced that the Supreme Market in Dorchester would be open for business in the morning (Sunday). Another voice promised that at eleven o'clock there would be a wrap-up on Hurricane Edna.

At this point I decided to take a stroll. The night was agreeable—moon showing through gray clouds, light rain, hurricane still to come. My stroll turned out to be a strange one. I started for the shore, thinking I'd look over things down there, but when I got to the plank bridge over the brook I found the bridge under water. This caused me to wonder whether my spring, which supplies the house and which is located in the low-lying woods across the road, was being unindated. So, instead of proceeding to the shore, I crossed the road and entered the woods. I had rubber boots on and was carrying a flashlight. The path to the spring is pretty well grown over and I had difficulty finding it. In fact, I'm not sure that I ever did find it. I waded about in the swampy woods for ten or fifteen minutes, most of the time in water halfway up to my knees. It was pleasant in there, but I was annoyed that I was unable to find the spring. Failing in this, I returned to the house, kicked off my boots, and sank back into radioland. The Bangor station predicted ninety-mile winds within half an hour, and I discovered a scrap of paper on which my wife had scribbled "Bangor 9437, 7173, and 2313"—emergency numbers taken down just as though we were really in telephone communication with the outside world. (The phone had been gone for a long time.)

At 8:44 the power failed, the house went dark, and it was a whole lot easier to see Edna. In almost no time the storm grew to its greatest height: the wind (NW by this time) chased black clouds across the ailing moon. The woods to the south of us bent low, as though the trees prayed for salvation. Several went over. The house tuned up, roaring with the thunder of a westerly wind. For a little while we were both battened down and battered down.

There are always two stages of any disturbance in the country—the stage when the lights and the phone are still going, the stage when these are lost. We were in the second stage. In front of the house, a large branch of the biggest balm-of-Gilead tree snapped and crashed down across the driveway, closing it off. On the north side, an apple tree split clean up the middle. And for half an hour or so Edna held us in her full embrace.

It did not seem long. Compared to the endless hours of the radio vigil, it seemed like nothing at all. By ten o'clock the wind was moderating. We lighted the dog up to her bed by holding a flashlight along the stairs, so she could see where to leap. When we looked out of a north bedroom, there in the beautiful sky was a rainbow lit by the moon.

It was Taylor Grant, earlier in the evening, who pretty well summed things up for radio. "The weather bureau estimates that almost forty-six million persons along the east coast have felt some degree of concern over the movement of the storm," said Mr. Grant. "Never before has a hurricane had that large an audience." As one member of this vast audience, I myself felt a twinge of belated concern the next morning when I went over to the spring to fetch a pail of water. There in the woods, its great trunk square across the path, its roots in the air, lay a big hackmatack.

I never did get to hear the wrap-up. ▪

BRAHMINS

Minority Report

JONATHAN KELLEY During his short life of 27 years, Jonathan Kelley showed considerable promise as a serious contributor to American humorous literature during the early nineteenth century. The Philadelphia-born Kelley became publisher of the *Boston Traveller*, which served as a base for the syndication of his comic sketches to the leading newspapers and periodicals of the nation.

His essay lampooning the lecture style of the preeminent literary figure of his day—Ralph Waldo Emerson—demonstrated both youthful bravado and a certain anti-intellectualism, which undoubtedly found an appreciative audience among provincial readers even in that era of determined self-improvement.

■ Of all the public lecturers of our time and place, none has attracted more attention from the press, and consequently the people, than Ralph Waldo Emerson.

Lecturing has become quite a fashionable science—and now, instead of using the old-style phrases for illustrating facts, we call traveling preachers perambulating showmen, and floating politicians, lecturers.

As a lecturer, Ralph Waldo Emerson is extensively known around these parts, but whether his lectures come under the head of law, logic, politics, Scripture, or the show business is a matter of much speculation; for our own part, the more we read or hear of Ralph, the more we don't know what it's all about.

Somebody has said that to his singularity of style or expression, Carlyle and his works owe their great notoriety or fame—and many compare Ralph Waldo to old Carlyle. They cannot trace exactly any great affinity between these two great geniuses of the flash literary school. Carlyle writes vigorously, quaintly enough, but almost always speaks when he says something; on the contrary, our flighty friend Ralph speaks vigorously, yet says nothing!

Of all the men that have ever stood and delivered in presence of a reporter, none surely ever led these indefatigable knights of the pen such a wild-goose chase over the verdant and flowery pastures of the King's English as Ralph Waldo Emerson. In ordinary cases, a reporter well versed in his art catches a sentence of a speaker and goes on to fill it out upon the most correct impression of what was intended, or what is implied. But no such license follows the outpouring of Mr. Emerson; no thought can fathom his intentions, and quite as bottomless are even his finished sentences. We have known "old stagers," in the newspaporial line, veteran reporters, so dumbfounded and confounded by the first fire of Ralph and his grand and lofty acrobating in elocution, that they up, seized their hat and paper, and sloped, horrified at the prospect of an attempt to "take down" Mr. Emerson.

If Roaring Ralph touches a homely mullein weed on a donkey heath, straightaway he makes it a full-blown rose in the land of Ophir, shedding an odor balmy as the gales of Arabia; while with a facility the wonderful London auctioneer Robbins might envy, Ralph imparts to a lime-box or pigsty, a negro hovel or an Irish shanty, all the romance, artistic elegance, and finish of a first-class manor house or Swiss cottage inlaid with alabaster and fresco, surrounded by elfin bowers, grand walks, bee hives, and honeysuckles.

Ralph don't group his metaphorical beauties or dainties of Webster, Walker, etc., but rushes them out in torrents—rattles them down in cataracts and avalanches—bewildering, astounding, and incomprehensible. He hits you with a metaphor so unwieldy and original that your breath is soon gone—and before it is recovered, he gives you another rhapsody on t'other side; and as you try to steady yourself, bim comes another, heavier than the first two; while a fourth batch of this sort of elocution fetches you a bang over the eyes, giving you a vertigo in the ribs of your bewildered senses; and before you can say "God bless us!" down he has you—cobim! with a deluge of high-heeled grammar and three-storied Anglo-Saxon, settling your hash, and brings you to the ground as though you were struck by lightning or got in the way of a thirty-six-pounder! Ralph Waldo is death and an entire stud of pale horses on flowery expressions and japonica-domish flubdabs. He revels in all those knock-kneed, antique, or crooked and twisted words we used all of us to puzzle our brains over in the days of our youth and grammar lessons and rhetoric exercises. He has a penchant as strong as cheap boardinghouse butter for mystification, and a free delivery of hard words, perfectly and unequivocally wonderful.

We listened one long hour by the clock of Rumford Hall one night to an outpouring of *argumentum ad hominem* of Mr. Emerson's—at what? A boy under an apple tree! If ten persons out of the five hundred present were put upon their oaths, they could no more have deciphered or translated Mr. Ralph's argumentation than they could the hieroglyphics upon the walls of Thebes or the sarcophagus of old King Pharaoh!

When Ralph Waldo opens, he may be as calm as a May morn—he may talk for five minutes, like a book—we mean a common-sensed, understandable book; but all of a sudden the fluid will strike him—up he goes—down he fetches them. He throws a double somersault backwards over Asia Minor—flip-flaps in Greece—wings Turkey—and skeets over Iceland; here he slips up with a flower garden—a torrent of gilt-edged metaphors that would last a country parson's moderate demand a long lifetime are whirled with the fury and fleetness of Jove's thunderbolts. After exhausting this floral elocution, he pauses four seconds; pointing to vacuum over the heads of his audience, he asks in an anxious tone, "Do you see that?" Of course the audience are not expected to be so unmannerly as to ask "What?" If they were, Ralph would not give them time to "go in," for after asking them if they see that, he continues:

"There! Mark! Note! It is a malaria prism! Now, then; here—there; see it! Note it! Watch it!"

During this time half of the audience, especially the old women and the children, look around, fearful of the ceiling falling in or big bugs lighting on them. But the pause is for a moment, and anxiety ceases when they learn it was only a false alarm, only:

"Egotism! The lame, the pestiferous exhalation or concrete malformation of society!"

You breathe freer, and Ralph goes in, gloves on.

"Egotism! A metaphysical, calcareous, oleraceous amentum of—society! The mental varioloid of this sublunary hemisphere! One of its worst feelings or features is the craving of sympathy. It even loves sickness, because actual pain engenders signs of sympathy. All cultivated men are infected more or less with this dropsy. But they are still the leaders. The life of a few men is the life of every place. In Boston you hear and see a few, so in New York; then you may as well die. Life is very narrow. Bring a few men together, and under the spell of one calm genius, what frank, sad confessions will be made! Culture is the suggestion from a few best thoughts that a man should not be a charlatan, but temper and subdue life. Culture redresses his balance and puts him among his equals. It is a poor compliment always to talk with a man upon his specialty, as if he were a cheesemite and was therefore strong on Cheshire and Stilton. Culture takes the grocer out of his molasses and makes him genial. We pay a heavy price for those fancy goods, Fine Arts and Philosophy. No performance is worth less of geniality. That unhappy man called of genius is an unfortunate man. Nature always carries her point despite the means!"

If that don't convince you of Ralph's high-heeled, knock-kneed logic or *au fait* dexterity in concocting flapdoodle mixtures, you're ahead of ordinary intellect as far as this famed lecturer is in advance of gin and bitters or opium discourses on—delirium tremens!

In short, Ralph Waldo Emerson can wrap up a subject in more mystery and science of language than ever a defunct Egyptian received at the hands of the mummy manufacturers.

In person Mr. Ralph is rather a pleasing sort of man, in manners frank and agreeable, about forty years of age, and a native of Massachusetts. As a lawyer he would have been the horror of jurors and judges; as a lecturer he is, as near as possible, what we have described him. ■■

Newport—
of Cottages and
Queens

CLEVELAND AMORY In recent years Cleveland Amory has established a reputation as America's foremost animal-rights activist. But he was better known to earlier generations as one of America's wittiest and most popular social historians.

A native of Boston, Amory chronicled the fables and foibles of America's social set in such works as *The Proper Bostonians* and *Who Killed Society?* In *The Last Resorts* Amory recounted the histories of the glamorous watering holes of the super-rich. The book contains many humorous tales about Newport, Rhode Island, where multimillion-dollar "cottages" served as summer retreats for the American aristocracy of the late nineteenth and early twentieth centuries.

■ Even Mrs. Belmont paled before the third member of Newport's Great Triumvirate, the irrepressible Mrs. Stuyvesant Fish of "Crossways." Mrs. Belmont was the *grande dame* of Newport's Golden Age but Mrs. Fish was its *enfant terrible*. More than any one figure of her times she is held personally responsible by old-time resorters for causing the breakdown of the classification of Society as she found it, and for causing the beginning of the end of the reign of the Four Hundred. For a lady who was by no means beautiful, who had only, as she herself put it, "a few million," and who cared little for the art or theater and less for music or literature, to accomplish such a feat was remarkable enough. It was more remarkable since Mrs. Fish never went to school, could not spell even the simplest words, rarely read even a newspaper, and, if she could manage to scrawl a dash-littered letter, she could not, if her life depended on it, make such a letter legible. She had, however, two vital assets, a quick wit and a sharp tongue, and with these went a large ambition. As she once told her daughter-in-law, "It doesn't make any difference what you decide to do in life, but you must do it better than anyone else." Mrs. Fish chose to be a hostess, and today, looking back, even her enemies agree that more people had more fun on more occasions *chez* Mrs. Fish than they had anywhere else. In the bargain, it went without saying, they would be insulted. That was to be expected; it was Mrs. Fish's way. Disliking the era in which she lived, she chose to spend her life making fun of it, and a vital part of her own having fun was making fun of others. In the end, the lady who could hardly write her own name not only wrote a new chapter in American Society but also became, of the old era, perhaps its greatest satirist.

Born in New York in 1853, the daughter of the New York lawyer, William Henry Anthon, she had as her first dislike in life her own name— one which she promptly changed from Mary Ann to Marian. From the beginning her friends never called her anything but Mamie. Her father died when she was twelve years old; her family, unable to afford New York City, moved to Astoria where, alone of the three children, Mamie was able to avoid the school system entirely. If not a beautiful girl, she had striking black eyes and inherited from her French ancestry a good deal of what was then called "come hither"; characteristically she married her childhood beau from back in New York City—a young man who had been born just three blocks from her. At that time Stuyvesant Fish worked for the banking house of Morton, Bliss & Company, where his father also worked. When a check in payment of the Alabama Claims was presented to the firm, the elder Fish signed the order in behalf of the government, the younger for Morton, Bliss. A man in the office, seeing the two signatures, remarked, "I see the Father and the Son, but where is the Holy Ghost?" The younger Fish stared at him. "That, sir," he said, "is the mutual trust and confidence that makes the whole transaction possible."

Young Mrs. Fish, who made a lifelong career of running her husband, did not share his fervor for his firm. When Morton, Bliss & Company interrupted her honeymoon, she never forgave them and shortly persuaded her husband to enter the service of the Illinois Central. Of this club, the so-called "Society Railroad" of the day, Fish became president in 1887; he held the position until 1906, at which time, Mrs. Fish having feuded with Mrs. E. H. Harriman, he was blackballed.

In between managing her husband and raising three children, Mrs. Fish also took care of Society. Moving to Newport in 1889 from "Glenclyffe," her home in Garrison, New York, she spent several summers renting cottages and then, in 1900, on the hill beyond Bailey's Beach, she built her famous "Crossways." A distinguished French nobleman once said to her, in the manner of titled foreigners angling for invitations, that he had heard she had a beautiful villa in Newport. "You have been misinformed," replied

Mrs. Fish. "I have just a plain white house." Actually "Crossways," a handsome white Colonial cottage with four large Corinthian columns in front, was no castle to rival "The Breakers" or "Marble House" but it was by no means plain. And neither, Newport was shortly to learn, were the entertainments in it. Mrs. Fish had not one ballroom, but two. Despite the fact that the downstairs of "Crossways" could be transformed into what amounted to an all-ballroom floor, Mrs. Fish had an extra ballroom built on behind. Rebelling at the two- and even three-hour dinners of the times, Mrs. Fish had them served in fifty, or even forty, minutes. Her record was an eight-course dinner in thirty minutes flat. At this dinner footmen were so anxious to meet the deadline that participants recalled it was necessary to hold the plate down with one hand and eat with the other. Elisha Dyer, during the fish course, took a bone from his mouth and by the time he put it down, the meat course was in front of him. Mrs. Fish's other dining innovation was the serving of champagne, in preference to wine, from the oysters on. "You have to liven these people up," she said. "Wine just makes them sleepy."

Mrs. Fish's greetings to her guests were as unique as her service. "Howdy-do, howdy-do," she would say impatiently, pushing the newly arrived guests at Mr. Fish with a look of keen annoyance. "Make yourselves at home," she would add. "And believe me, there is no one who wishes you were there more than I do." One guest had a special greeting. "Oh," said Mrs. Fish, surprised, "I'd quite forgotten I asked you." The conclusions of her parties were equally curious. One guest made an excuse to leave early. "I promised I would be home by . . . " he began. "Don't apologize," broke in Mrs. Fish. "No guest ever left too soon for me." Once bored with one of her own parties, she had the orchestra play "Home, Sweet Home" before the guests' carriages had even been called. An enthusiastic beau begged for one more two-step. "There are just two steps more for you," said Mrs. Fish, "one upstairs to get your coat and the other out to your carriage." A lady went out and sat down to wait for her carriage. The footman came in to report that the port-cochere was windy and the lady was furious. "Let her stay there," said Mrs. Fish. "She'll cool off better out there than she will in here." Ladies' luncheons were her particular bêtes noires. "Here you all are," she said greeting one, "older faces and younger clothes." At another time she gave a luncheon for fifty ladies and through it all sat upstairs, refusing to come down. Finally her maid begged her at least to come down and say good-by. "But, Mrs. Fish," she said, "you invited them two weeks ago." Mrs. Fish waved her maid away. "Tell them I've changed my mind," she said.

On an individual scale Mrs. Fish's insults were even more cherished—though she never could remember names and addressed everyone as "Pet" or "Sweet pet," "Lamb" or "Sweet lamb." She was particularly acid on the favored feminine topic of babies. A lady asked her, concerning a large and constantly expanding Newport family, if she had seen Mrs. So-and-so's last baby. "Pet," replied Mrs. Fish, "I don't expect to live that long."

On another occasion Mrs. Fish was asked if she knew another lady was pregnant. "Lamb," she said, "I do. Isn't it disgusting?" When the new word "propaganda" was being widely used, a lady confided to her that she was distressed because she could not have a baby. Mrs. Fish was bored. "Perhaps," she said slowly, "you haven't got the proper gander." On the question of house guests she was particularly outspoken. Even Harry Lehr, who served her as court chamberlain as Ward McAllister had Mrs. Astor, was not above occasional reproach. One day after his marriage to Mrs. Dahlgren, a group at "Crossways" were trying to guess each other's favorite flower. "I know Mamie's," said Lehr quickly, "the climbing rose." Mrs. Fish smiled. "And I yours; pet," she replied, "the marigold." One day Lehr introduced her to the Englishman Tony Shaw Safe who had come to the resort as manager of a polo team and stayed on to marry a wealthy Newporter and hyphenate his name from Shaw Safe to Shaw-Safe. He was particularly insistent on being called by the full hyphenation. "Howdy-do, Mr. Safe," Mrs. Fish blithely greeted him. "I'm sorry to call you Mr. Safe but I've forgotten your combination."

Other guests were even more summarily treated. One of Lehr's friends complained that there were not enough bath towels. "I had to dry myself on a bath mat," he said. "Pet," replied Mrs. Fish, "you were lucky not to be offered the doormat." Moncure Robinson had been in Europe three months. On landing in this country he came directly to "Crossways" and started in the front door. Overhead, Mrs. Fish on the balcony spotted him. "Are you in for lunch?" she called down abruptly. "Well, I really don't know," he replied. "Well," said Mrs. Fish, "I'm out." Sumner Gerard, visiting at another Newport cottage, complained he had stayed a week and had seen his hostess only once. "I wish I could run my house as well," said Mrs. Fish. She particularly detested people who asked her the details of her menage. One lady asked her how large "Crossways" was. "I really can't tell you," said Mrs. Fish. "It swells at night." The same lady also asked her how many laundresses she employed. "I have six white ones who work all day," replied Mrs. Fish, "and six black ones who work all night. Being black, you see, you can't see them."

As a feudist Mrs. Fish was unequaled and she particularly enjoyed her altercations with other Newport hostesses. Mrs. John Drexel had a male secretary who was her inseparable companion. One day a friend of Mrs. Drexel came up to Mrs. Fish. "Mamie, have you seen Cousin Alice?" she asked. "I've looked everywhere in the house," she added anxiously. "No," replied Mrs. Fish. "Have you looked under the secretary?" ■

Pequod Island Days

JOHN P. MARQUAND *The Late George Apley*, which won a Pulitzer Prize for John P. Marquand in 1938, was the most successful of his novels satirizing upper-class New Englanders. The story is told in the form of a memoir by Horatio Willing, Boston academic and family sychophant. His relentlessly upbeat portrayal of a crumbling society whose cultural and political dominance comes up against the leveling forces of twentieth-century New England and America becomes a self-satirizing narrative.

We watch as the pathetic Apley tries unsuccessfully to escape the aristocratic and Puritan trappings of his heritage. In this excerpt, for example, his attempts to shed the smothering influences of the domineering women in his life by fleeing into the Maine wilderness are routinely frustrated, all under the nose— but wholly beyond the comprehension—of the obsequious narrator, Willing.

The Establishment of a Beloved and Challenging Institution

Pequod Island Camp and the life on that remote jewel of an island nestled in the clear blue waters of one of Maine's wilderness lakes has been described by the present writer in his memorial, "Pequod Island Days," which was distributed privately a few years back to those fortunate enough to know the spot. At the risk of injecting his own personality, a few selections from this work by the present writer are quoted, as they are so deeply concerned with Apley.

Well I remember the first day that anyone saw Pequod Island and thought of it as something more than a stopping place on a wilderness journey. It was in the latter part of a September afternoon, in the cool before sunset, that the canoes of three tired campers and their guides first broke the stillness of the waters of Pequod Lake after Half Mile Carry. In the party was our host, George Apley; Winthrop Vassal; and myself. Our guide was Norman Rowe, as fine a man as ever handled a canoe in white water, and one who, although he did not know it then, was for many years to be the guide, philosopher, and friend of every pilgrim to Pequod Island. There is little need to describe him here, for we all know him, a typical Yankee product of the woods, endowed with the quiet patience and the tolerance that is born of open spaces. We all know that drawling, singsong speech which George Apley was able so perfectly to imitate. We all know the dry, tolerant humor with which he regarded us "sports," as he called us. We have often seen him in later years at storytelling time around the campfire, with his perennial quid of tobacco tucked inside his cheek, exchanging pleasantries with his employer and dear friend; and the rapport between this son of Boston and this rough-handed, clear-eyed product of forest and stream was in many ways as amazing as it was beautiful—but perhaps it was not amazing after all. The son of Boston and the son of Maine were both sons of New England who shared a common philosophy. It has sometimes amused me to speculate how Norman Rowe might have developed had he been brought up in Apley's own environment. At any rate, his exterior never for a moment concealed the sterling traits of a gentleman, for he had many of the same qualities which President Emeritus Eliot perceived in his rough fisher friend farther up the Maine coast, and of which he wrote so eloquently.

We were weary indeed as the canoes neared the golden bow of beach that fringed the wooded slopes of Pequod Island, but it was a carefree, happy weariness. As we went for a dip in the lake while the guides busied themselves expertly with putting up tents, cutting soft beds of balsam boughs, and preparing trout, coffee, and flapjacks for supper, we were alone in a wilderness of woods and water, alone save for the mournful call of the loons and the splash of an occasional fish. Once seated about the campfire, according to his invariable habit of good fellowship, Apley directed the guides to sit among us instead of modestly withdrawing into a corner by themselves. He had the faculty, inherited perhaps from his seafaring ancestors, of putting this type of person entirely at his ease, so much so that one had the illusion that Apley was one of them. He drew Norman Rowe into fanciful accounts of the habits of moose and beaver; and as Norman Rowe's imagination became stimulated through his own narration, George Apley's eye had that sly twinkle which those who knew him in the woods so well remember. When Norman had finished his story of a tame beaver at a lumber camp who rang the dinner bell whenever he was hungry, George Apley said: "I believe you, Norman, we all believe you," and Norman shared in the hearty laugh at his expense. Then George Apley placed a hand in a friendly way on Norman's shoulder. "Norman," he said, "you are too good a man to lose; I am going to buy this island and I am going to put you on it."

That was the beginning of Pequod Island Camp.

Starting spontaneously, Pequod Island has never lost its spontaneity, and one loves to think that the aura of good fellowship which enfolded it that evening and the carefree gayety of that moment have never left it. Pequod Island has always been a place where one may drink deeply and gayly of unspoiled nature, and where one may commune with the forest about it. The great central cabin which now overlooks the beach, christened facetiously by George Apley the "Forum Romanum," with its enormous fieldstone fireplace and rawhide-seated chairs, was George Apley's own idea, as indeed was the arrangement of the outer cabins, each given the name for some building of classical Rome. These even included the dormitory of unmarried women, facetiously but racily called "The Hall of the Vestal Virgins." Thus, the whole island became in time an idealization of its owner's hospitality. It is true that each guest paid a nominal fee for his or her board and lodging, but this plan was only hit upon to free each visitor from a certain sense of obligation to the host. Simple though the life was at Pequod Island, the actual running expenses were vastly greater than any sums collected, and this difference was made up cheerfully by "Romulus" Apley, our host, a name which was facetiously given him by the present writer.

Everyone arriving at Pequod Island dock recalls the sign made in letters of rustic cedar twigs which so typifies the welcoming spirit of the place: ALL YE WHO STEP UPON THIS PIER, LEAVE THE WORLD BEHIND. In a sense this admonition has always been sedulously followed. The dross of the world we have known has always been left in the broad-beamed passenger launch, and only what is fine in the world, with an occasional unpleasant exception, has come to Pequod Island. Now and then, to be sure, an individual has stepped ashore who did not fit in, who could not share that carefree spirit, but he has never been asked again. It was George Apley's idea also that there should be no drinking and no smoking. As the sign over the fireplace in the Forum Romanum gayly said: "Wood smoke is enough." Incidentally, it was amazing how quickly everyone who arrived there was cured of his craving for tobacco.

It was first George Apley's idea that Pequod Island should be a haven for men, since he was under the illusion that its facilities were of too rough-and-ready a nature to appeal to the fairer sex. He was soon cheerfully to admit his error. After two years the fame of Pequod Island became so widely known in Boston that it could no longer serve exclusively as a retreat for the "mere male." On the third summer, perhaps out of sheer curiosity, Catharine Apley and Amelia Simmings asked to be included in the party; and they may have come to scoff, but they remained to pray. Much to Apley's surprise Pequod Island appealed to them also, and to them we owe much of the routine and tradition which still exist there today. The accurate social sense of Amelia Simmings and Catharine Apley has been largely responsible for the selection of divergent but congenial personalities, so that there has always been good talk and stimulating thought on Pequod Island. It was Catharine Apley's idea, so successfully carried out, that no one of the fair sex should give a thought to dress. The rules for costume which she rigidly laid down demanded a flannel shirtwaist, a khaki skirt, black cotton stockings, and black sneakers. After wading in the brook or climbing to the top of Eagle Mountain across the lake, this costume might be changed, but it was never varied. Thus it has often caused no small amusement among new guests to observe in the dining hall that the village girls from the nearby town, employed as waitresses at the camp in summer, are universally more expensively dressed than those upon whom they wait. It was due to Amelia Simmings that the routine schedule of camp activities, which the rising generation considers as firm as the laws of the Medes and the Persians, was first adopted. Since Amelia Simmings first arrived at Pequod Island, the rising bell has sounded at six-thirty, and it was she who thought of a derisive song to greet the tardy arrivals at table, the first lines of which must ring in the memory of every Pequod Islander.

> Late, late, we all have ate,
> And now a cold egg is your fate.

Amelia Simmings also arranged the institution of the After Breakfast Forum, to discuss, after a short prayer, the activities of the day. It was first her idea for George Apley to act as chairman of Parliamentary Meeting, but later Mrs. Simmings herself took over this office. Each day a variety of morning and afternoon projects were laid informally before the assembled company, old and young, so that there was something to meet each taste. The fishers, for example, might go to Sturgeon Cove, the berrypickers might betake themselves to the top of Eagle Mountain, the workers—for at Pequod Island there was always work to do—might be assigned to dam-building, wood-chopping, boat-painting, or trail-cutting. The "idlers" were customarily taken in hand by Professor Speyer, to sit quietly on the rustic benches beneath the trees of Indian Point, there to read some selections from good books. The youngsters—for here John and Eleanor Apley and many of their friends and contemporaries spent a large portion of their summers—might join any of these parties if they were not backward in their lessons. In the evening by the hospitable lamplight of the Forum the secretary of each group rendered its report for the day to the tune of friendly and whimsical mirth, and so Pequod Island would retire to well-earned and dreamless repose.

To one who reads these pages, but who has never been on Pequod Island, this program may seem simple, but in truth it was not. The personalities that took part, and who contributed so much besides to our charades and pageants, were what leavened an otherwise dull loaf. It is needless to say that many famous figures appeared on Pequod Island and that eventually an invitation there was like an accolade. Poetry, philosophy, music, art, and diplomacy, all have passed beneath the giant pines which guard the Forum's door. There has always been something provocative in the gay spirit of Pequod Island, but the feature one remembers best was the character of the host who ruled over it.

In all those years, particularly after the organization beneath the capable hands of Amelia Simmings and Catharine Apley, the spirit of George Apley was felt more than his presence—a genial, kindly, but retiring spirit. As time went on his love for the woods and solitude became more and more pronounced, and he organized a group within the group at Pequod Island, known as the "camping crowd." The camping crowd was always directly under control of Norman Rowe and frequently with its canoes and tents left the island for days, and sometimes weeks, for little-known parts and for untouched beaches and streams. On one matter George Apley was always firm. Neither Catharine nor Amelia could interfere with the camping crowd. This was made up always of men, generally of his clubmates, and later his son John Apley and his college friends were admitted to the group.

> You know [he wrote his friend, Dr. Sewell, by then a famous abdominal surgeon] how much I love Pequod Island. I fully realize that a part of its charm is that it makes other people happy, and I leave much of that to Catharine and Amelia. The Robin Hood festival which my dear mother arranged herself this year was particularly delightful, and so are the talks and the singing in the evening, but now and then I have a feeling which I am brave enough to express only to you and a few others. I had thought on first coming to Pequod Island that we might get away for a while from certain things, that we might have a moment's breathing space, a respite from what we know so well and love so much. I suppose that this was rather too much to hope for. It sometimes seems to me that Boston has come to Pequod Island. I suppose we cannot escape from it entirely, nor do we really wish to, but I know what you and I like: the dripping water from a canoe paddle, the scent of balsam, the sweet smell of pond lilies and mud, the weariness of a long carry. These things are still on tap at Pequod Island. Norman and I have the canoes ready, and you can either go with me or talk with Professor Speyer. Personally, my summer is under canvas, with a few days in camp in which to recuperate, and then off again. Yet, even in those trips we move in circles, we move in circles and come back. I wish to goodness my life were not always a circle. I wish I were not always resting beneath the umbrella of my own personality. You must bear with me when I say this, because you know me better than most, you know it is a mood and I'll soon get over it. The

mood is on me tonight only because I have listened to several hours of intelligent conversation, and I am not a very brilliant person. Sometimes here on Pequod Island and back again on Beacon Street, I have the most curious delusion that our world may be a little narrow. I cannot avoid the impression that something has gone out of it (what, I do not know), and that our little world moves in an orbit of its own, again one of those confounded circles, or possibly an ellipse. Do you suppose that it moves without any relation to anything else? That it is broken off from some greater planet like the moon? We talk of life, we talk of art, but do we actually know anything about either? Have any of us really lived? Sometimes I am not entirely sure; sometimes I am afraid that we are all amazing people, placed in an ancestral mold. There is no spring, there is no force. Of course you know better than this, you who plunge every day, in the operating room of the Massachusetts General, into life itself. Come up here and tell me I am wrong.

Mr. Wong writes me from New York that he has a dozen new bronzes from the Han Dynasty. He will send them to Boston and I must look at them. I wish to heaven I had not started collecting them; it seems as hard to tell what is a real bronze as it is to tell who is a real person. Come up soon and explain this to me.

A letter written some years later to his son is in a somewhat different vein.

Dear John:—

I am sorry that you consider it advisable not to be with us here at Pequod Island for your usual month this summer, but instead to visit your college friends at Bar Harbor. There is an atmosphere of money at Bar Harbor which I, personally, have never liked, and I hope that you are not going there solely for that reason. It seems to me that you and the other young people whom I know are not as contented as I used to be at your age. I suppose it is because the world is moving faster. I was aware myself of this change when your mother and I gave up our carriage and began using an automobile.

What really worries me, however, about your not going to Pequod Island is that I am afraid you are neglecting a certain duty which you owe to others. Our little community at Pequod Island requires the coöperation of everyone to keep it together, and this coöperation, as I well know, not infrequently entails a certain sacrifice of personal inclination. Nevertheless, it is my obligation and yours, as my son, to make our guests here happy. You must be lenient with certain eccentricities. Believe me, I can understand how you feel about many of the requirements of your Aunt Amelia, because I agree with you that some of them are ridiculous. Frankly, I have sometimes wished that I were not invariably aroused at

half-past six. I have often wished that I could spend the day doing exactly as I pleased, but I know now that such a wish is a luxury
and a weakness. As time goes on it will become more and more
evident to you that you are a part of a society whose dictates you
must obey within certain prescribed limits, and in every walk of life
we must give way to the common will. Yes, there are certain things
one does and others one does not do. One of the things which you
and I must not do is to neglect our duties at Pequod Island.

I am afraid you will learn before you are much older that this
general principle will run through much of your life. Take our downtown lunch club for instance—it comes into my mind as just such
another group which has its customs and its manners. You will find
when you become a member, as you doubtless will when you take
up business in Boston, that you will not be cordially received at
certain of the tables where the same people have customarily eaten
for the last thirty years. Furthermore, you will discover if you go
downstairs to smoke in the room reserved for the purpose that you
should not linger there long over your cigar, whether you have
anything to do for the next hour or not. This, of course, is a trivial
example, and I simply give it as an illustration to show that you and
I cannot and should not change established customs.

I want to tell you one thing more, John, and some day you will
know how right I am. There are certain duties one cannot escape.
I do not know just why. I consider this quite often without arriving at any just rationalization. It is, I think, because you and I have
been born into a certain environment with very definite inherited
instincts. We cannot escape that environment, John, because it is a
part of you and me. You can leave Pequod Island for Bar Harbor, but
Pequod Island will nevertheless remain a part of you. You can go to
the uttermost ends of the earth, but, in a sense, you will still be in
Boston; and this is not true alone with you and me; it has been the
same with others. For many years after the discovery of the Sandwich Islands, all Americans touching there were known to the
natives as Bostonians. Believe me, this was not entirely an accident; in my opinion these individuals stood out in the childlike
minds of the Polynesians as more distinct than other American
nationals. They had brought something of Boston with them, just as
you and I will bring it with us, always.

This is an inescapable fact but one, I believe, that we should
be rather proud of than otherwise. It is something to be an inte-
grated part of such a distinct group. It is somehow reassuring; at
any rate you can go to Bar Harbor, John, but you cannot get away
from Pequod Island. . . .

It is interesting to observe that John Apley himself appended a note
to this letter which reads: "By God, you can't." ∎

Inflexible Logic

RUSSELL MALONEY Writer, editor, and book critic Russell
Maloney (1910-1948) was born in Brookline, Massachusetts, and
educated at Harvard. After graduation in 1932 he proceeded to
bombard *The New Yorker* with so many gags, anecdotes, and
sketches that the magazine invited him to join its staff.

He turned out prodigious quantities of material for the
magazine—under his own name, anonymously, and over many
pseudonyms. Speaking jocularly of his output and of the
magazine's demanding standards, he once said he had "written
and had printed in *The New Yorker* something like twenty-six hundred perfect anecdotes."

Maloney later branched out to write short stories, articles,
and humorous commentaries for all of the top magazines of his
day and to review books for *The New York Times* and CBS Radio. Of
all his writings, Maloney is perhaps remembered best for this
piece from *The New Yorker*.

■ When the six chimpanzees came into his life, Mr. Bainbridge was thirty-
eight years old. He was a bachelor and lived comfortably in a remote part
of Connecticut, in a large old house with a carriage drive, a conservatory, a
tennis court, and a well-selected library. His income was derived from
impeccably situated real estate in New York City, and he spent it soberly,
in a manner which could give offence to nobody. Once a year, late in April,
his tennis court was resurfaced, and after that anybody in the neighborhood was welcome to use it; his monthly statement from Brentano's seldom ran below seventy-five dollars; every third year, in November, he
turned in his old Cadillac coupé for a new one; he ordered his cigars, which
were mild and rather moderately priced, in shipments of one thousand,
from a tobacconist in Havana; because of the international situation he
had canceled arrangements to travel abroad, and after due thought
had decided to spend his traveling allowance on wines, which seemed
likely to get scarcer and more expensive if the war lasted. On the whole, Mr.

Bainbridge's life was deliberately, and not too unsuccessfully, modeled after that of an English country gentleman of the late eighteenth century, a gentleman interested in the arts and in the expansion of science, and so sure of himself that he didn't care if some people thought him eccentric.

Mr. Bainbridge had many friends in New York, and he spent several days of the month in the city, staying at his club and looking around. Sometimes he called up a girl and took her out to a theatre and a night club. Sometimes he and a couple of classmates got a little tight and went to a prizefight. Mr. Bainbridge also looked in now and then at some of the conservative art galleries, and liked occasionally to go to a concert. And he liked cocktail parties, too, because of the fine footling conversation and the extraordinary number of pretty girls who had nothing else to do with the rest of their evening. It was at a New York cocktail party, however, that Mr. Bainbridge kept his preliminary appointment with doom. At one of the parties given by Hobie Packard, the stockbroker, he learned about the theory of the six chimpanzees.

It was almost six-forty. The people who had intended to have one drink and go had already gone, and the people who intended to stay were fortifying themselves with slightly dried canapés and talking animatedly. A group of stage and radio people had coagulated in one corner, near Packard's Capehart, and were wrangling about various methods of cheating the Collector of Internal Revenue. In another corner was a group of stockbrokers talking about the greatest stockbroker of them all, Gauguin. Little Marcia Lupton was sitting with a young man, saying earnestly, "Do you really want to know what my greatest ambition is? I want to be myself," and Mr. Bainbridge smiled gently, thinking of the time Marcia had said that to him. Then he heard the voice of Bernard Weiss, the critic, saying, "Of course he wrote one good novel. It's not surprising. After all, we know that if six chimpanzees were set to work pounding six typewriters at random, they would, in a million years, write all the books in the British Museum."

Mr. Bainbridge drifted over to Weiss and was introduced to Weiss's companion, a Mr. Noble. "What's this about a million chimpanzees, Weiss?" he asked.

"Six chimpanzees," Mr. Weiss said. "It's an old cliché of the mathematicians. I thought everybody was told about it in school. Law of averages, you know, or maybe it's permutation and combination. The six chimps, just pounding away at the typewriter keys, would be bound to copy out all the books ever written by man. There are only so many possible combinations of letters and numerals, and they'd produce all of them—see? Of course they'd also turn out a mountain of gibberish, but they'd work the books in, too. All the books in the British Museum."

Mr. Bainbridge was delighted; this was the sort of talk he liked to hear when he came to New York. "Well, but look here," he said, just to keep up his part in the foolish conversation, "what if one of the chimpanzees finally did duplicate a book, right down to the last period, but left that off? Would that count?"

"I suppose not. Probably the chimpanzee would get around to doing the book again, and put the period in."

"What nonsense!" Mr. Noble cried.

"It may be nonsense, but Sir James Jeans believes it," Mr. Weiss said, huffily. "Jeans or Lancelot Hogben. I know I ran across it quite recently."

Mr. Bainbridge was impressed. He read quite a bit of popular science, and both Jeans and Hogben were in his library. "Is that so?" he murmured, no longer feeling frivolous. "Wonder if it has ever actually been tried? I mean, has anybody ever put six chimpanzees in a room with six typewriters and a lot of paper?"

Mr. Weiss glanced at Mr. Bainbridge's empty cocktail glass and said drily, "Probably not."

Nine weeks later, on a winter evening, Mr. Bainbridge was sitting in his study with his friend James Mallard, an assistant professor of mathematics at New Haven. He was plainly nervous as he poured himself a drink and said, "Mallard, I've asked you to come here—brandy? cigar?—for a particular reason. You remember that I wrote you some time ago, asking your opinion of . . . of a certain mathematical hypothesis or supposition."

"Yes," Professor Mallard said, briskly. "I remember perfectly. About the six chimpanzees and the British Museum. And I told you it was a perfectly sound popularization of a principle known to every schoolboy who had studied the science of probabilities."

"Precisely," Mr. Bainbridge said. "Well, Mallard, I made up my mind. . . . It was not difficult for me, because I have, in spite of that fellow in the White House, been able to give something every year to the Museum of Natural History, and they were naturally glad to oblige me. . . . And after all, the only contribution a layman can make to the progress of science is to assist with the drudgery of experiment. . . . In short, I—"

"I suppose you're trying to tell me that you have procured six chimpanzees and set them to work at typewriters in order to see whether they will eventually write all the books in the British Museum. Is that it?"

"Yes, that's it," Mr. Bainbridge said. "What a mind you have, Mallard. Six fine young males, in perfect condition. I had a—I suppose you'd call it a dormitory—built out in back of the stable. The typewriters are in the conservatory. It's light and airy in there, and I moved most of the plants out. Mr. North, the man who owns the circus, very obligingly let me engage one of his best animal men. Really, it was no trouble at all."

Professor Mallard smiled indulgently. "After all, such a thing is not unheard of," he said. "I seem to remember that a man at some university put his graduate students to work flipping coins, to see if heads and tails came up an equal number of times. Of course they did."

Mr. Bainbridge looked at his friend very queerly. "Then you believe that any such principle of the science of probabilities will stand up under an actual test?

"You had better see for yourself." Mr. Bainbridge led Professor Mallard downstairs, along a corridor, through a disused music room, and into a large conservatory. The middle of the floor had been cleared of plants and was occupied by a row of six typewriter tables, each one supporting a hooded machine. At the left of each typewriter was a neat stack of yellow copy paper. Empty wastebaskets were under each table. The chairs were the unpadded, spring-backed kind favored by experienced stenographers. A large bunch of ripe bananas was hanging in one corner, and in another stood a Great Bear water-cooler and a rack of Lily cups. Six piles of typescript, each about a foot high, were ranged along the wall on an improvised shelf. Mr. Bainbridge picked up one of the piles, which he could just conveniently lift, and set it on a table before Professor Mallard. "The output to date of Chimpanzee A, known as Bill," he said simply.

" '*Oliver Twist*, by Charles Dickens,' " Professor Mallard read out. He read the first and second pages of the manuscript, then feverishly leafed through to the end. "You mean to tell me," he said, "that this chimpanzee has written—"

"Word for word and comma for comma," said Mr. Bainbridge. "Young, my butler, and I took turns comparing it with the edition I own. Having finished *Oliver Twist*, Bill is, as you see, starting the sociological works of Vilfredo Pareto, in Italian. At the rate he has been going, it should keep him busy for the rest of the month."

"And all the chimpanzees"—Professor Mallard was pale, and enunciated with difficulty—"they aren't all—"

"Oh, yes, all writing books which I have every reason to believe are in the British Museum. The prose of John Donne, some Anatole France, Conan Doyle, Galen, the collected plays of Somerset Maugham, Marcel Proust, the memoirs of the late Marie of Rumania, and a monograph by a Dr. Wiley on the marsh grasses of Maine and Massachusetts. I can sum it up for you, Mallard, by telling you that since I started this experiment, four weeks and some days ago, none of the chimpanzees has spoiled a single sheet of paper."

Professor Mallard straightened up, passed his handkerchief across his brow, and took a deep breath. "I apologize for my weakness," he said. "It was simply the sudden shock. No, looking at the thing scientifically—and I hope I am at least as capable of that as the next man—there is nothing marvelous about the situation. These chimpanzees, or a succession of similar teams of chimpanzees, would in a million years write all the books in the British Museum. I told you some time ago that I believed that statement. Why should my belief be altered by the fact that they produced some of the books at the very outset? After all, I should not be very much surprised if I tossed a coin a hundred times and it came up heads every time. I know that if I kept at it long enough, the ratio would reduce itself to an exact fifty percent. Rest assured, these chimpanzees will begin to compose gibberish quite soon. It is bound to happen. Science tells us so. Meanwhile, I advise you to keep this experiment secret. Uninformed people might create a sensation if they knew."

"I will, indeed," Mr. Bainbridge said. "And I'm very grateful for your rational analysis. It reassures me. And now, before you go, you must hear the new Schnabel records that arrived today."

During the succeeding three months, Professor Mallard got into the habit of telephoning Mr. Bainbridge every Friday afternoon at five-thirty, immediately after leaving his seminar room. The professor would say, "Well?," and Mr. Bainbridge would reply, "They're still at it, Mallard. Haven't spoiled a sheet of paper yet." If Mr. Bainbridge had to go out on Friday afternoon, he would leave a written message with his butler, who would read it to Professor Mallard: "Mr. Bainbridge says we now have Trevelyan's *Life of Macaulay*, the Confessions of St. Augustine, *Vanity Fair*, part of Irving's *Life of George Washington*, the Book of the Dead, and some speeches delivered in Parliament in opposition to the Corn Laws, sir." Professor Mallard would reply, with a hint of a snarl in his voice, "Tell him to remember what I predicted," and hang up with a clash.

The eleventh Friday that Professor Mallard telephoned, Mr. Bainbridge said, "No change. I have had to store the bulk of the manuscript in the cellar. I would have burned it, except that it probably has some scientific value."

"How dare you talk of scientific value?" The voice from New Haven roared faintly in the receiver. "Scientific value! You—you—chimpanzee!" There were further inarticulate sputterings, and Mr. Bainbridge hung up with a disturbed expression. "I am afraid Mallard is overtaxing himself," he murmured.

Next day, however, he was pleasantly surprised. He was leafing through a manuscript that had been completed the previous day by Chimpanzee D, Corky. It was the complete diary of Samuel Pepys, and Mr. Bainbridge was chuckling over the naughty passages, which were omitted in his own edition, when Professor Mallard was shown into the room. "I have come to apologize for my outrageous conduct on the telephone yesterday," the Professor said.

"Please don't think of it any more. I know you have many things on your mind," Mr. Bainbridge said. "Would you like a drink?"

"A large whiskey, straight, please," Professor Mallard said. "I got rather cold driving down. No change, I presume?"

"No none, Chimpanzee F, Dinty, is just finishing John Florio's translation of Montaigne's essays, but there is no other news of interest."

Professor Mallard squared his shoulders and tossed off his drink in one astonishing gulp. "I should like to see them at work," he said. "Would I disturb them, do you think?"

"Not at all. As a matter of fact, I usually look in on them around this time of day. Dinty may have finished his Montaigne by now, and it is always interesting to see them start a new work. I would have thought that they would continue on the same sheet of paper, but they don't, you know. Always a fresh sheet, and the title in capitals."

Professor Mallard, without apology, poured another drink and slugged it down. "Lead on," he said.

It was dusk in the conservatory, and the chimpanzees were typing by the light of student lamps clamped to their desks. The keeper lounged in a corner, eating a banana and reading *Billboard*. "You might as well take an hour or so off," Mr. Bainbridge said. The man left.

Professor Mallard, who had not taken off his overcoat, stood with his hands in his pockets, looking at the busy chimpanzees. "I wonder if you know, Bainbridge, that the science of probabilities takes everything into account," he said, in a queer, tight voice. "It is certainly almost beyond the bounds of credibility that these chimpanzees should write books without a single error, but that abnormality may be corrected by—*these!*" He took his hands from his pockets, and each one held a .38 revolver. "Stand back out of harm's way!" he shouted.

"Mallard! Stop it!" The revolvers barked, first the right hand, then the left, then the right. Two chimpanzees fell, and a third reeled into a corner. Mr. Bainbridge seized his friend's arm and wrested one of the weapons from him.

"Now I am armed, too, Mallard, and I advise you to stop!" he cried. Professor Mallard's answer was to draw a bead on Chimpanzee E and shoot him dead. Mr. Bainbridge made a rush, and Professor Mallard fired at him. Mr. Bainbridge, in his quick death agony, tightened his finger on the trigger of his revolver. It went off, and Professor Mallard went down. On his hands and knees he fired at the two chimpanzees which were still unhurt, and then collapsed.

There was nobody to hear his last words. "The human equation . . . always the enemy of science . . . " he panted. "This time . . . vice versa . . . I, a mere mortal . . . savior of science . . . deserve a Nobel . . . "

When the old butler came running into the conservatory to investigate the noises, his eyes were met by a truly appalling sight. The student lamps were shattered, but a newly risen moon shone in through the conservatory windows on the corpses of the two gentlemen, each clutching a smoking revolver. Five of the chimpanzees were dead. The sixth was Chimpanzee F.

His right arm disabled, obviously bleeding to death, he was slumped before his typewriter. Painfully, with his left hand, he took from the machine the completed last page of Florio's Montaigne. Groping for a fresh sheet, he inserted it, and typed with one finger, "*Uncle Tom's Cabin*, by Harriet Beecher Stowe. Chapte . . . " Then he, too, was dead. ■■

PASSING THROUGH

Away from It All

CHARLES W. MORTON Charles W. Morton made a living in the 1940s and 1950s writing brisk, slightly crotchety essays on American life for various popular magazines of the day. Of his sardonic style, it was written that "Morton's sense of indignation never blows up into steam but sizzles along quietly—and pungently—as he writes on everything from the pretensions of summer vacationers in Maine (who out-native the natives) to various phenomena of modern education."

■ The etiquette of Maine summer resorts is exacting. There are places, so I am told, where a man with a new Cadillac and plenty of silky gabardines can move in without attracting unfavorable comment. But the ways of Poland Spring or Bethel will not interchange with the standards of Penobscot Bay, for example, and the rule seems to be that the more exclusive the resort, as a general thing, the more primitive one's style of living—if, that is, one is to get on agreeably with the rest of the community. It took me two full seasons at Little Chokecherry Island before I felt I really knew my way around—learned not to put my foot in it, so to speak. Even so, I made a few ghastly slips.

One of the bad ones happened on my first afternoon on Little Chokecherry—cocktails at the Barclays', twenty or thirty people (mostly New York real-estate money, I believe). The Barclays do themselves very well in town and at Nassau, and I've seen quite a bit of them over the years. I could tell by the cars outside that the party was a good one: several Model Ts, an early Chevrolet with the steam still blowing through the radiator cap, and an Apperson Jack Rabbit—about a '13, I judged. My own 1928 Model A needed no apologies; but I was in fast company for a newcomer, no doubt about that.

I had turned up with a perfectly correct outfit—dirty blue jeans (and none of your prefaded stuff, either), a couple of old shirts with the sleeves cut off at the elbow, black oilskin jacket, and a pullover. I had a pair of brown pumps with leather bows—scuffed and nicely out of shape—that drew admiring comments from the Little Chokecherry crowd. I could talk Down East fairly fluently, and I could even toss off a phrase or two from the Nova Scotia coast. Everything was going nicely until the telephone question took me by surprise. Fortunately for me, the conversation with Barclay was not overheard.

"You know," he said, "we have no telephone on Little Chokecherry."

I answered in my best Down East accent, but unthinkingly, "Thet's tew bad."

Barclay looked at me coldly.

I spoke up before he could say anything. "Sorry, old man, but did I understand you to say that you have a telephone here on Little Chokecherry? I should have thought you'd want to protect a place like this—"

Barclay thawed somewhat. "Naturally we do *not* have a telephone here," he said.

"Exactly," I answered, "and I was bound to be blunt about it when I thought you said you had." It was lame, perhaps; but it was quick, and apparently it worked.

"As for telegrams," Barclay went on, "why, it actually takes longer for a telegram to get here than it does for ordinary mail. A telegram has to go to the office at North Banbury. Then it's telephoned to the general store at Griggsport, on Big Chokecherry. Then, if the storekeeper doesn't forget all about it, the mail boat *may* bring it across." We both laughed heartily.

In dealing with a chap like Barclay, I've found that a direct attack is often effective. I knew the mail boat came every Monday, and I wanted to retrieve that gaffe of mine about the telephone, so I now said, "And only one mail boat a month!"

The cockiness went out of Barclay. "No," he said, "we're not quite so fortunate as that. As a matter of fact—"

I interrupted him just to rub it in, "Well, twice a month is not bad," I said. By the time Barclay had confessed that the boat came every week, I was able to simulate amazement and some hauteur. "You people have done rather well," I said, "in keeping this place to yourselves. But I am not convinced that all this hubbub of a mail boat every week is necessary."

Barclay tried to explain it away on the grounds that the natives insisted on the weekly delivery of mail, and that was the first and only time I had any trouble with him.

It was just as well, in a way, that I went through the telephone drill with Barclay at the very beginning, for almost everyone else I met on Little Chokecherry tried it on me. I gathered it was a standard test for all strangers. My mailboat riposte, however, proved to be invaluable in helping me through that difficult first week.

I steered clear of the natives on the island from the start. They were a problem, and there had been many ups and downs, I gathered, before I arrived. Natives had been something of a fad for a time, a few seasons back, when the Coggeshalls—oil money, the wife's, I mean—were making a fuss over an old chap who lived on Gull Point. They picked him up as a stunt; there was quite a flurry about him. He was invited everywhere that summer. The trouble with him—and indeed with most of the natives—was that they insisted on rigging themselves out for the square dances in white shirts, neckties in some cases, and their women managed to make themselves look like so many hothouse plants.

And then the natives became standoffish, if you please, about some of the New Yorkers—felt we ought to clean up for the dances, or wear more clothes, or something along that line. The upshot was that our crowd and the natives drifted apart, and I am not sure it wasn't the best way out for all concerned.

It was on Big Chokecherry, the next year, that I nearly got myself into a bad fix. We had nothing to do with the summer crowd there; the place wasn't really an island, since you could reach it by a bridge and a long causeway, and all sorts of people went there. As Barclay used to say, all Big Chokecherry lacked was a Ferris wheel and a public bathhouse.

I'd gone to Big Chokecherry to do some marketing (and to make a few phone calls, if the truth be known). I thought I'd drop in on a friend who had a place not far from Griggsport. He had a water's-edge location, infernally hard to find, and I wasted a lot of time getting there. Where I made my first mistake was in telling him so. It seemed to set him up no end.

"Some people in Boston wrote me the other day that they never were able to find this house," he said rather smugly. "We have some perfectly wild shoreline of our own here on Big Chokecherry, without chasing all the way out to sea to other islands."

I let it pass. After all, I'd laid myself open to it. I didn't even pick him up on his implication that Big Chokecherry was an island. Herrick—that was his name (good family, but no money to speak of)—set about making a cocktail. It was toward the end of the afternoon, dark in the woods there, and Herrick reached up and turned on the lights: electricity. It was a new ball game then and there.

Herrick pretended to be unconcerned about the lights and went ahead pouring drinks, and I decided to say nothing. I kept staring at the lights. Finally, I reached up and turned the lights off, then on again. I looked at Herrick.

"It's one of those Delco outfits," he said, "but it breaks down every so often. We have to keep a few Aladdin lamps on hand."

I decided to put Herrick in his place. "Delco," I said, "and Aladdin lamps? Maybe so. We like to get away from that sort of thing. Candles and plain oil lamps are good enough for Little Chokecherry. Next, I suppose, you'll be telling me you have a flush toilet here."

Herrick colored. I knew instantly that he did have a flush toilet. But he was a cool head in the pinch. "I wonder how the Red Sox are getting on," he remarked casually. "We're so cut off here."

That was where I made my worst blunder of all those seasons at Little Chokecherry. "Game and a half behind Detroit," I said. "I listened in last night. Sox won, five to three, in ten innings."

"Listened in!" Herrick pounced on me like a terrier. "*Listened in*! Do you mean to tell me you have a radio on Little Chokecherry?"

There I was, trapped. I could have bitten my tongue off. "It's only an old battery set, and the batteries are so weak you can hardly hear it," I began.

But Herrick would not be denied. "With all this talk about Little Chokecherry's being so 'unspoiled,' " Herrick said, "I am certainly amazed to—"

A tremendous crashing and banging in the kitchen saved the day for me. Herrick affected to hear nothing and kept right on jawing about the radio. But he was concealing something else besides a flush toilet, I felt certain. I tried a little Down East on him. "Tarnation, man," I shouted, "it sounds worse 'n a b'ar in a blueb'ry patch, I declare. Whut's amiss out yonder?"

"It's only the iceman," said Herrick.

I got up and switched the lights off and on. "On Little Chokecherry," I said to him, "even old Mrs. Barclay hauls her own ice, and she must be close to eighty."

As I drove back to Griggsport—I keep a Stutz Blackhawk with a dump-truck body on "the mainland," as we call Big Chokecherry—I realized that the radio would have to go. I'd been using it only on the sly, but the Herrick experience was enough for me. I knew he wouldn't talk, what with the Delco business and the iceman, and I buried the radio behind my woodpile that very night.

I was reminded of this episode last season, when another newcomer was running the gauntlet on Little Chokecherry. The fellow—some sort of Detroit money, so I'm told, and I never did get the straight of how he was allowed to rent the Old Cannery—turned up at the Coggeshalls' one afternoon. He may have been in college with Coggeshall, or perhaps it was school; I don't know. He was presentable enough—bare feet, striped dungarees cut off just below the knee, four-day beard, ragged sweat shirt—and he rode a belt-drive Excelsior motorcycle that couldn't have been a day later than 1910. He had been well coached, all right, and he was very much the fine gentleman until Coggeshall happened to mention East Quisquid. Coggeshall was in the middle of a cruising story and telling about having to lie at anchor, fogbound, and twiddle his thumbs for two whole days in East Quisquid harbor.

"Sorry you didn't look me up," said this Detroit fellow.

Coggeshall was just talking along. "Of course, nobody ever goes ashore at East Quisquid," he was saying just as this Detroit man spoke up like the blundering chatterbox that he was.

All conversation stopped right there. It was embarrassing, but there was nothing anyone could do.

"How do you mean, 'look you up'?" asked Coggeshall. "Were you anchored there too?" Coggeshall was giving the chap an out, a face saver, he told me later.

But the Detroiter was too brash to recognize it. "Not at all," he said. "I have a place there."

It would be hard to exaggerate the effect of such a statement on the kind of people who go to Little Chokecherry. East Quisquid, as everyone knows, has a beach and town water, and a man can hardly step out of his house without running into people he's never seen before. Ocean temperatures are said to be warmer there, too, and the place attracts just the sort of crowd you might expect it to.

Well, the fat was in the fire, and Coggeshall decided to dispose of the Detroit man then and there. "But isn't there a beach at East Quisquid?" he asked.

"Yes, a wonderful beach," the fellow replied. "My house is right on it. Almost in the sand."

Coggeshall went on, relentlessly. "Don't you find the sea much warmer there?"

"Oh, a great deal warmer—sixty-four one day last week. Perfectly delightful." Apparently there was no way of stopping this simpleton.

"Just one more question," said Coggeshall. "Am I right in believing that all those houses at East Quisquid *are on town water?*"

"Every one of them. There's a big standpipe up on Gull Mountain. Pressure is excellent."

Well, that was the end of *that* conversation. No one said another word to the Detroiter, and we all drifted off as quickly as possible. Of course, the thing was all over the island in no time.

I didn't see the Detroit man again after Coggeshall's party, and he left Little Chokecherry on the next boat. It would be hard to explain to him, I suppose, wherever he is today, that the distance between East Quisquid and Little Chokecherry is not merely something that can be measured on a map. ■

Quigley 873

FRANK SULLIVAN A long-time columnist for the New York *World*, Frank Sullivan employed his light, satiric wit in many fields. Perhaps best known for a compilation of clichés from various professions, he wrote several books (*Sullivan at Bay, Moose in the Hoose*) and magazine pieces, particularly for *The New Yorker*.

■ Perhaps no class of scientist is more apt to encounter the unexpected in the course of his work than the student of folklore. My wife and I appreciated this last summer when we discovered the refreshingly unique Lovers' Leap at Wassamattawichez Notch, New Hampshire, which for research purposes we have catalogued as Quigley 873.

My wife, Dr. Johanna Bracegirdle Quigley, and myself (Professor W. Hungerford Quigley) may possibly be recognized as coauthors of "The Role of the Lovers' Leap in American Folklore," the rather monumental study that, we flatter ourselves, has effected a sweeping change in thought on the subject since its publication a decade ago. We narrowed our field of research to the Lovers' Leap because it seemed to us not only a fascinating but a neglected aspect of folklore, and we have never regretted our decision. Dr. Johanna, a mite more thorough as a scientist than am I, has several times actually made the jump from a Lovers' Leap, just to get the feel of the thing, but on each occasion she used a parachute; I have been adamant on that point.

I might say a word or two here about Lovers' Leaps, for the benefit of readers unfamiliar with the colorful tradition. In North America, which is rich in precipices of all heights, the Lovers' Leap has reached its fullest flower, and in American folklore it is almost always a beautiful Indian maiden and a handsome young brave who, thwarted in their love by parental or tribal opposition, solved their problem tragically by leaping from a ledge at the top of the precipice to the rocks below. The scene later becomes known in legend as a Lovers' Leap. The investigations of Dr. Johanna and myself, up to our discovery of Quigley 873, had revealed 872 authentic Lovers' Leaps in the United States and Canada, and we thought we had exhausted the field. The jumps ranged from fifty to three thousand feet, and the leaping lovers represented every tribe in the country except the Seminoles of Florida. Florida, being very flat, affords no facilities for lovers desirous of leaping, and how the star-crossed Seminoles solve their difficulties is a nice problem that Dr. Johanna and I hope one day to probe.

It was during a motor trip in the White Mountains that we discovered Quigley 873. We were bowling along a road near Lake Wassamattawichez on an idyllic June afternoon when, rounding a bend, we saw before us, on the opposite side of the valley, a crag that we both realized instantly might be a Lovers' Leap, and one of the most perfect we had ever encountered— sheer drop, magnificent view, parking space. It had everything!

"It *must* be a Lovers' Leap, but I don't seem to recognize it," I said to Dr. Johanna. Was it possible that we had stumbled on a new Leap? We hardly dared hope.

Well, the thing was to find out, and to do this it was necessary, of course, to locate the oldest inhabitant of North Wassamattawichez, the village nestling in the valley below. My wife and I once differed, though not seriously, on the best method of verifying oldest inhabitants. If a birth certificate was not available, she favored a thorough physical examination by a competent physician; but oldest inhabitants, she found, often displayed a nettling resistance to such a test, and she finally gave up her method and adopted mine, which I do think works as well in the long run. My system is simply this: if a native sufficiently advanced in years uses "mebbe" for "maybe," "allus" for "always," and "sezee" for "says he," and if he recalls that his father carried him to the railroad station to watch Lincoln's funeral train pass by in 1865, then I ask him his age, deduct fifteen years from his answer, and accept him as a bona-fide oldest inhabitant.

Dr. Johanna and I soon found our man, a venerable patriarch named Jonas Atkinson, one hundred and four minus fifteen years old, and we engaged him in conversation over a mug of foaming ale at the quaint tavern in the village. By way of breaking the conversational ice, I asked him the traditional question demanded by protocol. "To what do you attribute your great age, Mr. Atkinson?"

"I allus sweat good," he replied, and, gazing into his already empty mug, added slyly, "An' I allus enjoy my ale."

I smiled and commanded the landlord to fetch more ale.

Dr. Johanna then took up the ball. "My husband and I were attracted by that odd-looking cliff yonder side of the valley," she said with assumed nonchalance. "Has it by any chance got a name?"

"Yep," said Mr. Atkinson, "It's called Lovers' Leap."

The astronomer who has found a new comet or the botanist who has uncovered a hitherto unknown trillium will recognize the excitement that filled us at this confirmation of our hope.

"Lovers' Leap, eh?" said Dr. Johanna, still with pretended indifference. "Whatever for?"

"Two Injuns leapt there a long time ago," said Mr. Atkinson.

"Dashed themselves to death on the rocks below, clasped in a last fond embrace?" asked Dr. Johanna, now scarcely able to control her excitement.

"Shucks, no, Sis," said Mr. Atkinson, "Nothin' like that."

Dr. Johanna and I exchanged perplexed glances. "You mean they jumped off that cliff and *lived?*" I asked.

"Didn't say they jumped offen it, Bub," said Mr. Atkinson. "I said they leapt."

"Well, what's the difference?"

"Well, sir, I'll tell ye—consarn it, I can't. M'throat's gone scratchy on me agin."

"Landlord, more ale!" said I.

"Thankee. Drat this foam. Most of it gits in a feller's beard. Sheer waste o' good ale. Well, sir, it was like this. This maiden an' this here brave from the Wassamattawichez tribe fell in love. Made a fine-lookin pair, too. He was an all-around athlete and could jump better'n any brave in the tribe, an' they called him Standin' High. She was almost as good as he was at track, so they called her Leapin' Trout. Well, things would o' gone all right, but her father promised her hand to an old buck that happened to have a lot o' wampum. So the kids decided to elope. One day they slipped away an' met down yander in the ravine, all set to light out fer the West. Well, they git jest underneath the cliff thar when who comes rushin' at 'em from one end o' the ravine but a mob o' her folks in hot pursuit. So Leapin' Trout and Standin' High started for th'other end o' the ravine, but who shows up thar but Got Wampum, th'old buck she was supposed to marry, with a mob o' *his* folks. Escape was cut off.

"Leapin' Trout pulled a pizened arrow out o' her quiver an' cried 'At least we can die together!' but her lover stayed her hand. 'Don't puncture yerself,' sezee. 'There is yet a way out.'

" 'Whar?' s'she.

" 'The cliff up thar,' sezee.

" 'Jump fifty feet straight up?' s'she. 'Are you crazy, Standin' High?'

" 'You can do it, with a little help,' sezee. 'I got an idea.'

"There was a log restin' a-teeter across a boulder. He told her to stand on the end that touched the ground.

" 'Now,' sezee, 'when I jump on th'other end, you'll shoot up into the air, and when you do, just hunch and scrunch yerself along all you can an' you'll make the top o' that cliff, understand? It's our on'y chance.'

" 'But you, Standin' High,' s'she, 'what'll become o' you?'

" 'Don't worry about me,' sezee. 'I'll take off right after ye. Come along. We got no time fer argufication.'

"They didn't, nuther, because by now mobs o' kinfolk was comin' down at 'em from both ends o' the gulch, whoopin' and yellin' like savages, and makin' a reg'lar garboil.

"So Leapin' Trout crouched on the grounded end o' the log. Standin' High sprang up onto a big boulder that was nigh. 'Git ready!' sezee. 'Git set! Go!' An' with that he jumps offen the boulder onto th'other end o' the log with all his might, an' up shoots the beautiful Indian maiden like a bat out o' hell. You know, the way the acrobats do it in the circus. An', by gum and by golly, she lands on the edge o' the cliff fifty foot above, teeters there a second, then grabs a bush and hauls herself to safety."

"And what became of Stanley High?" asked Dr. Johanna eagerly.

"*Standin'* High!" corrected Mr. Atkinson. "Well, he can't use the log. He ain't got no friend down thar to catapult *him* up. He has to rely on the stren'th the Lord gave him. So he grabs a fifty-foot pine trunk layin' nearby, gits a good runnin' start, takes off, an' sails into the air in as purty a pole vault as this nation ever see."

"Did he make it?" asked Dr. Johanna.

Mr. Atkinson turned purple and gave out gasping, choking noises. "Landlord, more ale!" I cried. "Hurry!"

Mr. Atkinson quaffed and the spasm passed.

"That ale didn't come a minute too soon, Bub," he said. "Thirsty work, spinnin' these legends."

"Yes, yes, Mr. Atkinson, but tell us—did Standing High make it?"

"Missed it by ten foot."

"A-a-h, what a pity!" Dr. Johanna mourned. "He fell back on the toma-hawks of his enemies?"

"I never said that, Sis. He got away all right. But he'd o' bin a gone goose if it hadn't bin fer J. Fenimore Cooper."

"J. Fenimore Cooper?"

"Yep. Standin' High was a great reader, fer an Injun. Allus claimed he learnt everything he knew about Injun lore from J. Fenimore, an' when he left home that mornin' he'd slipped his well-thumbed copy o' *The Deerslayer* into his pants pocket. That saved his life."

"How?" I asked.

"Well, when old Got Wampum reached the spot, jest after Standin' High took off fer the top o' the cliff, he gave a yell o' baffled rage an' let fly an arrow at his rival's retreatin' form. Old Got Wampum was a good shot."

"He hit Standing High?"

"Right where it done the most good, as things turned out. The arrow passed clean through Cooper's book an' penetrated Standin' High to a depth of mebbe half an inch. Not so deep as a well but deep enough to encourage, as the Bard would say. Standin' High gave a sharp cry an' sprang three more feet into the air."

"And that got him to the top of the cliff?" I asked.

"Nope. He was still shy seven foot."

"So he fell back on the arrows of his foes after all?"

"Not by a durn sight. He grabbed Leapin' Trout by the hair."

"By the hair?"

"Sure. Leapin' Trout had hair seven foot long, like that gal in the fairy tale."

"Rapunzel?" suggested Dr. Johanna.

"Don't mind if I do," said Mr. Atkinson quickly.

I said, "Landlord, more ale!"

"Thankee," said Mr. Atkinson. "Yarnin' suttinly makes a feller spit cotton. Yep, Leapin' Trout got a good hold onto a tree, let her hair down over the cliff, Standin' High grabbed the hair, an' she hauled him up."

"To safety?"

"Yes, Ma'am," said Mr. Atkinson.

"What an utterly charming legend!" said Dr. Johanna, brushing what I fear was a not quite scientific tear from her cheek.

"They didn't leap *offen* that cliff," said Mr. Atkinson. "They leapt *onto* it. I reckon this here's the on'y lovers' leap in reverse in this country, and the on'y one with a happy endin'."

"I can just see old Got Wampum, the disgruntled lover," I chuckled. "I'll bet *his* face was red."

"Why not? He was an Injun," said Mr. Atkinson.

"Did Stanley High and Running Broad live happily ever after?" asked Dr. Johanna.

"Her name was Leapin' Trout," corrected Mr. Atkinson. "Yep, they done all right. Toured fer years with the Pawnee Bill show and retired with a small fortune. I heard tell they had a grandson went to Yale, class of 1922, and he was the best one in all the colleges at vaultin' with the pole." ■

Lobster Unlimited

RUSSELL BAKER A native of Virginia, Russell Baker has written the "Observer" column in the *New York Times* since 1962. His witty observations on the American scene are done in the classic style of political humor established in the nineteenth century by such New England comic writers as Seba Smith and Charles Farrar Browne (Artemus Ward).

For purposes of this collection, however, a Baker piece with a more direct connection to New England seemed best.

■ Mouths watering for lobster, we came to Maine. "Got any lobster?" we asked the man at the pound. He said one thing he sure had was lobster. He picked two lobsters from a tank and held them out. They seemed much too small to make a meal for two people who had their mouths set for a real lobster dinner.

"We'd like something bigger." He returned to the tank, brought out two bigger lobsters and said, "These'll run about two pounds apiece. Don't often get 'em that big anymore these days."

The man obviously didn't know the appetite he was dealing with. One had to speak to him tartly. "Perhaps I have not made myself sufficiently clear. We are not looking for canapé spread. We are looking for lobster."

He gave us a hooded glance. "Two-pounders ain't enough?" he inquired. "How about a nice three-pounder?"

"Lobster, man! We want lobster, not bird food."

He smiled. "Well," he said, "I might just be able to give you what you're looking for."

It was our turn to smile. He called to a young man. "Bring out Old Sam," he said. The young man looked at us, then looked at his employer, then shrugged. After a considerable wait, he returned from a back room with a reasonably large lobster.

"This is Old Sam," said the lobsterman. "He'll run about seven pounds."

We were still not sure. "Do you think he'll make a full meal?"

The lobsterman looked us both squarely in the eyes. Not a muscle twitched in his face. "There's a lot of good eatin' on that lobster," he said.

We took it. Old Sam was put in a paper bag and driven home. We put on a pot of water. As it started to boil, Old Sam began to shake the paper bag, indicating an unhappiness with the proceedings. We ripped the bag and he came out thrashing. At the pound he had not looked like much, but on the kitchen table he had claws the size of Muhammad Ali's fists. We recoiled.

"Pick him up and drop him in the pot," each of us said instantly to the other. But Old Sam was touchy. As the cook's hand reached toward his carapace, he countered with a left hook and crossed with his right, nearly amputating an index finger. The two of us glared uneasily at him and he glared right back, and then it became apparent that even after we captured him there was going to be trouble, since the boiling pot was not big enough to contain half of him.

We decided to try it anyhow. We couldn't just let him push us around and take over the house. While one of us distracted him in the front, the other sneaked up behind him, grabbed his tail, swung him through the air and dropped him into the pot.

Boiling water splashed over stove and floor. Old Sam's tail rested momentarily in the steam, but his claws hung over the edge and he stared at us with an expression of absolute disenchantment, before hoisting himself over the side of the ineffectual pot and diving to the safety of the floor.

One of us screamed as he moved in for the attack, and two local men who happened to be passing on the beach ran up to investigate. They immediately grasped the situation.

"It's those people that bought Old Sam this afternoon," one of them said.

"Might have known it," said the other. He produced fishing line, threw a lasso around the lobster, trussed him tightly and rolled him on his back.

"If you're of a mind to boil Old Sam," his companion suggested, "better get rid of that saucepan and fire up a washtub."

They graciously assisted in this operation, and when the tub was at a rolling boil and the lobster had been safely immersed, one of them asked, "What are you going to do with Old Sam when he's boiled?"

"Eat him, of course."

"Mind if we bring a few folks over to watch?"

We certainly did mind. Hospitality has its limits. They shrugged and left, full of winks and sly grins.

That was seven days ago, and Old Sam is still with us. After the first night's meal, there was lunch of cold lobster claw. The second night, it was lobster salad from the carapace meat. The next day, cold lobster tail with mayonnaise. Then lobster roll. Then lobster stew. Then sliced lobster.

Periodically, grinning children stick their heads in the window and ask, "Getting near the end of Old Sam yet?" In town, solicitous Maine folks ask us if it looks like Old Sam will last us another week. It does. There's a lot of good eatin' on that lobster, a seven-pound lobster being the marine equivalent to a two-thousand-pound beef. Which gives rise to an idea. Maybe tonight, after everybody else has gone to bed, we'll sneak off to the highway and get a hamburger. ■

Foliage Season

SID McKEEN Massachusetts newspaperman Sid McKeen has been a reporter, editor, and columnist in Worcester from the time he first entered the job market at twenty-two following World War II. In addition to his work as an editor of the *Worcester Telegram and The Evening Gazette*, he has produced a weekly column for the *Sunday Telegram* for more than a quarter of a century. The column, "Wry and Ginger," has also appeared in several other New England publications.

■ I don't know why we go through this silly foliage ritual every year in New England.

Perfectly rational human beings driving all over the map to get a glimpse of colored leaves. Jamming motels and restaurants. Clogging the highways.

For what? Every town—practically every neighborhood—has a selection of foliage that's just as pretty as what's showing fifty to one hundred miles away in any direction.

Take Arthur Holmes's ash tree, for example. Arthur is a neighbor who lives about two hundred yards up the street from us. The big ash in front of his house is as handsome a tree every autumn as you'll find anywhere in North America, bar none. Joyce Kilmer would have gone crazy over it.

Two weeks ago, when most of the other trees in this part of the world were just starting to blush, Arthur's ash was already solid gold.

It would be a standout anywhere—up in the Green Mountains of Vermont, nestled among the Maine pines, along the Kancamagus Highway in New Hampshire, or somewhere on the Mohawk Trail. But getting the jump on all its peers as it does, it really commands attention.

My wife began making noises about a foliage trip not long after Labor Day.

"If we're going to do it," she pointed out, "we'll need to make overnight reservations early. Last year you couldn't find a motel room for love or money at the height of the foliage season."

"Why should we waste our money running all over the region when Arthur Holmes's ash tree will be turning any day now?" I countered.

"But his tree is just a block away," she said. "That wasn't quite what I had in mind for a foliage trip."

"I'll bet," I said, mostly to myself.

Now, we could sit in a certain spot in our living room and just enjoy Arthur's tree to the maximum. No expensive overnight trip. No heavy traffic. No nothing. We could even keep an eye on the TV while we savored Arthur's ash.

Well, it wasn't to be, of course. We had to do the American thing—go out on the road like everybody else, travel for miles and ooh and ahh the scenery just as if it were nicer than it is right in our own back yard.

"Isn't that just beautiful?" my wife said, pointing to a stand of maples as we bumped along the Massachusetts Turnpike, practically bumper to bumper with all the other foliage oglers.

"I'd say on a scale of 1 to 10, it rates about a 7½," I said. "Arthur Holmes's ash I'd give a 9."

She didn't speak for the next 23 miles.

I had to admit (to myself, at least) that some of the trees were excellent. But some of the enjoyment was rubbed out by the thought of the traffic we'd be hitting on the return trip home.

Why is it that we can't just settle for the nice things right around us, I wonder.

It reminds me of the town I was born in. The town is right in the shadow of one of the most beautiful mountains in the world. People travel from every state, every country, and every continent to climb it. Yet at least half the people who live there have never set foot on it. Their idea of a vacation is to get out and see the sights somewhere else.

We finally got through all the traffic and made it back home. On the way we passed Arthur's ash. It had lost most of its foliage now and was definitely on the way out for another year.

"Thanks for the trip," my wife said. "I really enjoyed it."

"I'm glad," I said, "but look at what we missed, being away." ■

Scarcely Anybody Gets Killed

JOHN GOULD Author, editor, columnist, and storyteller John Gould was born in Massachusetts but has lived almost all of his life in Maine, where his family roots run back to the seventeenth century.

A graduate of Bowdoin College, he joined the reporting staff of the *Brunswick Record*, leaving there to start his own newspaper, the *Yarmouth Town Times* and to develop his career as a writer of books and magazine articles. Gould went on to start another newspaper, the *Lisbon Falls Enterprise*, to write the long-running "Dispatch from the Farm" columns for *The Christian Science Monitor*, and to produce more than two dozen books of humorous stories about rural New England.

■ Now our quiet old acres come to life and the noise of the shotgun is heard in the land. It is hunting season in Maine. The happy housewife, singing "I'll Be Coming, Sister Mary" through a clothespin as she takes in the Monday wash, finds her damask tablecloth punched full of No. 6 holes, and the prudent husbandman wears red hat and shirt when he steps out to the privy.

It is a noisy time, the tumultuous cannonade mingled with the shrieks of the wounded and the groans of the dying, and all Maine citizens conduct themselves beyond the call of duty. In ordinary years we will bag more deer than we do hunters, and some years when the conditions are favorable hardly anybody gets killed.

Two years ago I was sitting where I am now, in a front window that gives onto the mailbox and highway, and my every attention was engrossed on a reply to a gentleman who had written to me about a sum of money. I had spelled "lousy" with a *w*, and was erasing my error when the First Battle of the Marne took place directly outside my window. The room is only eight feet square, but I trotted around it a good deal with one foot shoved in the wastebasket, and then I looked out to see what had occasioned this unrest on my part. A large, florid gentleman with St. Vitus's dance was leaning one elbow on my window sill and shooting with amazing rapidity into the general direction of north. Whatever he was shooting at was beyond the immediate panorama, and I had to move to look. As I did so, a spike-horn buck deer decided he had endured enough of life's misfortunes, and he gave up the ghost and died at the foot of an apple tree which we have always considered to be on the front lawn. I assumed that in spite of his obvious nervous condition the gentleman over whose shoulder I was peering had connected in some strange way and had, as the saying goes, "got his deer."

The gentleman continued to shoot off and on while I opened the window, and then I spoke to him softly and said, "You can stop shooting now, he's dead."

The gentleman then turned two glassy eyes upon me and said, with some degree of accuracy, "I got him! I got him!"

This appeared to be so, and I saw no reason to dispute it, so I said, "Put your gun on safety, you're all done for this year."

At this the gentleman fired two or three more times, lopping a large limb off the apple tree, and I reached out and pushed the safety catch on his firearm. Then when he pulled the trigger nothing happened. This surprised him and brought some light back into his eyes and caused him to hand me the gun, which I took inside the house and unloaded.

One thing about the chase that I have found amusing is the question of what you do now. The fun-loving sportsman who dons his gay garb, picks up his accouterments, and strikes out to slay the white-tailed deer is in pretty good shape until he shoots something. Immediately the frolicsome deer, who can bound across country like sin, is no longer a sporty quarry but suddenly becomes a couple of hundredweight of meat. A slaughterhouse is equipped to handle same, and in the proper place a venison carcass presents no great problem. But the hunter, hiding behind his Fish & Game Club badge, is no longer a hunter; he's a wholesale owner of fresh meat and he has to take care of it.

Somebody who has journeyed five miles into the uncharted fastnesses to shoot a three-hundred-pound buck is immediately very sorry that he was so ambitious. The deer that you chased out has to be carried back.

The gentleman leaning against my house told me he had never shot a deer before. I said, "Well, you have now," and I thought it was quite a witty remark. We unsheathed a knife and dressed out the deer, but the gentleman to whom the meat belonged didn't know how to do it, and he kept walking back and forth saying, "I got him, I got him." I noticed he was still holding his hands out, thinking he still held the rifle, and every little while his right index finger would twitch.

I hadn't intended to mention this, but I fell to thinking very few people have had the pleasure of just such an experience in quite such close surroundings. I am not of a shooting turn of mind myself, and the deer in my dooryard usually come and go as they please. We have to shoo them once in a while to get out to the henhouse, but they come right back. I resented this man's interrupting me in the middle of a sentence, but he had a license, and the deer belong to the people of the state.

A neighbor woman who saw a deer out her kitchen window ran to the gunrack and got a gun and shot the deer. It cost eighteen dollars to put the glass back, but she got him, and he weighed 235 pounds. Her husband was out hunting at the time, but he didn't get anything.

As a detached witness of this annual scene, I can report that the hunting season in Maine is less bloody than the antishoot faction makes out. It does give the undertakers a welcome flurry between the summer tourist season and early-winter pneumonia, but from the point of view of our dear woodland friends it is not too tough. I have an old bull partridge who lives up by the spring in my pasture, and every April when we are on the tag end of the maple syrup season he begins to drum and advertise that his hen is expecting. Our so-called partridge is actually a ruffed grouse, or—as the political naturalists in our Maine Development Commission continue to spell him—a *ruffled* grouse. Sometimes he is more ruffled than others, but you will find him in your Audubon book under the former name, and he is one of the finest birds we have. Unlike the imported pheasant, he stays where he belongs in the woods and never bothers pay crops up in the fields. So every April I know that my partridge is about to multiply, and I sneak through the bushes and try to catch him drumming. He inflates his breast, or at least swells it out somehow, and then beats his wings against himself rhythmically—gaining speed as he goes. The first blows are staccato, but on the end his finale is a whirr. He almost lifts himself off the ground in flight, and seems to hang by his toes to the log he sits on. After drumming he sits quietly or parades a little, and at intervals day after day he drums until the eggs hatch. People who don't know about drumming always think it sounds like a gasoline motor of some sort in the distance.

Well, what I'm coming at is that the partridge is always there in the spring, and he is there off and on all summer when I go up to pick berries, and then one day the hunting season is on and my woods are full of red-shirted sportsmen who are trying to shoot my partridges. All day the guns resound. A stratum of lead lies on the ground, the Getchell birches are riddled, and ever and anon the coroner comes and sits on somebody. Each morning the hunters come and whack the puckerbrush, and each evening they go home. But after the hunting season is over and I go up in my woods to catch a little firewood, I always find my partridges as before. They explode up from underfoot and scale away. And the next spring the old bull partridge is always drumming away in a uxorious trance, or *an* uxorious trance as the case may be.

It is the same with our deer. Somebody is always getting one by accident, but I notice that the deer I grow up with all summer are for the most part alive and well when it comes time to yard out in the cedars for winter. They sometimes look tired, but they are all right.

I've wondered if maybe my game isn't smarter than most. According to the official statements of our Fish and Game Commissioner, a lot of wildlife is done in every fall in Maine, but on the basis of my own domestic surveys there's little of it done in right here. I think my salubrious location and what Caesar would have termed the nature of the place contribute smartness to my wildlife. I can offer a case in point to support my opinion.

One night a knock came to our door and I opened it to find a band of 'coon hunters who wanted to know if our back woodlot abounded in said animal. I said we had a lot of them, that some days I kept stepping on them while I was working around. They asked if I cared to have them sport a little in that section, and I said yes, that if they'd wait until I got my boots on I'd go with them and watch. I said I'd been inside all day, papering a room, and a breath of air would do me good. So I checked to see that my last will and testament was handy and could be found should occasion require it, and we all went up on the beech ridge and down into the softwood growth.

They had a fine dog by the name of Duke, and he had a pedigree as long as the delinquent tax list in the town of Bowdoin. Duke had been imported from Ohio a short time before, and a great deal of interest was current over his skill. Duke was eager. They unsnapped him and away he went, bugling until the region resounded. The cry of a 'coon hound in the woods on a frosty night is a magnificent arrangement.

"What's he got?" somebody said.

Somebody else said, "Sounds as big as a cow!"

It struck me at the time that wondering what a 'coon dog would be chasing indicated doubt over the dog to begin with. I don't know much about Ohio 'coon dogs, but if I invested in one and paid the express on him, I would expect him to chase 'coons. This is only an opinion, and I may have the wrong slant.

Anyway, the bugling suddenly ceased, ta-ra, and back came Duke with his face stuck full of porcupine quills. We took him up to the house and spent the rest of the night pulling out quills. One of the sportsmen was a dentist, and he knew how to pull, so we let him pull. I understand they shipped Duke back to Ohio the next day, collect.

But you can't tell me my 'coons didn't rig up a scheme with that particular porcupine, and that while we were leading Duke home some forty or fifty intellectual 'coons weren't sitting around on pine limbs chuckling at a great rate. A dog that can't tell a porcupine from a 'coon is not so unusual as to be noteworthy, but one named Duke that has been shipped in from

Ohio at great expense ought to know a little more than the average. That's the only time I ever went 'coon hunting.

My observation is that game keeps increasing every year. Hunters come in droves to shoot my foxes, but at night the foxes come and steal my ducks. They claim foxes eat pheasants, but every year we have more and more pheasants and more and more foxes, and it's harder and harder to raise up ducks. One reason is that people out hunting foxes occasionally shoot one of my ducks.

I like wildlife. I like to roam the farm and see the animals and birds around me. Every once in a while somebody asks me why I don't post my land and stop this cruel slaughter. Well, one reason I don't is because I think the animals like the hunting season. It quickens their reflexes, and I think they find the season exciting. They keep their heads down, and hunting seasons come and go, and it adds piquancy to an otherwise uneventful life.

We have a favorite deer who likes our upper orchard. She's been around for years and brings up her young ones more or less in sight of the house. Sometimes we take summer visitors up along the wall and point her out. With her fawn, or sometimes twin fawns, she will be chewing on the orchard grass, and she'll lift her head and look at us and go back to eating. When the people go back to the cities they say, "Think of it! A deer right in the field back of the house!" I'd hate to have anything happen to this old girl.

Last year a fellow with an ammunition belt around his red jacket came, and he had a rifle that will shoot five miles. He went up in my orchard to seek out this doe. He found her and took a shot at her. The bullet whistled over our house and hit Smith's barn. Well, this fellow shot at the deer all afternoon. She would dodge behind a tree and eat until he found her again, and then while he shot a few times she would dodge behind another tree. She gave him a great variety of shots, and no two alike. Now and then the hunter would have to wait for his gun barrel to cool off, and we would see him sitting under a tree eating one of our apples. Along about dusk he came down and got in his automobile and drove away.

For the most part, I think that is about the way our hunting season works out. There's a lot of noise, and now and then we hear a bullet slap into the clapboards, and once in a while we have to stop husking corn and go up in the woods and bring out a wounded hunter. Bringing out a wounded hunter wouldn't be so bad if you didn't have to listen to his companion explain how he looked like a deer. The best one I ever heard was about a young fellow up back who shot his own mother while she was paddling a canoe down the river. She came down the river, and he up and shot her. He said he thought she was a partridge, and probably he did. When a fellow has a gun in his hand it's funny how many things look like a partridge. One time we were carrying a corpse out through a fence, and the fellow was explaining how his companion looked just like a deer. Jud Maybury was on one of the feet, and Jud asked, "Buck or doe?"

The fellow didn't know Jud was joking, so he said he kind of thought he looked more like a doe.

Jud wagged his head all afternoon and spent the rest of the season down cellar back of the furnace reading the Waverley Novels. Jud was never much of a reader, but he had to occupy his time.

We always feel badly, of course, when some of our pet game gets knocked off, but the untimely demise of our sportsmen is not looked upon as a great loss. To illustrate the Maine attitude toward this, I shall cite an instance of a couple of seasons back. I would not want people to think we are callous about it. In every instance the guilty hunter is subjected to the severity of a court trial, although when he is a member of the governor's council or something like that a certain deference is always shown to his capacity. (I had not intended to use the word capacity in such way that it would constitute a hilarious joke, but I can't control the attitudes of my readers, and if you so take it, so be it.)

Well, in this case I speak of, the gentleman had whanged his wife at a distance of about fifteen feet right between the eyes with a large caliber rifle, and she was mortified. The gentleman immediately deposed and stated that he thought she was a deer, and to make his position more secure he added that while he knew his wife had been out hunting with him, he had come to the conclusion, only a moment before, that she had gone home. Therefore, not expecting his wife to be in the vicinity, when he saw her it was the most natural thing in the world to presume that she was a deer.

This case was reported in the newspapers at the time substantially as I now retell it and is on record in our courts.

The judge in this case was, as you can see, forced to adjudicate a great deal. His decision was straightforward and to the point and quite in keeping with the high quality of jurisprudence now being enjoyed in Maine. He said that a gentleman out hunting with his wife has the right to presume, at any time, that she has gone home, and that if a husband so presumes, the wife is guilty of contributory negligence if she remains in the vicinity. This decision was widely applauded, and I understand that upon releasing the respondent, the judge invited him to give a humorous talk at the next meeting of the Bar Association. So you can see that the situation in the Maine woods is under control at all times.

I would like to say in concluding this discussion that the state is not unmindful of certain civil obligations to its inhabitants, and that a Representative Bubar from the town of Blaine arose in legislature recently and proposed that hunting license fees be increased by seventy-five cents, so the state would have a fund to pay five thousand dollars to the widow of any hunter shot in the woods. Mr. Bubar (I am not sure if I pronounce that correctly) was deadly serious, if I may be permitted a poetic expression. It is through such paternal evidences of interest that we know, from time to time, that our state government intends to look after us. If the bill should pass, I predict that after the first hunting season each surviving resident of Washington County will be driving a five-thousand-dollar automobile. ■■

Taxiing Toward
a Fun City

NATHAN COBB A native of Newton, Massachusetts, Nathan Cobb studied journalism at Penn State University before joining the staff of the *Boston Globe*, "covering anything from chicken factories in Maine to chicken dinners in Miami Beach." Primarily, however, Cobb has concentrated on turning out trenchant, often hilarious accounts of the life in Boston. Several of his urban commentaries appeared in a 1980 book, *Cityside/Countryside*, in tandem with pieces about rural life by Maine journalist John N. Cole.

■ Criticizing Boston's taxicabs is about as controversial as taking a stand against earthquakes, ax murderers, or the Third Reich. It is the constant sport of politicians and journalists, partygoers and shoppers. The litany of sins is regularly recited: the cabs are dirty, unsafe, expensive, and unreliable. Alas, the list is more accurate than not. The Boston taxi often performs like a runaway armored car, bouncing over potholes with its locked fare box and bulletproof partition rattling loudly. It frequently gives the impression that something rather large and bulky is rolling around inside its trunk. (The previous rider's suitcase? A body? Pray God, a spare tire?) Air conditioning is all but nonexistent, and Pepto-Bismol is required for digestive survival. The drivers themselves are generally friendly but often topographically confused. "We don't want rapists or sexual deviates driving cabs," an official of the City of Boston Cab Association was once quoted as declaring. However, most Bostonians would gladly travel to their destinations with a sexual deviate if only said driver could be counted on to know the way.

Yet such detractors miss the point. And so do all those people who get caught up in the city's annual "crackdowns" and "cleanups" of the local taxi industry. The fallacy in their reasoning lies within their basic premise, which states that the purpose of a Boston taxicab is to carry people from *here* to *there*. But that, of course, is not the principal function of such a vehicle. It's not for nothing that Governor Michael Dukakis would rather ride the Green Line to and from work.

What the Boston taxicab provides is an antidote to faceless, mechanized urban living. No two rides are the same. No two taxis take you from Point A to Point B via Route C. And even if they do, the fares are somehow different. To enter a taxi in the Hub is to embark on a magical mystery tour of assorted mechanical surprises and geographic wonders. It is common in some cities for cabbies to take unwary passengers for rides which are figurative as well as literal, meandering about town in order to increase their fares. This does not happen in Boston. Correction: the *meandering* happens, but it is not accompanied by scurrilous motives. You see, the only requirements for operating a cab here are a driver's license and a clean criminal record. Believing that the Statehouse is located in Mattapan is not considered a roadblock to employment.

I am not a particularly heavy cab user. But I would guess that I make between 100 and 150 trips a year, annually leaving $500 behind in the hands of my chauffeurs. I consider the money well spent. Only last week a cabbie asked me from the front seat if I wanted to look at some postcards. My prurient interests aroused, I inquired as to their nature. The cards that he slid under the partition were pictures of the kind one finds in the desk drawer of one's hotel room in Las Vegas. Filthy stuff.

I once drove with a cab driver who had a coatimundi riding shotgun. The animal, a South American raccoon, seemed put off by the careening taxi. It kept nervously nibbling on the front seat. Then there was the time my cab gave up the ghost in the Callahan Tunnel, and I had to drag my suitcase along the catwalk, inhaling exhaust fumes for half a mile. I have encountered at least two cabbies who didn't speak English and many more who didn't understand it.

But that's the fun of it, don't you see? In London, all the taxis look alike. In New York, all the drivers look alike. Boston is the taxicab badlands, the foaming frontier of rugged individualism where you jump aboard the stagecoach and hang on for the duration. Sitting in front of you is a hairy kid, a bald man, or a woman with an orange bouffant. What's the difference? Sit back and enjoy the ride to the airport. By the way, where is that? ∎

You Can't Get Here from There

JOHN N. COLE The rural half of the *Cityside/Countryside* collaboration with Boston's Nathan Cobb was supplied by John N. Cole. The Manhattan-born, Yale-educated Cole fished commercially off Montauk for a time, until he moved to Maine to become a newspaper editor and writer of books. His crisp, literate essays on country life, nature, and the environment have won a devoted following well beyond the borders of his adopted state.

■ By this time I can begin to believe it's over. The summer, I mean. Yes, there are the glories of a Maine September all around us; this is, I will argue, our finest season. Summer is also a climatic delight, especially here in Maine, but by this time each year I let myself wallow in the relief of knowing that it's gone. The traffic on Maine Street no longer chokes so that my daily trip takes thirty minutes instead of fifteen; the parking space in front of Day's News & Variety is not taken every morning when I stop for my daily newspapers; I do not wince now whenever the phone rings, hoping against hope that it won't be one more college roommate (how many did I have?), one more traveler who just wants to "visit for a minute" and stays the night with children and Russian wolfhound.

And, most of all, there is the restoration of domestic tranquility that comes when myself and The Lady no longer debate over who is going to give what directions to whom. I have no data on the topic, but I would wager a week's pay there cannot be more than a dozen couples in all New England who agree that each of the two knows how to give directions. I would argue and wager, on the other hand, that every husband thinks every wife has no orientation whatsoever, does not know where she lives, and can only succeed in getting touring visitors hopelessly lost whenever she attempts her endless narrative of "turn left at the cute little mailbox and then right—well, sort of right—at the lovely stand of rosa rugosa. . . . "

But for every husband who despairs enough to wrench the phone from the graceful hand of his otherwise exemplary helpmeet, there are the wives who will laugh out loud whenever the man of the house begins his "how you find us" spiel. "Go just four-tenths of a mile a bit east of south until you come to a large pine tree—and watch for the utility pole—and then west for another eight-tenths of a mile along the Point road until it forks to the north. . . . "

Both sorts of monologue (and the listener is usually trying to take notes with a hard pencil on a wet pizza plate) go on for most of a half-hour. When the visitor finally rolls into the yard, exhausted from a day on the hot highway and superlatively irritated by having had to stop fourteen times to ask suspicious strangers for directions, the direction-giver always inquires, "Did you have any trouble finding us?"

The answer, coming from a known freeloader who can see a cool drink and an evening meal vanishing if there is further discord, always replies, "No, none at all. The directions were just perfect." Then, whosoever bestowed the instructions turns to hapless spouse and says "See" through properly curled lip and with impeccable disdain. Thus the stage is set for yet another competition when yet another roommate (how many did I have?) calls and says he's on his way back from Nova Scotia and would love to drop by.

There was a time when I thought such directional discord was rampant only at our house, but having recently expanded my own swath as a traveling freeloader, I can report it is quite universal. So much so that I have made some attempt to analyze its causes in the interests of social history. It is not only the normal and healthy competition between couples which prompts the "direction syndrome" but also the little-noted fact that each of us sees our own home roads in quite different ways.

As individuals, we find ourselves looking hard at one tree, noting one garden, spotting one bird's nest, while our counterpart keeps track of the condition of one lawn, or the paint on another garage. Thus, when either tries to give directions, the other assumes he/she has taken leave of his/her senses.

I'm happy the summer and the arguments are over. Things got so bad I drew a map, had it copied, and mailed out at least half-a-dozen. The knowledge that they are out there, in circulation, has me terrified about next summer and remorseful that I didn't let The Lady's directions suffice for everyone. That way, none of the callers could ever have found the house. ■

CUSTOMS

Early Life

P. T. BARNUM Connecticut, called the "Nutmeg State" in sardonic reference to the reputation of its famous Yankee peddlers of the eighteenth century for selling wooden nutmegs, was the perfect birthplace for the American emperor of bunkum, Phineas Taylor Barnum.

The fabulous showman began his career exhibiting freaks and other exotic oddities, many of them fakes. He operated the pop-culture American Museum in New York, served as impresario for such enormously popular attractions as Tom Thumb and singer Jenny Lind, and founded a circus which he modestly labeled "The Greatest Show on Earth."

Barnum's autobiography proved to be every bit as lucrative as any of his other entrepreneurial undertakings, selling more than a million copies during his lifetime. Mostly self-congratulatory and moralistic, the book went through several editions, each ballyhooed as "completely revised," even though that meant no more than a new paragraph or footnote inserted here and there.

■ Like most people in Connecticut in those days, I was brought up to attend church regularly on Sunday, and long before I could read I was a prominent scholar in the Sunday school. My good mother taught me my lessons in the New Testament and the Catechism, and my every effort was directed to win one of those "Rewards of Merit," which promised to pay the bearer one mill, so that ten of these prizes amounted to one cent; and one hundred of them, which might be won by faithful assiduity every Sunday for two years, would buy a Sunday-school book worth ten cents. Such were the magnificent rewards held out to the religious ambition of youth.

There was but one church or "meetinghouse" in Bethel, which all attended, sinking all differences of creed in the Presbyterian faith. The old meetinghouse had neither steeple nor bell and was a plain edifice, comfortable enough in summer, but my teeth chatter even now when I think of the dreary, cold, freezing hours we passed in that place in winter. A stove in a meetinghouse in those days would have been a sacrilegious innovation. The sermons were from an hour and one-half to two hours long, and through these the congregation would sit and shiver till they really merited the title the profane gave them of "blue-skins." Some of the women carried a "foot-stove" consisting of a small square tin box in a wooden frame, the sides perforated, and in the interior there was a small square iron dish, which contained a few live coals covered with ashes. These stoves were usually replenished just before meeting time at some neighbor's near the meetinghouse.

After many years of shivering and suffering, one of the brethren had the temerity to propose that the church should be warmed with a stove. His impious proposition was voted down by an overwhelming majority. Another year came around, and in November the stove question was again brought up. The excitement was immense. The subject was discussed in the village stores and in the juvenile debating club; it was prayed over in conference; and finally in general "society's meeting," in December, the stove was carried by a majority of one and was introduced into the meetinghouse. On the first Sunday thereafter, two ancient maiden ladies were so oppressed by the dry and heated atmosphere occasioned by the wicked innovation that they fainted away and were carried out into the cool air, where they speedily returned to consciousness, especially when they were informed that, owing to the lack of two lengths of pipe, no fire had yet been made in the stove. The next Sunday was a bitter cold day, and the stove, filled with well-seasoned hickory, was a great gratification to the many and displeased only a few. After the benediction, an old deacon rose and requested the congregation to remain and called upon them to witness that he had from the first raised his voice against the introduction of a stove into the house of the Lord, but the majority had been against him and he had submitted; now, if they *must* have a stove, he insisted upon having a large one, since the present one did not heat the whole house but drove the cold to the back outside pews, making them three times as cold as they were before! In the course of the week, this deacon was made to comprehend that, unless on unusually severe days, the stove was sufficient to warm the house, and, at any rate, it did not drive all the cold in the house into one corner. ■■

Shaking Hands

EDWARD EVERETT Massachusetts-born, Harvard-educated
Edward Everett (1794–1865) was one of the fledgling American
nation's intellectual and political giants. He served by turns as a
minister, Greek scholar, editor (*North American Review*), politician,
diplomat, and educator.

Everett served for ten years in the United States House of
Representatives before being elected governor of Massachusetts
in 1835. Six years later he was appointed United States minister to
Great Britain, returning to become president of Harvard. In 1852
he succeeded Daniel Webster as United States secretary of state.

He wrote constantly throughout his long and busy life, turning out a variety of material from serious biographies to—as can
be seen here—engaging humorous essays.

■ There are few things of more common occurrence than shaking hands.
Yet I do not recollect that much has been written on the subject.

Among the ancients, I have been unable to find any distinct mention
of *shaking hands*. They joined but did not shake them. Although I find
frequently such phrases as *jungere dextras hospitio*, I do not recollect to have
met with that of *agitare dextras*. I am inclined to think that the practice grew
up in the age of chivalry when the cumbrous iron mail in which the knights
were cased prevented their embracing and when, with fingers clothed in
steel, the simple touch or joining of fingers would have been but cold
welcome. A prolonged junction was a natural result to express cordiality. As
it would have been awkward to keep the hands unemployed in this position, a gentle agitation or shaking might have been naturally introduced.

How long the practice may have remained in this rudimental stage, it
is impossible in the silence of history to say. There is nothing enabling us
to trace the progress of the art into the forms in which it now exists among
us. I shall pass immediately to the enumeration of these forms.

1. The *pump-handle* shake is the first that deserves notice. It is executed by taking your friend's hand and working it up and down through an

arc of fifty degrees for about a minute and a half. To have its true nature, force, and distinctive character, this shake should be performed with a fair, steady motion. No attempt should be made to give it grace, and still less vivacity. The few instances in which the latter has been tried have universally resulted in dislocating the shoulder of the person on whom it has been attempted. On the contrary, persons who are partial to the pump-handle shake should be at some pains to give it an equable, tranquil movement, which should on no account be continued after perspiration on the part of your friend has commenced.

2. The *pendulum* shake may be mentioned next, as being somewhat similar in character but moving, as the name indicates, in a horizontal direction. It is executed by sweeping your hand horizontally toward your friend's and, after the junction is effected, rowing with it from one side to the other according to the pleasure of the parties. The only caution in its use, which needs particularly to be given, is not to insist on performing it in a plane strictly parallel with the horizon when you meet a person who has been educated to the pump-handle shake. I had two uncles, both estimable men, one of whom had been brought up in the pump-handle shake, and the other had brought home the pendulum shake from a foreign voyage. They met, joined hands, and attempted to put them in motion. They were neither of them feeble men. One endeavored to pump and the other to paddle. Their faces reddened; the drops stood on their foreheads. It was at last a pleasing illustration of the doctrine of the adjustment of forces to see their hands slanting into an exact diagonal—in which line they ever afterward shook. But it was plain to see there was no cordiality in it, as is usually the case with compromises.

3. The *tourniquet* shake derives its name from the instruments made use of by surgeons to stop the circulation of the blood in a limb about to be amputated. It is performed by clasping the hand of your friend as far as you can in your own and then contracting the muscles of your thumb, fingers, and palm to produce the proper degree of pressure. Particular care ought to be taken, if your own hand is as hard and big as a frying pan and that of your friend as small and soft as a young maiden's, not to make use of the tourniquet shake to the degree that will force the small bones of the wrist out of place. A hearty young friend of mine who had pursued the study of geology and acquired an unusual hardness and strength of hand and wrist by the use of the hammer, on returning from a scientific excursion gave his gouty uncle the tourniquet shake with such severity that my young friend had the satisfaction of being disinherited as soon as the uncle got well enough to hold a pen.

4. The *cordial grapple* is a shake of some interest. It is a hearty, boisterous agitation of your friend's hand, accompanied with moderate pressure and loud, cheerful exclamations of welcome. It is an excellent traveling shake and well adapted to make friends.

5. The *grievous touch* is opposed to the cordial grapple. It is a pensive junction followed by a mild, subsultory motion, a cast-down look, and an inarticulate inquiry after your friend's health.

6. The *prude major* and *prude minor* are nearly monopolized by ladies. They cannot be accurately described but are constantly noticed in practice. They never extend beyond the fingers and the prude major allows you to touch even them only down to the second joint. The prude minor gives you the whole of the forefinger.

I might go through a long list of the *grip-royal*, the *sawmill* shake, and the shake with *malice aforethought*, but these are only combinations of the three fundamental forms already described as the pump-handle, the pendulum, and the tourniquet. In like manner, the *loving pat*, the *reach romantic*, and the *sentimental clasp* may be reduced in their main movements to various combinations of the last three types given in the list.

I should trouble you with a few remarks in conclusion on the mode of shaking hands as an indication of character, but through my study window I see a friend coming up the avenue. He is addicted to the pump-handle. I dare not tire my wrist by further writing. ■

How to "Lose" Real Estate

PHILBROOK PAINE A New Hampshireman through and through, Philbrook Paine was born in Dover, grew up on a salt-water farm in Durham, and was educated at Phillips Academy and the University of New Hampshire. He became a writer, following in the footsteps of his father, Ralph D. Paine, a successful author of boys' books and sea stories. As a wire service reporter, magazine writer, and newspaper columnist, Paine has written extensively—and often humorously—about the life and character of his native state.

■ Few people in New Hampshire ever sell any land. If worse comes to worse, they "lose" it, or "they let it go." Sometimes, if the profit has been enormous, they "had to let it go," implying that only fate or the hand of God had compelled them to part with such treasure.

There was a widow in Durham at one time whose eyes would overflow with tears when she told friends on the way to the bank how she had "lost" her dear little bungalow. This was after she had been trying to sell it for six years, and her profit had been miraculous.

Exchanging real estate is a game of wits and half-wits, perfectly understood by both sides, and played according to strict rules. The trick is never to let the other fellow know what you are really up to. The buyer, for example, has his own jargon. "I could take it off your hands" indicates that the prospective purchaser is dying to buy.

Sometimes an outsider and a native come to terms quickly, the former being naive and unfamiliar with real estate protocol; but transactions between two natives often consume five years or more. I have been through the process, so I speak from experience.

In 1957 I began negotiating for the purchase of a field in front of my house that consisted of twenty-eight acres. Much of it was swampy, low land, in need of ditching, that joined my property only fifty feet from the front door. It had belonged to a former neighbor who for forty years had never objected to our cutting brush near the wall in order to maintain our view of the river.

But then in 1950 he had "lost" it to a man named Les Russell for what was considered at that time a respectable sum of money, especially since a tractor could not go onto the land until late July. As real estate, this field was typical of the New Hampshire term, "Especially suitable for the crows to fly over." It contained a cemetery and some flat-lying stones on which the earliest date was a weathered 1738.

But when we began remodeling the old homestead in 1957, I made my first pitch to Les about buying the field. It was an extremely shrewd approach. I went out to his house where he lived alone and asked him if it would be all right to cut down some of the young locust trees that were growing in his field and obstructing our view.

At first he would not commit himself to an outright yes or no, but we were able to set up a meeting for the following Saturday. He arrived at ten o'clock and stayed until noon. We examined the trees. We sat on a stone wall and smoked. We stared into space. Eventually he said that he would let me know. When something like this had come up with the former owner of the field, he had always said, sure, go ahead and cut the brush. It's a nuisance. But I must have appeared suspicious to Les. Perhaps he thought that I had discovered some new and lucrative market for thorny locust brush.

In view of later developments I suspect he consulted his lawyer. But about a month later he came down and said that he guessed it would be all right if I cut some of his brush. I was very grateful. In another year I hoped to approach him about the possibility of buying the land. This, however, was the opener.

A year later I went back to see him about some rocks that had fallen off our boundary wall, and this, too, called for an on-site inspection meeting. We appraised each rock to make sure that I was not trying to purloin some of his. New Hampshire is not called the Granite State without good reason, and there should be enough rocks for everybody. But a continuous war rages between the city population and the country folk over stone walls. The former seem to feel that stone walls belong in the public domain. Do anything you wish to a rural dweller except swipe a stone of his wall. Hack down his bittersweet, throw bottles in his fields, but never get caught touching a boundary line.

This meeting with Les turned out satisfactorily for both of us. I tried to give the impression of a man completely disinterested in that particular twenty-eight acres. In fact, I stressed the problems confronting us in restoring the old homestead to a livable place. Vast sums of money were being paid out to carpenters, well-drillers, plumbers, painters, and driveway specialists. There certainly would be nothing left for the purchase of more land. Les comprehended perfectly.

"There isn't enough money in the world to buy that field," he said before departing, although I had in no way intimated that I had ever thought of purchasing it. It was plain that we both now understood each other. By some sixth sense he knew that I was trying to take it off his hands, and I was aware that the field could be "lost," but only for a formidable price. Therefore, I decided to let the crows fly over it for awhile.

Along about August of that year, after the field had been mowed, Les began playing some of his high cards. Sundays were his days to survey that particular piece of property, and he often walked the boundaries to see if I had removed any of his stones. This brought him close to the house, and usually I was right there waiting for him.

"Hey, Les," I'd say. "Come on over the wall. I want to show you this old car I'm restoring." I found that I was trying to reassure him that there was enough money in the world to buy his old field . . . if I wanted to. Actually, it was sort of a balancing act. On the one hand I was trying to play solvent enough to buy the field, but at the same time I was going to some lengths to demonstrate how previous reckless expenditures on such things as wells, tractors, and old cars had brought us all to the doors of the poor-house. Again, Les comprehended perfectly.

"I'm thinking about putting in a trailer park down there," he said one day.

This was a hard one to field on such short notice, but I did the best I could. "Seems logical," I said. "There's money in trailer parks. I just did a feature story on them. I know."

"About forty trailers, I reckon."

"Easily," I agreed. "Right down there on the flat area between us and the river." Apparently I had trumped his ace.

"Or forty houses," he said. "Half-acre lots. A builder in Dover has looked it over."

I was well aware that forty houses were an impossibility unless the future owners were willing to commute to work by boat in the spring, so I agreed that this was a splendid idea, too. Les was disheartened by my reaction and didn't reappear again until the next summer.

By this time I had evolved a real plan. I would discover indirectly how much he had in mind to charge per acre. This would give me a rough idea of how much he proposed to ask for the whole piece. So I did an idiotic thing. I committed myself.

"Les," I said one day on the wall, "have you ever thought of selling part of this field?"

He answered, "Oh, no," so quickly that I knew that he had been thinking of it seriously, probably during the whole winter.

"Say, just a couple of acres down on the river," I said. "I couldn't afford to pay much."

A crafty, outer-space look came over his face, typical of the New Hampshire trader. "What do you want a couple of acres for?" he asked, fixing his eye on an invisible constellation in the sky.

This was a touchy moment in our relationship. What I said next would either start the deal on its way to a final conclusion, or it would terminate it for another year.

"I want to raise raspberries," I said. At the time I had no way of knowing that four real-estate developers had already approached him with similar schemes for raising hay and strawberries, obtaining a place to "pasture my daughter's horse," and for duck hunting.

I had never underestimated Les's cunning, but I wasn't immediately aware of how badly I had tripped until he stood up, brought his gaze back to earth, and leered, "You're a real-estate developer, aren't you? I knew it all along."

"Nothing could be further from the truth," I declared stoutly. "I've always wanted to raise raspberries."

"Then why don't you raise them on your own place?" he interrupted.

Well, he had me there. On a previous séance near the stone wall, I had invited him to view a field which I had cleared behind the barn. There was space enough there to raise more raspberries than the whole town could eat. "It's not flat enough," I said lamely.

In view of subsequent events, this legitimate attempt at deceit had been a costly mistake. Les could now surmise that I wanted his field purely for "protection." And in New Hampshire real-estate jargon there is no more expensive word. Through headstrong impulsiveness I had painted myself into a corner. The only thing to do now was to play dead.

In the meantime the town had been assessed by the State Tax Commission, and Les's field had been valued at eight thousand dollars. Three possible waterfront lots accounted for most of this. The crows were still contentedly flying over the rest. But as a view it was doing admirably.

During these preliminary skirmishes innumerable experts on New Hampshire real estate had given me advice. "Find out if he needs money," one of them counseled me. So I inquired around town. The results were dismaying. Apparently I was dealing with a man so dumb that he had virtually retired at the age of forty-five. The result, some people said, of having bought the right pieces of land at the right time. His field in front of the house was obviously one of these.

Another friend offered to try to buy the land for me. He said that Les and he were on fairly friendly terms and that he would try to discover what price Les actually had in mind.

Les's reaction was predictable. "You been talking to Paine?" he asked. "Or do you want to raise raspberries, too?" My friend reported that Les had added a crafty smile to this reply and had gone off well pleased with himself.

Thereafter, the fourth year of the negotiations passed uneventfully. Whenever Les stalked around his field, I kept out of sight. Even when he baited me by hacking away at some brush close to the wall, I refused to be drawn into combat. I was a man who had lost interest. But Les knew better.

Enter now a real-estate broker with a purpose. Through the village grapevine he had heard of my desire to "take the field off Les's hands." The realtor thought that the field could be "lost."

"Phil," he asked, "have you ever thought of making Les an offer?"

"Look," I said, "how do you make an offer to a man like that? I don't think he knows what he wants for that field."

"You're probably right," the realtor said, "but let's try to read his New Hampshire mind. Everybody has a price. Suppose we establish one for him."

"How?"

"Well, look at it this way. The field is assessed for eight thousand dollars, according to the town report. That's our base point. Remember now, we are putting ourselves in Les's place. Is it true that you tried to buy two acres from him?"

I said that it was.

"Add a thousand for that. Now we have nine thousand. I believe that you said that you had shown him the antique car in the garage."

"I did."

"Ten thousand. Did you show him the remodeled house?"

"Unfortunately, yes. Moreover, the fellow who drives the lumberyard truck cuts the hay from the field."

"Which means, of course, that Les knows within a few hundred dollars, give or take a little, how much you have spent on the restoration. Add five hundred. Did you tell Les about the well?"

"Yes," I said. "In fact, I guess I bragged a little. It may not be the deepest and most expensive well in New Hampshire, but it must rank among the top ten."

"Add another five hundred," said the realtor. "We now have an offer of eleven thousand. I think we are getting somewhere near Les's figure. Has he seen your boat?"

"I know he has. He called it a yacht."

"Too bad, but it can't be helped. Add another five hundred," said the realtor cheerfully. "By the way, is there anything else that you can think of that might have been worth five hundred? Think hard and try to remember."

"Well," I said. "Well, there was this day when Les and I were sitting on the wall and one of my wife's friends drove in and parked her Cadillac in the drive. The timing couldn't have been worse."

"No, it couldn't," agreed the realtor. "But it can't be helped. That adds another five hundred, which brings us up to an even twelve thousand. Add six hundred for my commission, and we have Les's price of twelve thousand, six hundred. Are you willing to pay that much?"

"Not on your life," I said indignantly. "Look at that field. It's a miserable piece of real estate, half under water most of the year, situated directly across from the town disposal plant, and it doesn't even raise good hay. By the furthest stretch of the imagination it is worth about twenty dollars an acre. Even that's pretty high."

"In other words," said the realtor smoothly, "you would pay twelve-six for it?"

"Never," I said. "Would you?"

Then he sprang his trap. "As a matter of fact," he said, "I've been thinking about it seriously for some time. If you don't want it, I do. Six or eight houses down there on the waterfront might not look too bad. You'd get used to it in time. And I'd pick myself up some change in the deal." That realtor knew a thing or two about "protection" too.

With that, I had to admit defeat. Trying to outsmart one New Hampshireman was hard enough, but two were too many. "Okay," I said. "Make the offer, and if possible tie it down this afternoon. A trailer park was bad enough, but six houses on the waterfront . . . why, we wouldn't be able to see the river at all. Twelve-six."

Curiously, that was exactly the figure Les had in mind. The realtor relayed the news back to me by telephone. Could I meet them at the Dover Court House two weeks from Saturday to sign the papers? I said that I could.

When we gathered at the Register of Deeds office, we were a solemn trio, but the saddest was Les Russell. He had "lost" his field. The realtor had made an educated guess at what it had cost him in 1950, and I was still in shock. But then Les said something that cleared the air.

"Phil," he declared, "there was one thing I was going to speak to you about. But now it doesn't make any difference."

"What was that, Les?"

"Weren't you pushing that stone wall over a little into my field every year? Changing the boundary?"

I was nonplused for a moment, but then I recovered. "You're right, Les," I said. "It was one of my hobbies. I did it at night with a yoke of oxen." ■

The Yale Hour

PARKE CUMMINGS Parke Cummings was born in a Boston suburb, educated at Harvard, and moved south to Westport, Connecticut, where he happily earned a living writing magazine articles for publications ranging from *The Saturday Evening Post* to *The New Yorker*. His specialties were humor and sports (Cummings's books included *The Dictionary of Sports*, *American Tennis*, and *Baseball Stories*). He managed to combine both of his interests in the following piece.

The Yale Athletic Association
Gentlemen:

I have just learned that you are prepared to sell the broadcast rights to your six home football contests this fall, the sponsor of the advertised product to pay you twenty thousand dollars for the privilege. I am forming a company to market a new product, and I should like to make various inquiries as to the cooperation we might expect—and also make a few suggestions as to how we would want the program handled if we can come to an agreement.

First of all, our product is a concentrated beef extract, packed in cans, which we have named Steako. It is not, as you might assume, a liquid, nor a jelly, but a solid of the consistency of hash—although it contains no potatoes or other foreign matter. It is simply a concentrated steak, made from the best sections of the animal, and hence has great health-giving qualities for both children and grown-ups. Its advantages over the old-fashioned steak are obvious, it being easy to chew, requiring no carving. It can be heated in the can very quickly and hence eliminates grills, greasy pans, and the fear that it may be overdone or underdone. Steako comes in three varieties—rare, medium, and well done—so in all cases the consumer simply heats the can in boiling water for ten minutes and has his Steako cooked just as he likes it.

You stated that you would in no case consider the sponsor of a product that might reflect on Yale's name—such as liquor, cosmetics, or (I presume) drugs. I agree heartily with your stand and am sure that you will concede that Steako makes an ideal tie-up, both with football and with Yale football especially. The tradition of the Yale football player trained on beef is an illustrious one in the history of American sports, and I am sure that Yale, as a modern up-to-date university, would be anxious to further the cause of a modern and up-to-date way of consuming beef.

So much for the product, and now I want to get a few details straight. I presume that the six games will start at the usual time and will in no case be canceled because of inclement weather or, most important of all, campaign speeches. Sponsors lately have become pretty fed up with having their programs interrupted on account of this last, and we would want a guarantee against this eventuality. Naturally, we assume that you supply the contestants, uniforms, coaches, band, cheerleaders, etc., and will attend, as formerly, to all details of seating and caring for the customers.

Several men in our company—not college graduates, I may say— were of the opinion that the Yale players should be garbed in special uniforms to emphasize our product. They were willing to adhere to the traditional blue jersey, but one of them suggested that across the front of each jersey should be inscribed the words Yale Steakies. However, I refused to hear of this, and you may be assured that your players may be garbed in any fashion you see fit. Possibly, as a compromise, something might be done about the cheerleaders' costumes, but I do not feel that we need go into that right now.

Speaking of tie-up, however, it did occur to me that it might be well to get that in on the containers of our product. I think Steako cans should be blue and that the word Yale should be displayed prominently thereon— though not, of course, as prominently as Steako. I also considered having a picture of a bulldog on the can but decided that it might give the public the impression that our product was a dog food.

Instead, I have another idea. Each can of Steako might have on it a picture of one of the members of the Yale squad. Then, at the end of the season, any Steako customers who could produce eleven empty cans containing the pictures of the eleven players who started the Harvard game might receive some sort of prize. This might develop into quite an interesting contest. I would like to hear your reactions on this.

I think this plan might also stimulate more people to attend the games, and now I want to clear up the attendance problem. We are willing to have you and the athletic association of the team Yale happens to be playing attend to the distribution of tickets, except that the Steako company would expect to be given one hundred seats for its officials, its advertising agents, etc., at each game. These would not be in the Yale cheering section, but would have to be reasonably good seats near the center of the field.

Steako will not interfere with the conduct of those who attend the games. In other words, if Dartmouth or Army should happen to score a touchdown, we should not in the least object to fans in their cheering sections voicing all the approval they care to. We wouldn't feel—although Steako is in a sense tied up with Yale—that this would be prejudicial to our product. I just want to emphasize that we are willing—nay, anxious—that the game itself, including the spectator angle, should go on just as though there were no sponsor. While we should like to have Yale win, we cannot insist on it, although, of course, the record of the team might be some consideration when the time came to renew for the 1937 season.

On the other hand, we think that all games should be a good show. Nowadays the big broadcast hours don't only sound well, but they are also a good spectacle for those in the studio audience. So although, as I have said, we wouldn't want to interfere with the game itself, we feel that there should be some interesting sidelights. We would probably form a Steako quartet which could render songs when time was taken out or between the halves. Also, I imagine we will have a pretty girl or two, dressed for football with coonskin coats, etc., who would sing out on the field between the halves.

That brings us to the band. Rather than getting Whiteman, Koste-lanetz, or somebody like that, we are wondering to what extent the Yale band would be willing to cooperate with us. We are prepared to offer an extra five thousand to have that organization known as the Yale Steako Band, and to wear appropriate costumes designed by us. For a certain percentage of the time we would be willing to have it play songs of its own choice—which would be Yale football songs and those of the oppo-nents–but we would expect it also to give renditions of our own choosing.

I was thinking particularly that new words, tying up Steako, might be written for some of the famous old Yale football tunes like "Boola Boola," "Bulldog, Bulldog, Bow Wow Wow," or "Goodnight, Poor Harvard." For instance, just as an example, the Steako quartet might gather in front of the band and, instead of "Bulldog, Bulldog, Bow Wow Wow," might sing, "Steako Steako, boy oh boy"; or the theme of "Goodnight, Poor Harvard," might be changed to "Goodnight, Poor Butcher"—selling the idea, of course, that Steako spells finis to the old-fashioned butcher with his tough, hard-to-cook steaks. Of course, we wouldn't do this too often, as the public nowadays won't stand much of it, but we might use it as a theme song at the beginning and end of the program. It would be mighty good radio, I think. The first thing the listener would hear would be the Yale band playing a few bars of "Bulldog, Bulldog," and then the quartet, good and snappy, would come in with "Steako, Steako, boy oh boy!" I think it would put the listeners right in the mood at the very start.

I do not think it would be necessary for people in the cheering section to sing these parodies, and Steako doesn't want to interfere with their privilege to shout and sing whatever they like. Of course, we would appreciate applause from them after a rendition by our quartet or torch singer, or laughter after a comic song. Probably the cheerleaders could hold up "Laughter" or "Applause" cards.

I am looking forward to an early reply from you about my various inquiries and suggestions. If we get together on this, I think we can supply six swell Saturday afternoons of entertainment and thrills for radio listeners, as well as making the public Yale- and Steako-conscious.

Very truly yours,

PARKE CUMMINGS

Appendix

■ Sources for the Mark Twain "introduction" are as follows:

"There is no more sin . . . " (*Mark Twain's Speeches*, 1910); "A successful book . . . " (*Mark Twain's Letters*, 1917); "Humor is only a fragrance . . . " (*Mark Twain in Eruption*); "The humorous story . . . " (*Literary Essays*, "How to Tell a Story"); "Humor is the great thing . . . " (*Literary Essays*, "What Paul Bourget Thinks of Us"); "Humor is mankind's greatest blessing." (*Mark Twain, A Biography*, by Albert B. Paine); "There is no lasting quality . . . " (*Celebrities Off Parade*, W.D. Orcutt, 1935); "The human race . . . " (*The Mysterious Stranger*).

Permissions

■ Inclusion of works by the following authors was made possible by the generous permission of these authors, publishers, and representatives: